Nationalism, Historiography, and the (Re)Construction of the Past

Nationalism, Historiography and the (Re)Construction of the Past

Edited by Claire Norton

New Academia Publishing, LLC
Washington, DC

New Academia Publishing, 2007

Printed in the United States of America

Library of Congress Control Number: 2006932672
ISBN 978-0-9787713-1-7 paperback (alk. paper)

New Academia Publishing, LLC
P.O. Box 27420, Washington, DC 20038-7420
www.newacademia.com - info@newacademia.com

Contents

Nationalist Art and Performance

The Remembering of the Past to Construct the Nation in Post-Ottoman States

Illustrations

Preface

The papers in this book originated from a conference organized by myself and Marios Hadjianastasis entitled *Nationalism, Historiography and the (Re)Construction of the Past* held at the University of Birmingham on 10-11 September 2004. The conference was conceived in an interdisciplinary spirit and the intention was to examine the relationship between nationalism and conceptions of the past via a variety of different media and in diverse geo-political contexts. The participants, through a series of detailed case studies, explored how the employment of nation-state dominated discourses have caused a re-imagination of the past, and also how the past has been re-constructed to accord with nationalist agendas.

The collection of edited papers presented here do not look at the evolution of particular nationalisms, but rather concentrate on the impact that nation-state dominated cartographies have had on the manner in which the past is re-constructed and remembered. A comparative and multidisciplinary approach is again adopted and is exemplified in the authors' focus on diverse means by which the past is constructed. The chapters do not exclusively focus on the relationship between, for example, art or literature and national identity, but take a broader perspective and examine academic writings, art, museums and heritage sites, archaeological remains, folktales, myths of origin, and theatrical spectacle. Moreover, the authors' case studies are drawn from across the globe including, Rwanda, South Africa, Yemen, Uzbekistan, Greece, Hungary, Italy, Bulgaria, Turkey and the former Yugoslav Republics.

The book consists of an introductory article by Prof. John Breuilly based upon his keynote speech at the conference, and eleven chapters organized under four sub-headings: Museums, Monuments and Cultural Property: Creating a National Heritage; Myths of Descent, Race and Contemporary Politics; Nationalist Art and Performance; and, Remembering the Past to Construct the Nation in Post-Ottoman States. As can be seen from the sub-headings the chapters have generally been organized thematically rather than according to the nations or nationalisms under discussion.

Breuilly's introduction looks at the development of nationalist historiography from the late eighteenth century onwards. He explores the notion of a nationalist historiography and examines in depth certain key features common to nationalist historiographies: myths of origin, the role of the 'other', and golden ages. His chapter also considers the difference between nationalist and national historiographies, the role of historians as interpreters of nationalist movements and how culture in a broad sense is also subject to the process of nationalization.

The first sub-section includes articles by Arthurs, Flynn and King, and Tanaka which all explore the heritage industry (museums, monuments and the repatriation of historic objects), the manner in which representations of the past are intertwined with (re)constructions of national identity and how meaning is inscribed in, and ascribed to, archaeological artifacts. Arthurs examines how a single collection of archaeological objects in Italy has been variously presented and re-constructed in a museum context over the course of the twentieth century. Through this analysis he explores the ways in which different twentieth-century Italian regimes—Liberal, Fascist, and Republican—conceived of Rome's place within the teleology of national history. Flynn and King consider how two heritage sites central to apartheid iconography have been refashioned in the post-apartheid era. In particular they focus on how this refashioning does not seek to eradicate or replace the segregated white-dominated history of the apartheid era, but rather presents a deliberate counterpoint to it. These two sites therefore act as a metaphor for the status of the public past in post-apartheid Africa, where old sites, memories and identities exist side by side with new ones. Tanaka explores the link between archaeological objects and the construction of national identity. Specifically he concentrates on how the idea of place overrides the idea of ethnicity in claims by the Turkish state for the ownership and the repatriation of objects from classical antiquity.

The second sub-section concentrates on the manner in which myths of descent are used in a nationalist context to justify or create present political realities. Bruunbauer analyses myths of non-Slavic or autochthonous origins popularized in the last two decades in the former Yugoslav Republics in order to discern their relation to ideological and political currents and perceived threats to particular nations. Turner also explores myths of autochthonous descent, but in a Rwandan context. He examines pre-genocide anti-Tutsi representations of the past in which Tutsis are depicted as foreign usurpers in conjunction with post-genocide attempts to rewrite Rwandan history and use it as a basis of national unity.

The third section concentrates on the role that art and theatrical performance have in nationalist reconstructions of the past. Stohrer discusses how the Yemenite government, since unification in 1990, has attempted to create a homogeneous national culture and shared remembrance of the past through public performances by the National Folklore Ensemble. She analyses how one particular performance at a celebration for the tenth anniversary of unification attempts to construct a single image of a unified Yemen; past and present. Okada looks at the intersection of art and nationalism in the context of the ex-Soviet Republic, Uzbekistan. She explores how one example of state-sponsored public art designed to reflect the complicated history of Uzbekistan and its long journey to independent status, has experienced various re-incarnations as the legitimizing ideology of the state has undergone subtle changes in the past two decades. Hadjipapa, in contrast, concentrates on the manner in which both Bulgarian and Greek artists have appropriated the iconography of religious art and employed it in a new context in order to pursue nationalist ambitions.

The fourth and last section is concerned with how states arising from the fragmented Ottoman Empire have (re)constructed or re-contextualized elements of the past to legitimize their own claim to nation status. Soileau concentrates on how Turkey has appropriated or re-constructed the Islamic saints of Haji Bektash Veli, Mevlana Jalaluddin and Yunus Emre as great Turkish humanists thus reflecting and reinforcing Ataturk's shift to the secular and progressive in his imagination of the Turkish nation. Norton examines predominantly Hungarian academic histories of the Ottoman-Hungarian border lands. She analyses historians' depiction of the Hungarian community as a 'natural' entity which pre-existed the Ottomans and remained linguistically, ethnically and culturally distinct from other peoples in the area, as an attempt to teleologically justify the existence of the nation state of Hungary. Lastly, Paleou focuses on the use that the Greek Left made of remembrances of both the struggle for independence against the Ottoman Empire in 1821 and the national resistance movement against Axis occupation in the Second World War. She examines the manner in which the left-wing journal *Review of Art* commemorated and remembered these events in various editions in the 1950s and 1960s and how they attempted to link these events to their continuing struggle for social liberation and justice in Greece.

It remains to thank the Institute of Archaeology and Antiquity at the University of Birmingham for hosting the conference and also for their financial support for both the conference and the publication. In particular, Dr. Ruth Macrides and Prof. Vince Gaffney were generous with both their time and support. I would also like to thank all the contributors for firstly making the conference such an enjoyable and intellectually stimulating occasion and secondly for their efforts in revising and editing their papers for this volume.

Claire Norton
St. Mary's College, University of Surrey, October 2006.

1
Nationalism and Historians
Some Reflections. The Formation of National(ist) Historiographical Discourse

Prof. Breuilly

It seems fair to assume that members of human groups, at least as soon as they come into contact with other groups, coin group names. There are two kinds of names: common nouns for types of groups and proper nouns for specific groups. So for example, in Latin there is the common noun *gens, gentis* which is variously translated into English as race, family, clan, tribe, people and nation. Then there are proper names, for example those used by Tacitus to denote the Germans who in turn were differentiated with more specific group names. Bede, the 'father of the English' combined common and proper nouns when he referred to *gens Anglorum*: the English people.[1]

Insofar as we have a long history of such names and many accounts which purport to tell us about the histories of the groups so named, one might think that national historiography is something one can trace back to Tacitus and possibly further, maybe to Herodotus. However, I would reject such an assumption on the following grounds.

1. Insofar as there were specific groups identified, these were characterized as what we might call tribes or ethnies, usually in implicit contrast to the more powerful, literate, urban-centered, state societies from which the writers were drawn. It was these outsiders who portrayed the 'customs' of such peoples.[2]

2. The chronicles of such groups, if they existed, portrayed little more than the deeds of their political and military elites.

3. Such accounts, whether by insiders or observers, were not written on the basis of a critical examination of primary sources.

4. In these accounts history is not understood as a secular process in which human beings make their own history and in turn that history changes human nature. Rather the historic process is subject to divine shaping or, independent of the will of gods or one God, is a stage on which unchanging human nature is confronted with recurrent challenges, providing present witnesses with exemplary stories of good and bad conduct and character.

A national historiography involves rather different assumptions.

1. The nation is the most important human group, binding together sub-national groups such as families and classes while at the same time dividing humanity.

2. The nation is the source of identity and values. The unique nation is the key historical actor, not general human nature or gods.

3. The nation can only be truly understood from within and that involves a study of the actions and products of the nation, its language, literature, art, folklore. That requires immersion in the material the nation has produced over the course of its history.

4. History is not just the chronicle of wars and states, of the deeds of great men; these only convey meaning when seen as emanating from the nation.

Nation as an historical category and secular historiography as a profession were closely bound together and their linked emergence can be located in the late eighteenth century. Central is the figure of Johann Gottfried Herder (1744-1805) who both exemplified but also reacted against enlightenment historiography. He exemplified it with his concern to understand human beings in terms of their own nature and their history as something they themselves produced. He reacted against the cosmopolitan presumptions of an essential human nature and the rational individual by stressing that human beings were culturally shaped, above all through the various and incommensurable languages they spoke.[3]

These historiographical developments accompanied the formation of sharply bounded states which appealed to the idea of popular or national sovereignty from the time of the American and French revolutions. Subsequently one can observe the construction of two kinds of national histories: state centered and culture centered. This distinction can be linked to other distinctions subsequently applied to types of nationalism: historic/non-historic, civic/ethnic, eastern/western, political/cultural.[4]

Just as these polarized typologies of nationalism have been challenged, so too can one challenge the historiographical distinction.[5] Certainly it would be misleading to suggest that *cases* can be assigned to *types*. One can observe both kinds of historical writing at work in particular cases. Thus Herder and those who followed him sought to write culture-centered histories, paying much attention to custom and folklore, music and art, and above all language, for example in their treatments of German history. At the same time, historians such as Heinrich von Treitschke and the Prussian school of historians focused attention on diplomacy and war. The distinction works as a broad one between different kinds of historical writing. It also points to an intellectual problem for nationalist historians: how to connect together these rather different historical accounts.

In the best historical work there is always some combination of the two approaches. However, one can crudely conceive of a continuum: at one end state-centered history predominates; at the other end culture-centered history. I would also suggest that a key element shaping where historical work appears on this continuum is the actual historical relationship between state and nation. Thus state centered history for a long time dominated the structure, if not the content, of English/British and French historical writing while culture-centeredness was more central in much Slav and Rumanian historical writing. In the first type of case, a national state preceded the age of nationalism and the state was regarded as the formative influence on that age. In the second, nationalism represented itself as the creed of a 'stateless' people making claims for self-determination against the existing state. A third, possibly intermediate type of case, is where a 'nation' whose elites could identify with a high culture and local political dominance, nevertheless were subordinate within a larger political framework such as the Poles of post-partition Poland or the Germans and Italians of pre-unification Germany and Italy. This helps explain why Herder, with his focus on 'folk' rather than 'elite' culture, had a much greater influence on Slav than German nationalist historiography.

The subject is complicated by the fact that conceptions of state and culture themselves vary in space and time, as do interests in the specific institutions which can function as the vehicle of national historical narrative, such as towns and churches, peasant communities or noble elites, workers or the bourgeoisie. Thus the 'state' was treated in nineteenth century British historiography mainly as a constitutional concept which focused on internal conflict whereas in German historiography it was approached from an idealist tradition which had little to say about internal conflicts and more about the need to assert state (general interest) 'over' society (particular interests) and in relation to other states. With cultural approaches there is a distinction between historians with an explicit concern for 'high' culture as expressive of the nation (e.g., Dante as the quintessential Italian writer) and with 'folk' culture as the true reflection of the nation. Finally, most nationalist historiographies are riven by disputes, for example between pro- and anti-revolutionary French historians, or the Whig and anti-Whig approaches to English history.[6]

Therefore, what constitutes "nationalist" historiography is itself a highly diverse intellectual field. Its unity is constituted by the way in which it centers the historic process on the unique nation rather than in any particular way it then presents such a history. For such a discourse to take the form of academic historiography it had to be linked to a distinct set of methods associated with the formation of a profession. In the field of mainstream history the most important methodological development was the notion that the archive was the central resource of the historian and that training as an historian should concentrate on how one understood and used archives. Standard accounts rightly focus on the work and influence of Leopold von Ranke (1795-1886) as the first 'professional' academic historian. They also note his particular views about states as the key actors in history and nations as the principal human grouping of post-Roman Europe.[7]

The professionalization of German historiography which greatly influenced subsequent developments was closely associated with the process leading to German unification. The attempt to combine state and culture centered accounts of this process is exemplified in the unfinished history of nineteenth century Germany by Heinrich von Treitschke with the inter-cutting chapters on Prussian state action and German cultural history. Juxtaposition, however, is not genuine connection and already one can discern a major intellectual problem in nationalist historiography, namely how to connect a politics labeled nationalism with a culture labeled national. The various pseudo-solutions proffered, including juxtaposition and teleology (an event has meaning in terms of the national becoming which follows that event) are also hallmarks of nationalist historiography of very diverse kinds.

Similar structures of argument, if with different content and political contexts, can be observed elsewhere. Michelet, the French historian, sought to bring the civic national historiography of the French revolution into a close relationship with popular conceptions of the French nation. In England the Victorian insistence on a continuous English history from before 1066 to the present day argued by Stubbs and Freeman and others again called for efforts to connect political to popular, state centered to cultural history.[8] At the same time the insistence on the nation as the source of values, of culture, promoted the historicization and 'nationalization' of a range of other disciplines such as art history, literature, law, linguistics and economics. This was part of a debate carried on with more rational, generalizing methods of inquiry, for example between classical political economy and historical economics.[9]

The impact of what might be called the 'historicist' approach went beyond academic historical writing.[10] The very notion that art, music, and literature are expressions of the nation, if taken seriously, will also shape the way such activities themselves are practiced and presented. The 'nationalization' of landscape, for example, led to new enterprises in visual art. Just as Benedict Anderson has argued that 'print capitalism' underpinned national imagining, or at least diffused such imaginings to mass audiences, so might one argue that 'lithograph capitalism' could do the same for visual imaginings of the nation.[11] Just to take one example: the

English artist William Turner was paid a huge sum of money by a commercial art publisher to produce a set of representations of 'English' (and Welsh; it is interesting that Wales was not considered separate from England in the way that Scotland was) landscapes which were designed to be turned into lithographs which in turn were mass produced for a mass middle-class clientele.[12]

Practice was closely linked to presentation. In the early and mid-nineteenth century are founded numerous 'national' museums and art galleries. Admittedly in the successful imperial states such museums were frequently filled with objects acquired from abroad; one thinks of how 'unBritish' are the holdings of the 'British' Museum or the art pillage carried out by Napoleon to stock the Louvre. But even in these imperial cases, the art is frequently represented as exemplars of different national cultures or civilizations rather than of some a-historical aesthetic. Art was organized on national and historical lines. A new profession of art curators was formed, both to apply these historical principles but also, as with Turner's lithographs, to make such objects accessible to a growing middle-class audience which could not be presumed to share in an implicit high culture which would make what they were looking at immediately comprehensible. There is, of course, something deeply problematic about a national culture which needs professionally explaining to its members.

A national art gallery should exhibit national art. For living artists this means art should be *about the nation* as much as *expressive of the nation*. One can see this in the art exhibition "Myths of the Nations" which ran some years ago in Berlin. In terms of geography the exhibition covered all of Europe and in terms of chronology the events depicted stretched from the defense of Thermopylae in 480 BCE to the German-Danish war of 1864. However, the paintings themselves were all made between the French revolution and the First World War, indeed most of them in the middle third of the nineteenth century.[13]

One can see the same national and historicist influences at work in music and architecture, as well as in such disciplines as linguistics, archaeology. The view of the world as divided into nations with long and distinct histories only became a popular and then a 'natural' one in the nineteenth century. Furthermore, it was a highly uniform view. As the "Myths of the Nation" exhibition makes clear, whether painting Hermann destroying Roman legions or Nelson dying at Trafalgar or the assassination of William of Orange, the paintings are remarkably similar as historical epics in a realistic style designed to convey the impression that these events had actually taken place while at the same time mythologizing them.

The growth of national historiography therefore was part of a more general nationalization of culture which shaped the practices of many arts and spawned numerous intellectual professions, all of which presented the nation as a real but also spiritual object in time and space.

Nationalism and Nation-State Formation

One part of the explanation for this nationalization of culture and historiography is to do with the emergence of nationalist movements and efforts, whether successful or not, to re-shape post-Napoleonic Europe into a series of nation states. Whether one sees nationalist discourse as an essential condition for the rise of nationalist politics or simply as an instrument of such a politics is a matter I must leave aside here.[14] Here I will just focus on the specific role of historians. In many instances historians were themselves major figures within national movements. One thinks of Thiers, Guizot and Lamartine in France, Palacky in the Czech movement, the leading figures in the Prussian school of history such as Sybel and Treitschke, and of Thomas Macaulay who not only wrote a best-selling national history but also for a while shaped British educational policy in India. Historians also figured prominently in the events which led to the second wave of nation-state formation following the First World War, for example Thomas Masaryck and the formation of Czechoslovakia. These men played a double role: on the one hand, their historical work communicated a powerful view of the nation as a real force operating through time; on the other hand, they occupied leading political roles in national movements.[15]

In addition to the historian as intellectual inspiration for, or political activist in, national(ist) movements, there is also the role of the historian as interpreter of nationalist achievements. New nation-states demanded a history which explained their success as arising out of something more than the accidents of war and great power politics. In turn they provided historians privileged access to their own archives as well as honoring them and appointing them to key academic positions. Such historians wrote state-centered accounts not only because there was a state to celebrate but also because they could work with state-generated and state-preserved archives. Historians of as yet stateless nations, or of failed nationalist movements, had to work with different kinds of materials and tended to produce more culture-centered accounts. It would be interesting to engage in a comparative study which investigated whether there was typically a shift from culture to state as there was a shift from stateless to state-nation. However, I should reiterate the point made earlier that all nationalist historiographies combine cultural and political elements and there are tensions if not open contradictions and debates within each such historiography.

By the early twentieth century these fairly novel national views of history had hardened into conventional understandings. In nation-states they formed the staple of school history. Only this can make sense, for example, of the brilliant historical satire *1066 and All That* by Sellar and Yeatman.[16] Here the idea of national history as dimly (and therefore wrongly) remembered school lessons can only work *precisely because that is how the readership actually learnt that history*. The very triumph of the nation-state, compulsory mass education and official school history rendered nationality a banality, something beyond dispute, even when mocked. That banality has in turn been promoted in other, everyday ways in contemporary mass culture, providing an essential foundation for the rapid shift to a more explicit and political nationalism at times of crisis.[17]

These stages of development from promoting nationalist movements and demands to celebrating a new nation-state to banality vary chronologically and from case to case. Thus, whereas long-established nation-states generally represent their national history as heritage and color, these co-exist with nationalist movements elsewhere seeking separation from a larger state and also with new nation-states trying to establish themselves within the international community. There is also a complex set of relationships between different national historiographies at different stages of development. Thus, for example, English historians by the early twentieth century took English/British national history for granted and imagined that the rest of the world could or should eventually follow this example. This shaped the way they wrote the history of 'other nations'. Such historians often repudiated 'nationalism', seen after 1918 as a nasty, extremist form of politics. Yet at a deeper level they extolled the claims of national diversity and independence. Thus, for example, G. M. Trevelyan detested Mussolini and Italian fascism, but saw it as a rejection rather than continuation of the values represented in the Risorgimento, in particular in the figure of Garibaldi, the subject of a three-volume biography.[18]

Even after the Second World War, with the breakdown of European hegemony and the formation of two rival global blocs each dominated by a world power subscribing to universal principles (liberalism, socialism), and a sense that the age of nationalism was now over, nevertheless the two blocs were structured as a series of territorial nation-states. Indeed, with European de-colonization accelerating into the 1960s there were many more such states than ever before. Nationalism was dead, long live the nation-state.[19] In a way this 'naturalized' the concept of the nation which was apparently detached from contested politics. Historiography followed. It was now natural to write history along national lines, a series of parallel trenches with just the occasional peek over the parapet, especially when one's own trench was overrun. Nineteenth century 'Polish' history, for example, is written in terms of the foreign occupation of Poland and the struggle against that occupation. The idea that one could write the history of Galicia as a part of Habsburg history, of Russian Poland as part of Russian history and of Posen and East and West Prussia as part of Prussian history is largely marginalized, even if that was the way perhaps the great majority of 'Poles' experienced matters through the nineteenth century.[20]

To have one's national history is, therefore, regarded as an important, indeed indispensable element of genuine freedom and independence. Where it has not been constructed, this is regarded as a deficiency. For example, school history in many former British colonies continues to be taught as an older and conventional Eurocentric history. A few years ago I found myself at a secondary school in a small town in north-west Zambia. A very poor region of a very poor country, the school could barely afford any books or other teaching materials. Its history syllabus was based on that provided by an English examinations board. When I held a couple of sessions on that syllabus with the students, I found myself discussing with them the wars of German unification and the origins of the First World War. My immediate reaction was one of dismay and indignation; why were these students not being provided with material on the history of their own country? My second reaction was that if I considered national(ist) historiography as limited and tendentious, something to be transcended in my own land, why should I advocate it for another? The only defense I can offer is that if there is one thing worse than having to learn the history of one's own 'nation', it is being compelled to learn that of another.

The construction or re-construction of national pasts continues apace today. One very active site is to be found in post-communist Eastern Europe where there is a tension between aspirations to westernize and to register a distinct identity. Clearly the official Marxist and Soviet view of the past which prevailed until 1991 will not serve in the Ukraine or the Baltic states. More generally, significant regime change calls for changes in historiography. A fascinating process is in train, for example, in post-apartheid South Africa where there is a tension between the desire to transcend the race-centered historiography of the apartheid regime and to juxtapose the newly celebrated values of the black majority against those of the defeated minority.[21]

Historians have perhaps been less prominent in anti-colonial post-1945 nationalist movements and nation-state formations. Partly this is because intellectually history has lost ground to other disciplines. For example, the discipline studied by the leading Kenyan nationalist, Jomo Kenyatta, was anthropology, a discipline he deployed directly in his early political activity, notably in his defense of the practice of female circumcision amongst the Kikuyu. Another factor may be the professionalization of politics which marginalized the role of 'amateurs' such as academics. More important was the grounding of independence claims in universalist values of freedom and independence rather than cultural diversity and self-determination, coupled with the sense of the artificiality of colonial boundaries and therefore of histories which accorded any meaning to those territories. There may also have been a concern that a culture-oriented history would prove divisive by drawing attention to significant cultural differences within new states as well as solidarities which reached across state borders. But even here one observes a nation-building process which included the cultivation of history as well as assertions of indigenous values against those of the west. This could in part build on western intellectual traditions themselves and indeed, historians from Europe often played a major role in the construction of national histories.[22]

In the case of post-communist national historiographies in Eastern Europe there were various resources on which one could build. One was a pre-communist national historiography as available in the Baltic states and the Warsaw Pact states. The cultivation of national culture and identity in the non-Russian Soviet Republics also provided resources, although historical writing had to align itself with Soviet and communist themes.[23] Yet the mere existence of a national republic did not itself guarantee the capacity to produce an influential and persuasive post-communist national past, as is clear when one compares Belarus with the Ukraine.

A final and vital source of national historiography was produced in non-western countries which were not formally subordinated to western imperial rule. In cases where the history of the pre-modern polity was one of a non-western imperial civilization, for example the Ottoman, Chinese and Mughal empires, there were great problems in 'nationalizing' a past which had recognized separate communities within the polity. Intellectuals did difficult work in seeking to take over some western notions of modernity and national identity and grafting these on to imperial values. In some cases the imperial past was simply rejected, for example the radical Turkish nationalist response to Ottomanism and even Islam, although there helped by the rapid ethnicization of the shrinking empire as 'Turks' fled the newly independent states of the Balkans and in turn expelled 'non-Turks' to their various 'national' homelands such as Greece and Bulgaria. The problem in China was less one of ethnic or confessional heterogeneity than of how to preserve any values from the past while stressing the need for popular sovereignty and social transformation along communist lines. The problem could be in part avoided by focusing instead on foreign enemies (above all, the Japanese) or by ethnicizing class relations, a common process in the steps leading to the mass murder of 'class enemies.'[24] In the case of the Mughal empire, the crisis which led the final phase of British rule to culminate in partition meant that such a possible historiography was blocked by the development of either secular (Congress) versus Hindu historiography in India and an Islamic emphasis in Pakistan. I am too ignorant of Bangladeshi historiography to know how far any concept of Bengali identity has been used as the basis of more recent historical writing.

Probably the most successful nationalization of a non-western history took place in Japan. Ethnic homogeneity, island isolation and the restoration of formerly discredited imperial institutions provided resources for a persuasive national historiography which was arguably unique in the non-western world. Yet underlying all these cases one can see a tendency, in modern world history, to shift from what might be called communalism or micro-ethnicity to macro-ethnicity and to nationalize either religious or civilizational characteristics.[25]

The Typical Features of Nationalist Historiography

The central assumptions of nationalist historiography is that there *is* a nation and that its existence and character can be substantiated through historical study. This is more obviously plausible in some cases (e.g. the 'English') than others (e.g. the 'Zambians') and so the actual historical record in part shapes the strategies deployed by nationalist historians. Nevertheless, there are similar features in a wide range of nationalist historiographies and I will briefly pick out a number of these.

Origins

When and where did the nation originate? In part the answer is about locating some original moment, ideally as far back as possible. So, for example, there are debates concerning the Anglo-Saxon origins of the English. In the simplest approach the Angles and Saxons are seen as the original ancestors who drove out earlier inhabitants and settled the country. In more sophisticated versions the creation of a fairly centralized Christian kingdom by the late Anglo-Saxon period is seen as setting the framework and values within which subsequent national history took place. In a yet more sophisticated version some medieval historians outline a process of 'ethnogenesis' in which, for example, Bede's *History of the English Church and People* (written c.731 C.E.) shapes a subsequent elite culture which increasingly conceives of itself as English, a culture which continues to survive across the 1066 divide.[26]

In German nationalist historiography Tacitus and his text *Germania* (c. 98 C.E.) has served a similar function. Rediscovered in the late fifteenth century, its ethnographic accounts of the 'Germans', including physical descriptions, were taken up in anti-Papal (anti-Rome, anti-Italy) discourses during the Reformation. Numerous other 'barbarian' ethnic groups such as the Franks could be used in similar ways. One finds something similar in the Daco-Roman arguments about Rumanians or the Hungarian myths based upon the movements of the Magyars.[27] Indeed the basic 'ethno-national' map of Europe can be related to the ethnographies generated by the Roman Empire and Romanized elites subsequently. Nationalist historians took these ethnographic stories fairly literally to create myths of origins.[28]

The story is more complex beyond Europe. In some cases there was a plausible history on which to draw such as that of the Chinese empire or the Japanese emperor system, especially helped by the relative ethnic homogeneity of the peoples of these areas. In areas of European settlement there was instead a denial of the features of an original people to earlier inhabitants. North America, Australia, New Zealand, southern Africa were depicted as 'empty' lands and the lack of settled agriculture or centralized political systems was taken to mean that the indigenous peoples lacked claims to a distinct homeland. The history of origins now became the history of original white settlement. The Great Trek, for example, works as an origin myth in Afrikaaner nationalism just as does the original Puritan landing on the eastern coast of North America. Australia was 'founded' with the arrival of the first fleet in 1788 and Columbus 'discovered' America.

In other cases it is necessary to look not to a distinct place or 'nation' but to more diffuse ethnic origins. As the Ottoman Empire gave way to the Turkish Republic, for example, so the notion of a Turkic people was constructed. The recent exhibition (2005) *The Turks: a Thousand Years of History* mounted at the Royal Academy locates the 'origins' in what is today western China around 700 C.E. This 'people', rather similar to the image of *Volkswanderungen* in the period of Roman imperial decline and collapse, then moved westwards into more settled and 'advanced' cultures, turning to Islam as European barbarians turned to Christianity. But just as it is important to French or German nationalist historians to detach nationality from Christianity, so it is vital for Turkish historians to detach national origins from Islam.[29]

The concern with origins is only dispensed with in cases of 'new nations' which formed within recently constructed boundaries drawn by European empires, starting with Spanish and Portuguese America, and later in much of Africa and Asia. Even then one finds shifts to ethnic identities which either support existing state boundaries (for example, in attempts to construct Mexican identity) or which are used to challenge those boundaries (e.g. the 'nationalization' of Islamic identity to justify the construction of Pakistan, but then in turn the construction of Bengali nationality to justify the separation of East from West Pakistan). This sets up further dynamics, e.g. a Hindu nationalist search for an ethnic (or rather, racial) original. At the same time, the destabilizing consequence of such constructions can lead in turn to a *denial* of origins, to a secular and civic national myth which deliberately restricts origins to a very recent time, usually founded in the struggle for independence.

Debates about origins are also linked to internal tensions within particular nationalisms. For example, the debate amongst Rumanian nationalists as to whether 'Rumanians' already resided in the country before Roman conquest or whether their origins are as those who settled along with the establishment of empire can be linked to more recent political differences.[30] The argument about whether Franks or Gauls are the true ancestors of the French, whether Normans blended with the Anglo-Saxon or suppressed English origins have similar purposes.[31]

Finally, the actual historical record shapes how origins are established. Where there is long political continuity there is a tendency to write of dominant, historical nations (English, French, Spanish) and to find a line of continuity, above all in rulers and their institutions. Where there is political discontinuity, but cultural dominance, there is a tendency to look to a high culture (Italian, German) around which a nation-state can be built. Where there has been political and cultural subordination there is a tendency to turn to 'folk' culture as the basis of national identity and history, as one finds amongst Slav nationalist writers of the nineteenth century.

But these are variations on a common theme. Each historiography will pick up on all or any of these features to establish origins. The common feature is that something which really has nothing to do with modern ways of thinking and acting 'nationally' will be identified as a founding moment, a national origin.

Threat and Resistance

The nation in part is constructed in relation to the 'other'. Arguably writers like Herodotus and Tacitus were establishing the identity of Greeks and Romans in their ethnographies of 'barbarians'. The 'barbarians' then used these Greek or Roman constructs in their political responses to various kinds of imperial rule and that was then projected back by nationalist historians of the modern period. How far these really represented 'us/ them' relations at the time is debatable.

The other is not merely different, but is a threat. As the threat is differently constructed, so then is the nation. Colley, for example, has argued that the shift from an English to a British identity was helped by the post-Reformation perception of the major Catholic powers – Spain, then France - as threats to the Protestant peoples of England, Scotland, Wales and (parts of) Ireland: that is, the Britons.[32] As the other changes constantly, so does the reference point of nationalist historiography. For much of the nineteenth century, for example, it was Catholic cum atheist-revolutionary France which was seen as the major threat in both British and German historical writing. With French defeat and German unification there was a marked shift, signaled finally in the world wars of the twentieth century. Enmity between the white Protestant cultures of Britain and Germany meant a shift in the conception of the nation, away from religion and skin color and towards notions of civilization and culture respectively.

The other could also be internal. In many ways this was a more deadly enemy. Catholicism was especially dangerous because there was a substantial British Catholic population in Ireland. The strident nationalism of the new German state after 1871 also targeted Catholics as lacking in 'national culture' as well as owing loyalty to a 'foreign' power, the Papacy. Bourgeois nationalism also identified socialism as a cosmopolitan creed leading the national working class astray, an idea later deployed against socialist internationalism and then the Soviet Union. In all these cases there were notions of purity: the pure language, the pure culture, the pure faith. In Christian nations the latter concern could also lead to an anti-Semitic strain in historical writing of the kind one finds on the right in Germany and France by 1900. Allied to race concerns it could in turn generate biological versions of historical writing.

Decline and Disappearance

An inconvenient feature of many national histories was that the nation frequently was defeated and even disappeared. Nationalist historians could ingeniously turn defeat into a national virtue. French historians, for example, insisted that the defeat of Vertingetorix by Caesar had the long term effect of integrating the French into a true civilization, unlike the barbaric Germans who remained outside the civilizing work of Rome. (German nationalists, of course, argued the precise opposite). It was an argument taken up by fascist defenders of Vichy France with the Third Reich serving as a modern equivalent of Rome. It helped if defeat was at least heroic and glorious as in the Serbian depiction of the 1389 Battle of Kosovo, or Jewish representations of the defense of Masada.

Much more difficult were the times of forgetfulness. Many nationalist intellectuals in the early nineteenth century saw their task to 'awaken' their nation from its long sleep. First, they had to identify the nation in terms of 'objective' characteristics which people shared, even if not as a conscious touchstone of national identity. Language was the central feature and there was much in the way of codifying, compiling dictionaries and grammars and seeking to create a national literature. The very success, in some cases, of these projects (in the sense of a shift from this intellectual stage to first elite and then popular political movements) could be taken as a verification of the intellectual act of faith. However, it was vital to insist that these pioneers 'uncovered' or 'awakened' the nation, they did not 'invent' or 'imagine' it.

Golden Ages

If defeats could be used at least as moments of heroic resistance, golden ages could serve to demonstrate the heights which the nation could reach. Late nineteenth and twentieth century English nationalist historians and literary scholars looked back for example to Elizabethan England as pioneer of an earlier imperial age, a moment of cultural greatness (above all in the figure of Shakespeare) and of survival against powerful enemies. Czech nationalist historians, starting with Palacky, centered their attention upon Jan Hus and the Hussite movement with its revival of Czech and its success against overwhelming odds. Renaissance Italy, Bourbon France, Kievan Russia, the Sweden of Gustavus Adolphus, and classical Greece: one can identify many such golden ages.

A problem was that such golden ages often sat uneasily with later nationalist purposes. For the Greek Orthodox church, pagan classical Greece was hardly a model. Renaissance Italy and classical Greece might represent glorious civilizational achievements but they were also regions divided into city-states which frequently warred with one another. Many of the heroes of these ages unfortunately seemed concerned with non-nationalist values (for example, Gustavus Adolphus and the cause of Protestantism) or at least indifferent to national issues. Heinrich Himmler found it regrettable that the Teutonic Knights, with their vow of chastity, failed to realize the mission of populating Eastern Europe with fine specimens of the Aryan race.

National Character

If there is a national identity it should also be embodied in a national character. This is a crude concept when applied to the stereotyped 'other' but usually took on a more nuanced form in relation to the national self. A good example can be found in Krishan Kumar's depiction of the "moment of Englishness" in the late Victorian and Edwardian period.[33] The focus is on an idealized version of the rural south: an a-political world of the village, fairness, and social harmony. It clearly is a reaction against industrial, urban and imperial Britain. National character privileges social types: the peacetime occupations of the village, well supported by the folk song and dance revival movement. By the inter-war period this was a dominant cultural tone, exemplified in the imagery and beliefs of a major politician such as Stanley Baldwin, or the involvement of one of the leading historians of the day, G. M. Trevelyan, in the early years of the National Trust.

Yet there was always debate. Against the 'little Englandism' of the folk movement, or writers like Hilaire Belloc and G.K.Chesterton, there was the British and imperial tone set by a writer such as Kipling. It has recently been argued that the 'little England' theme loomed much larger in the culture of the period although this is less clear at elite than popular levels.[34] One finds a similar debate in the historiography with someone like Seeley deploring the internal focus of so much 'English' history and insisting on a global, imperial framework instead. One can note a similar complexity in historiographical debates of this period in Germany and France with an imperial-national and an anti-imperial-national aspect. It seems to me to be a general characteristic.

Tension Between 'Essence' and 'Change'

The constant presence of such debates points to tensions within the nationalist framework. On the one hand the nation is presented as a fixed, a-historical category. This is most clearly expressed in the race idea, but also in notions of fixed vices and virtues, or one golden age which one should seek to recover, in essence if not detail. Yet at the same time the nation is seen to be a historical category which changes over time. Modern nationalists could see the absurdity of bourgeois figures dressing up as Hermann or Hus, Alfred or Vertingetorix. One way of trying to handle the tension was to insist on a spiritual continuity which took on different historic forms and scales. Thus the British parliament owed its origins and basic values to the Saxon hundreds, but clearly was a modern institution. The Afrikaaner could draw inspiration from the Great Trek even if now the task in the middle of the twentieth century was to achieve control over an urban economy. The necessary vagueness of such ideas enabled historians much room for maneuver.

Tension Between Institutions and Culture

Institutions offer the best framework for a historical account stressing continuity over a long period of time. Institutions provide both an identifiable structure which transcends generations and also produce the very evidence on which any credible modern historical writing must base itself. This is above all the case with governmental institutions. National historiography crystallized around modern nation-state institutions and naturally such historians looked to the earlier history of these institutions for their sources and their focus.

A long institutional history then makes possible a persuasive national historiography. England is a case in point. Here is a territorial polity to be traced back at least to the late Anglo-Saxon period and which is the principal vehicle of national history. So when G. R. Elton writes a history of 'England' in a series called history of 'peoples' he focuses almost entirely on monarchy and parliament.[35] When John Roberts came to write the preface as general editor for the various volumes that made up the *New Oxford History of England* he could state succinctly that:

> the institutional core of the story which runs from Anglo-Saxon times to our own is the story of a state structure built round the English monarchy....[36]

It becomes progressively more difficult where no such government over a long period can be identified. Sometimes therefore historians shift their attention to other institutions such as churches, guilds, and town governments which are taken to characterize a national history. Some Italian nationalist historians, for example, saw the glory of Italy in its city-states, even if these divided the nation (and only covered a part of the country). Sometimes a 'core' state is identified which 'grows' like the French monarchy or, much more recently, the Prussian state, but these frequently map badly on to the 'national'. In many cases there is not even such a core institution. At that point historians retreat to non-institutional history, starting (if appropriate) with elite culture, even if only in remote pasts, and then moving to folk and popular culture. However, this then raises the general problem that the nation – conceived as an inclusive group with a distinct culture and character – is difficult to relate to elite institutions and political history. All rich national historical accounts seek to combine the two – a 'pure' ethnic/cultural or a pure civic/political nationalism only work as fantasies – but the two make uneasy bedfellows.

Documentation and Constraints

One of the constraints upon all but the most crude and manipulated nationalist historical accounts relates to the acceptance of standards concerning the existence and use of sources. Thomas Masaryck, for example, recognized that certain documents cited to support an argument about Czech national identity in the medieval period were forgeries. Such constraints are largely negative: one cannot lay claim to historical events or personages on the basis of false documents. However, especially when dealing with poorly documented periods, nationalist historians can speculate as to how the gaps in the evidence and thus a chain of argument might be 'filled'. Furthermore, much nationalist historiography is based on 'identity' arguments; that is, what some event or person would have meant to people in terms of how they identified themselves. Given the absence of reliable evidence about identity questions such claims cannot be tested. Put the two together and one can read many pages of historical work which make unverifiable claims for, say, national sentiment in England and France during the Hundred Years War, or what most 'Germans' thought about Napoleon during the 'war of liberation'. In many cases the historiography works in a circular way; once one accepts that a particular building style or form of dress or event has a national meaning, then further examples can be adduced to strengthen the national argument. Sometimes sources double as direct testimony and contextual support. We know very little about Bede's England other than what he tells us, so Bede becomes a major source for the kind of England that existed at the time which in turn, quite naturally, supports specific claims he makes about the English. At the same time one can ignore inconvenient evidence, for example that the archaeological material from Bede's time does not register differences between the societies he classified as different.

Finally all historians have to make decisions about what is 'significant' or 'typical' and these decisions are not based on the sources but on the interests and mode of argument of the historian. A nationalist approach to the past will naturally shape such decision making.

National and Nationalist Historiography

The weaknesses of nationalist historiography are usually fairly obvious. It is teleological in that it sees implicit in the early stages of a national history the ripening of the later stages, and often regards that later ripening as some kind of final cause. Hegel's cunning of reason becomes the cunning of the nation. Nationalist historical writing is usually very presentist, making specific claims about the past on the basis of specific concerns in the present and anticipated future. It is often manipulated in blatant political fashion. Consequently it changes rapidly as present circumstances change.

National historiography is stronger. By national historiography I mean a view of the nation as the framework within which historical study takes place and historical accounts are ordered. The 'nation-as-frame' is not the same as the 'nation-as-historical agent' which is the nationalist approach. Given the dominance in the modern era of a world ordered by nation-states and the widespread success of "banal nationalism" which takes national identity for granted, a natural category, it is not surprising that historiography, especially for the more modern period, finds it difficult to avoid the national. Professional history arose in symbiosis with the nation-state and is appropriately organized. Historians define themselves as French, German, American or whatever, meaning not their own nationality but the identity of the field of history they study. (Though it is also the case that most French historians are French, most British historians are British, etc.). Many professional associations and journals are based on these identifications (English Historical Review, American Historical Review, French Historical Studies, etc.). Even historians who identify themselves in other ways (e.g. as economic or social historians, as comparative historians, as historians of gender or class) often fit their studies into the national frame or make trans-national comparisons which treat the nation as the comparator unit. The systems of higher education in which professional history formed are also nationally distinct in their organization and modes of training, which in turn gives a distinct character to national historiography. Finally, given that the greatest historical interest is in the most recent period, one which saw the apparent generalization of the nation-state form across the world, national historiography seems a perfectly appropriate way of organizing historical inquiry. It does not make much sense for earlier periods but one finds the national grid still being deployed for the medieval and even ancient periods.

Trans- or supra-national issues in the contemporary world (e.g. in ecological problems or cultural and elite transfers) are helping to generate new forms of historiography which break with the nation-as-frame.

There is a revival of interest in world history and in forms other than the 'history of civilizations' which have earlier predominated.[37] For the most part, however, the national approach continues to dominate. It means that at times of tension or crisis, this historiography can quickly be pushed in a nationalist direction, rather like nationalism can quickly move from a 'banal' to a 'hot' form.[38]

Contestation

In nationalist historiography the nation is presented as a consensual category: there is basic unity within the nation (except for traitors and internal enemies, but these are not truly national and their identification and defeat contributes to unity). This unitary society is pitted against the world beyond it. In fact, however, nationalist historiography is always a contested field unless authoritarian government represses such disputes. Obviously there are differences *between* nationalist historiographies; a Czech and a German, a Rumanian and a Hungarian nationalist history are bound to conflict. More interesting is conflict *within* nationalist debates. Jacobin and royalist accounts of French history are equally nationalist but in contradictory ways. Given the presentist and teleological nature of nationalist historical writing, this is simply a reflection of contemporary political conflict in which all parties claim the nation, and therefore its history, as their own. Whenever one hears a politician preach the case for presenting a consensual account of one's national history which will promote pride and strong identity, one should bear this point in mind. People only agree on national history when history no longer matters to them; when it has become picturesque heritage or tourist fare.

Not only is there contestation at any one time but also shifting positions over time. For example, English nationalism as a political programme and related historiography was for some time absorbed into or subordinated to a British imperial project and, therefore, history. The same point applies to any imperial nationality; the Germans in the Habsburg Empire, the Russians in the Romanov and Soviet empires, the 'Turks' in the Ottoman Empire. However, the decline or even collapse of empire sees a rapid shift into nationalist forms; the rise of Russian nationalism in the post-Soviet period, Turkish nationalism towards the end of the Ottoman empire, German nationalism in Austria once the Habsburg empire collapsed, a renewed concern with 'English' identity given the loss of overseas empire and the success of non-English devolution within the British Isles.

Another type of case comes with the collapse of regimes which had suppressed national historical accounts or imposed one particular version.

New regime require new, often national histories. Thus post-apartheid South Africa deposes Afrikaaner and race accounts, even if there is no fully developed alternative nationalist account yet prepared. Post-Soviet states turn to a Ukrainian or Armenian or Lithuanian national history.

Less dramatically, the shift from one kind of state to another produces changes. Spanish nationalist historiography has changed dramatically with the transition from dictatorship to democracy. A 'European Union of the regions' buttresses the concern with small, regional nationalisms even if these sometimes only take a cultural form and do not make political demands. The defeat and partition of Germany led to new ways of writing national history. Even a shift from a left to a right wing government can lead to corresponding shifts of emphases in national accounts. There simply is no agreed nationalist account of any national history.

The Confusion of 'Is' and 'Ought'

Why expend so much energy in showing that Albanians were in 'Kosovo' before the Serbs, that Jews occupied a largely empty Palestine, which corresponds to territory occupied by Jews in the accounts of the Old Testament, that Rumanians were a distinct group of pre-Roman natives or alternatively Roman settlers? Apart from the notion that a strong sense of identity must be rooted in history, the assumption is that demonstrating an 'is' – or rather a 'was' – concerning the national past enables one to assert an 'ought' in the national present and future. This is the morality of possession: to 'own' history is to establish claims. Ironically, though with only limited success, so-called 'first nations' or 'indigenous peoples' have managed to exploit this morality against the western societies which displaced them, claiming special recognition in Canada, the USA, Australia and elsewhere. The notion of 'apologizing' for the deeds of past societies is based on the same assumption. It is linked to the idea that political claims should be based on the 'natural' (nations are natural) whereas that which is 'artificial' is inauthentic. The desire to 'naturalize' political claims and institutions is widespread in contemporary culture and gives otherwise implausible nationalist historiographies much persuasive power.

Conclusion

It is easy enough to identify the typical fallacies of nationalist historiography: the arbitrary assumption of some a-historical essence which underlies historical change and development and the teleology which sees the end of national history as implicit in its earlier stages. However, when nationalist historiography is diluted into national historiography – a frame rather than an essence or agent, a set of constraints rather than a destiny – it is more difficult to identify these weaknesses. Given that in the modern period nationalism as politics, as sentiments and as intellectual doctrines has become increasingly important, a nationalist view of the past acquires a certain plausibility. When wedded to powerful political interests and values it can shape people's view of the past.

Beyond the empirical and individualizing critiques typical of the procedures of the historian, how can one confront these problems in historical writing? In my view it is necessary to have a general understanding of *why* nationalist historical writing exists and that means understanding how and why nationalism has come about. There is a rich and complex debate on this matter which I cannot consider here. Some of the positions in that debate in my view mirror the fallacies of nationalist historiography, such as primordialism which assumes the enduring, long historical character of nation and nationalism.

My own position is that of a modernist.[39] I argue that nationalism is most significant as a politics which has altered the nature of the global political system in the last two hundred years and that this politics is related to ways in which state and society have become modern. The modern system of sovereign, bounded and (theoretically) democratic states has generated as a mirror image a view of the world as divided into self-determining, distinct, bounded and inclusive societies called nations. It is a powerful political image and in many ways it has a self-fulfilling quality but ultimately that is all it is. Therefore it has no purchase at all on pre-modern history (which is what vitiates all long-run national as well as nationalist historical accounts) and some purchase in the modern era insofar as these have been shaped by nationalist movements, sentiments or ideas. Even then one should see the limited, changing and contested nature of these politics, sentiments and ideas and also the varied and contingent relationships between the three kinds of events. In that way one is able not only to be skeptical about any nationalist history but able to explain just why such debatable claims are made, and often in a persuasive way.

Notes
[1] Cornelius Tacitus, *The Agricola and the Germania,* translated and introduction by H. Mattingly, translation revised by S. A. Handford (Harmondsworth: Penguin, 1970); The Venerable Bede, *A History of the English Church and People,* translated and introduction by Leo Sherley-Price, revised by R. E. Latham (Harmondsworth: Penguin, 1968).

[2] For the way Rome created ethnic labels for "barbarians" which the latter then appropriated for themselves, see Peter Heather, *The Fall of the Roman Empire: A New History* (London: Macmillan, 2005). For medieval English ethnography see John Gillingham, *The English in the Twelfth Century: Imperialism, National Identity, and Political Values* (Woodbridge: Boydell Press, 2000).

[3] F. M. Barnard, *Herder's Social and Political Thought: From Enlightenment to Nationalism* (Oxford: Clarendon Press, 1965).

[4] Friedrich Meinecke introduced the distinction between *Staatsnation* and *Kulturnation* in *Cosmopolitanism and the National State* (Princeton, NJ.: Princeton University Press, 1970) originally published in 1907. The distinction was applied to the study of nationalism by Hans Kohn in his pioneering work *The Idea of Nationalism: A Study in its Origins and Background* (New York: Macmillan, 1944) reprinted with an introduction by Craig Calhoun (New Brunswick: Transaction Publishers, 2005). The notion was developed in formal political theory terms by John Plamenatz, "Two Types of Nationalism," in *Nationalism: the Nature and Evolution of an Idea*, ed. Eugene Kamenka (Canberra: Australian National Press, 1973).

[5] The distinction is criticised in a series of essays in *Nationalism in Europe during the Long Nineteenth Century*, ed. Timothy Baycroft and Mark Hewitson (Oxford: Forthcoming).

[6] A useful collection of essays for western Europe is Stefan Berger, Mark Donavan, and Kevin Passmore eds, *Writing National Histories: Western Europe since 1800* (London: Routledge, 1999). Berger is coordinating a large research project which should soon be publishing a series of books on the professionalization and nationalisation of historical writing in Europe.

[7] Generally on German historiography see Georg Iggers, *The German Conception of History: The National Tradition of Historical Thought From Herder to the Present* (Middletown, CT.: Wesleyan University Press, 1968).

[8] Robert Gildea, *The Past in French History* (New Haven and London: Yale University Press, 1994); Steven Kaplan, *Farewell, Revolution: The Historians' Feud: France, 1789/1989* (Ithaca and London: Cornell University Press, 1996); John Burrow, *A Liberal Descent: Victorian Historians and the English Past,* (Cambridge: Cambridge University Press, 1981).

[9] See Erik Grimmer-Solem, *The Rise of Historical Economics and Social Reform in Germany 1864-1894* (Oxford: Oxford University Press, 2003).

[10] I use the term "historicism" to mean the view that all human activity is through-and-through historically conditioned and, therefore, beyond the understanding of any generalising discipline such as political economy.

[11] Benedict Anderson, *Imagined Communities: Reflections on the Origins and Spread of Nationalism* 2nd ed. (London: Verso Press, 1991).

[12] See the catalogue for the 2003 exhibition: James Hamilton ed., *Turner's Britain*, (London: Merrell, 2003). For romantic painters one should not exaggerate the "national"; the "regional" also had its place in the conception of a special sense of place in which landscape and people are bound together in unique ways.

[13] See the catalogue: Monika Flacke, *Mythen der Nationen: Ein europäisches Panorama* (Munich and Berlin: Koehler and Amelang, 1998). The early stages of the politicisation of art in relation to a national state is considered in the second part of the book by Holger Hoock, *The King's Artists: The Royal Academy of Arts and the*

Politics of British Culture 1760-1840 (Oxford: Oxford University Press, 2004). The impact of a historicist and national view on the art museum in Germany is presented in James Sheehan, *Museums in the German Art World From the End of the Old Regime to the Rise of Modernism* (Oxford: Oxford University Press, 2000).

[14] For nationalists the nation must precede nationalism which is its expression. For many non-nationalist historians and theorists there must be some prior national cultural formation on which political nationalism can build. Anthony Smith writes of "ethno-symbolism" as a set of myths, memories, customs etc. which provide this foundation. Miroslav Hroch envisages nationalism as developing first as an intellectual and cultural movement before it can go on to take political form. Instrumentalists, at the other extreme, consider nationalist discourse as an opportunistic rhetoric which can be quickly learnt from others and applied to new situations if this appears advantageous. These debates are closely linked to, but distinct from, those regarding the modernity or otherwise of both nations and nationalism. For good surveys of such debates see: Anthony D. Smith, *Nationalism and Modernism* (London: Routledge, 1998); Umut Özkirimli, *Theories of Nationalism: A Critical Introduction* (London: Macmillan, 2000); Paul Lawrence, *Nationalism: History and Theory* (London: Longman, 2005).

[15] For a number of the central European figures, see Monika Baár *The Historian and the Nation in the Nineteenth Century: The Case of East Central Europe* (Oxford Historical Monographs Series) (Oxford: Oxford University Press, forthcoming).

[16] Walter Carruthers Sellar and Robert Julian Yeatman, *1066 and All That: A Memorable History of England; Comprising, All the Parts You Can Remember Including One Hundred and Three Good Things, Five Bad Kings, and Two Genuine Dates* (London: Methuen, 1930).

[17] The seminal work on this aspect of the subject is Michael Billig, *Banal Nationalism* (London: Sage, 1995).

[18] I developed this argument in "Historians and the Nation," in *History and Historians in the Twentieth Century*, ed. Peter Burke (Oxford: Oxford University Press, 2002): 55-87.

[19] Arguably the ethnic or cultural element could be downplayed at this time. On the one hand, ethnic cleansing in Europe, including that of the Germans in eastern Europe after 1945, made it possible to ignore ethnicity as a source of identity in most cases. On the other hand, the anti-colonial movements, seeking independence within the boundaries of the colonial state, stressed political freedom rather than race or ethnicity. Nevertheless, such elements quickly emerged both in the national historiography designed to boost the existing state and even more as a way of representing the claims of "stateless nations" within such states.

[20] For Poland see Norman Davies, *God's Playground: A History of Poland Vol. 2: 1795 to the Present* (New York: Columbia University Press, 1982). What is interesting is that when Davies came to write general histories of Europe and then Britain, he sought to abandon this national approach, even avoiding the word Britain in the title of the latter work. Idem, *Europe: A History* (Oxford: Oxford University Press, 1996) and *The Isles: A History* (London: Macmillan, 1999).

[21] See the chapter by M. K. Flynn and Tony King "Renovating the Public Past: Nation Building, Symbolic Reparation and the Politics of Heritage in Post-Apartheid South Africa," in this book.

[22] For example, Terence Ranger in the historiography of East-Central Africa, especially Tanzania and Zimbabwe. Just to complicate matters further, this historical work with its stress on African initiative was in part influenced by the "history from below" movement in Britain in the 1960s - above all, the path-breaking work of E. P. Thompson, *The Making of the English Working Class* (London: Gollancz, 1963). And in turn this non-European perspective had an influence back upon European historiography, for example in Ranger's co-editing with Eric Hobsbawm of the collection of essays *The Invention of Tradition* (Cambridge: Cambridge University Press, 1983) which has gone through numerous reprints.

[23] The Soviet constructions of non-Russian republics and the celebration of nationality and ethnicity, key factors in providing both a political and a cultural basis for the post-Soviet national states, nevertheless tended to focus on ethnography rather than history, especially as such history would tend to take an anti-Russian form. To that extent national historians in the new national states had to start afresh.

[24] For the ethnicisation of Turkish identity in relation to the Armenians, and of class enemies in communist countries, see now Michael Mann, *The Dark Side of Democracy: Explaining Ethnic Cleansing* (Cambridge: Cambridge University Press, 2005).

[25] Mann, *The Dark Side of Democracy*, makes much of the micro- to macro-ethnicity shift. A superb recent history which puts notions of "archaic globalisation" and the nationalisation of religious and civilizational differences at the heart of its account, is C. A. Bayly, *The Birth of the Modern World, 1780-1914: Global Connections and Comparisons*, (Oxford: Blackwell, 2004).

[26] I consider some of these arguments in "Changes in the Political Uses of the Nation: Continuity or Discontinuity?" in *Power and the Nation in European History*, ed. Len Scales & Oliver Zimmer (Cambridge: Cambridge University Press, 2005): 67-101.

[27] See Heather, *Fall of the Roman Empire*, and also Martin Thom, *Republics, Nations and Tribes* (London: Verso, 1995).

[28] See Patrick J. Geary, *The Myth of Nations: The Medieval Origins of Europe* (Princeton, NJ.: Princeton University Press, 2002).

[29] It is interesting that the catalogue for this exhibition has prefaces from the British and Turkish Prime Ministers and clearly the exhibition is closely linked to the timing of the Turkish application to join the European Union. *Turks: A Journey of a Thousand Years* ed. David J. Roxburgh (Royal Academy of Arts, London, 2005).

[30] The dispute mattered even under communism in Rumania. See Katherine Verdery, *National Ideology Under Socialism: Identity and Cultural Politics in Ceausescu's Romania* (Berkeley: University of California Press, 1991).

[31] See Burrow, *A Liberal Descent*; K. Pomian, "Franks and Gauls" in *Realms of Memory: Rethinking the French Past. Vol 1: Conflicts and Divisions*, ed. Pierre Nora, trans. Arthur Goldhammer, (New York: Columbia University Press, 1996).

[32] Linda Colley, *Britons: Forging the Nation, 1707-1837* (New Haven and London: Yale University Press, 1992).

[33] Krishan Kumar, *The Making of English National Identity* (Cambridge: Cambridge University Press, 2003).

[34] See Bernard Porter, *The Absent Minded Imperialists: What the British Really Thought About Empire* (Oxford: Oxford University Press, 2004).

[35] G. R. Elton, *The English* (Oxford: Blackwell, 1992).

[36] I quote from the preface to K. Theodore Hoppen, *The Mid-Victorian Generation 1846-1886* (Oxford: Clarendon Press, 1998), vii.

[37] See Bayly, *The Birth of the Modern World*, as well as Benedikt Stuchtey and Eckhardt Fuchs eds, *Writing World History: 1800-2000* (Oxford: Oxford University Press, 2003).

[38] These are distinctions made by Billig, *Banal Nationalism*.

[39] On debates between modernists and non-modernists see Anthony D. Smith, *Nationalism and Modernism: A Critical Survey of Recent Theories of Nation and Nationalism* (London: Routledge, 1998).

MUSEUMS, MONUMENTS AND CULTURAL PROPERTY
CREATING A NATIONAL HERITAGE

2
(Re)Presenting Roman History in Italy, 1911-1955

Joshua W. Arthurs

The Museo della Civiltà Romana (MCR, Museum of Roman Civilization), located on the southern outskirts of Rome, is unique among the Eternal City's innumerable antiquities museums.[1] Whereas the venerable halls of the Vatican collections or the Capitoline, with their glittering patrimony of marbles and bronzes, celebrate the aesthetic triumphs of antiquity, the MCR presents visitors with "...objects from family life, customs, work implements...faithful testimony of the life of a people who, despite the distance of the centuries, are in essence so close to us...."[2] Many guide-books attest to the Museum's "excellent and comprehensive exhibits" and its ability "to put Rome's scattered fragments and artifacts into context very helpfully."[3] Composed entirely of reproductions—plaster casts, scale models, photographs and maps—the MCR is considered one of the capital's most thorough and informative museums, an ideal first stop for tourists seeking a primer in Roman history.

At the same time, however, some of elements of the Museo della Civiltà Romana are immediately disquieting. The *Time Out Guide to Rome* notes its "vast blank walls and massive straight columns;" *Let's Go: Rome* warns that "if there was ever an intimidating museum façade, this is it."[4] A large table in one room converts prices from an ancient Roman market into Italian Lire—a double anachronism, given the advent of the Euro and the fact that the Lire are listed at their 1937 value. These and many other elements point to the Museum's previous incarnation as the Mostra Augustea della Romanità (MAR, Augustan Exhibition of the Roman Spirit), created by the Fascist regime in 1937-1938 to commemorate the bimillenary of the emperor Augustus' birth. The majority of the objects on display were acquired during this period, and the imposing neoclassical edifice which houses the collections was originally projected as part of the Esposizione Universale di Roma (EUR, Universal Exhibition of Rome) of 1942, an unrealized "Olympiad of Civilizations" marking the twentieth anniversary of the "Blackshirt Revolution." While the present site of the

MCR was constructed after the Second World War—inaugurated in 1952 and completed in 1955—it adheres closely to blueprints produced in the late 1930s.

The shadow of Mussolini's Italy therefore looms large over the installations, with their monumentality and severe whiteness; however, the institutional roots of the MCR stretch back even further. The Mostra Augustea was itself an elaboration of a 1911 archaeological exhibition (the Mostra Archeologica) organized by the renowned archaeologist Rodolfo Lanciani as part of an international exposition commemorating the fiftieth anniversary of Italian unification. Although it operated on a far smaller scale, the Mostra Archeologica represents the point of origin for a trajectory marked by tremendous continuities, in terms of the objects on display, methodological and institutional principles, and personnel.[5]

The development of the Museo della Civiltà Romana therefore spans Italy's tumultuous twentieth century, offering a compelling case study in the ways in which different regimes—Liberal, Fascist, and Republican—conceived of classical Rome's position within the nexus of Italian national history, and how this in turn both informed and reflected the display of archaeological objects. What valence did the Roman past hold across the radical transformations that occurred between the eve of the First World War and the aftermath of the Second? How were identical artifacts deployed and re-deployed in these multiple contexts? How did the archaeologists of the 1930s attend to the task of "Fascistizing" an exhibition created during the Liberal era, and how, subsequently, did the Museum's postwar curators handle the heavy burden of the Fascist past?

To date, the historiography on this subject has been fairly unanimous in drawing sharp distinctions between the bombastic excesses of the Mostra Augustea della Romanità and the more legitimate representation of history in the Mostra Archeologica of 1911 and the present-day Museum. The Fascist-era exhibition is often depicted as the apogee of the regime's "cult of Rome," a rhetorical, pseudo-scientific exercise whose primary purpose was "not historical reconstruction, but recruiting the past for the present."[6] Conversely, while some observers have identified a degree of "moderate and contained provincial triumphalism" in 1911, and recognized an anticipation of the imperial rhetoric of the 1930s, Lanciani has been lauded for his scientific rigor and for assembling a collection of archaeological reproductions "which to this day present the public with an understanding of ancient life, with extraordinary immediacy and accessibility."[7] Similarly, the MCR is seen as conserving "the most scientifically valid part of the Mostra Augustea," functioning as an important center for the study of antiquity, once shorn of its Fascist excesses.[8]

While my intention is by no means to valorize any aspect of the

Fascist-era project—which was indeed heavily marked by the militarist and expansionist rhetoric of the regime—I believe that the assessment above is problematic in several respects. First, it seems to rest on a less than nuanced conception of the relationship between science and politics, or practice and discourse. This study seeks to demonstrate the extent to which both sides of these binary oppositions are inextricably intertwined and mutually constuitive. Secondly, the characterization of the Mostra Augustea della Romanità as an "ideological" endeavor—in contrast to both its predecessor and its successor—overlooks both the "scientific" aspirations of its organizers and the extent to which both its precursor and successor were also highly imbued with nationalist and imperialist discourses. Finally, the path leading to the current Museo della Civiltà Romana was marked not only by the shifting political landscape of modern Italy, but also by considerable institutional continuities that render simple dichotomies problematic.

In short, I am interested in understanding how we perceive the relationship between the display of the past, ideology (especially with regards to nationalism), and archaeology as a disciplinary practice. Why do we consider one representation of history more "nationalist" or "ideological" than another? At what moment is meaning inscribed in, and ascribed to, archaeological artifacts? Where do science, representation and politics intersect?

"The Indelible Testimony of Latin Greatness": the Mostra Archeologica of 1911

As previously mentioned, this story begins with the 1911 international exposition marking the fiftieth anniversary of Italian unification.[9] In keeping with other expositions and World's Fairs of its day, the *Cinquantenario* was conceived as a celebration of progress, technology and the achievements of bourgeois civilization. This theme resonated particularly strongly in Italy: after fifty years of unity, *Italietta* ("little Italy") continued to lag far behind in economic, social and technological development, and was eager to improve its position on the periphery of European modernity. Accordingly, exhibitions in Turin and Rome would demonstrate Italian accomplishments in every endeavor, from public hygiene and commerce to sport and archaeology. The event, in the words of its promoters, would serve as a stage upon which

the Third Italy, in its daring self-assurance, in the audacity of its ineluctable will, affirms its existence, its unity, to the entire

world…with Rome, the Eternal City, at its head, the cradle of its
civilization, the center and heart of its new destiny.[10]

While the Rome exposition's main pavilions were situated on the
northern edge of the city, the Mostra Archeologica was located to the east,
in the Baths of Diocletian outside Stazione Termini. To many observers,
this locale was as significant as the installations themselves. For centuries,
the ancient Baths had been occupied by wine-sellers, blacksmiths' shops
and other unsavory establishments. Such reminders of Italian backwardness were particularly distressing for the exposition's organizers, as "the
disgraceful sight…gives foreigners an unfavorable indication of how we
attend to the task of preserving this marvelous monument."[11] Restoring
the monument to its original state, argued the mayor, "would be widely praised abroad, where cultured persons are unable to fathom how in
Rome we tolerate such disfigurements of the glorious ruins…."[12] In short,
the excavations were "an undertaking that both science and national de-
corum demand."[13]

Just as the "reclamation" of the Baths was conceived in terms of the
restoration of national dignity, Rodolfo Lanciani believed that the Mostra
Archeologica was motivated by an analogous "triple purpose":

> We tried, above all, to reconstruct a picture of Roman civilization
> under the Empire, asking each of its thirty-six provinces to con-
> tribute some reminder of the benefits it received from Rome in
> various aspects of civic and private life, and especially in terms
> of public works. Then we began the task of restoring to Her—in
> copy form, of course, of course—the artistic treasures that have
> been carried away since the Renaissance, to enrich museums in
> other countries. Thirdly, we have tried to reconstruct monuments
> and statuary groups that the vicissitudes of time have broken and
> scattered.[14]

These goals were explicitly reflected in the composition and organization of the installations. The visitor's itinerary began with a series of three
rooms, devoted to Eternal Rome (featuring personifications of the city and
other divinities), to the *Imperium Romanum* (with mile-markers and columns from distant lands, stressing the extent of Rome's expansion) and
to the Divine Augustus, the founder of the Empire. Having emphasized
the imperial mission emanating from the capital, the rest of the exhibition
was organized on the basis of the ancient provinces, paralleling the national pavilions featured elsewhere in the city. In other words, rather than
France, Germany, Hungary and so on, visitors toured "the three Gauls,

the two Germanias, the two Pannonias, the two Moesias, Dacia, the three Spains, Mauretania, Numidia, Britannia, Belgium, Batavia, and Egypt."[15] One room featured a scale model of fourth-century Rome, built by the French architect Paul Bigot, which offered a leisurely promenade through the ancient city:

> a stroll through imperial Rome thus becomes the easiest and most delightful of things. You are a visitor? Enter the city through the Via Appia, follow Via Nova, bathe in the Baths of Caracalla....Who wouldn't want to devote at least a day of their lives to enjoy the spectacle of imperial Rome, to live for an instant as a contemporary of Trajan and Marcus Aurelius, to roam the streets, the Fora, and the temples of the metropolis, all magically resurrected?[16]

For Lanciani and his colleagues, this resurrection of imperial Rome, particularly as reflected in the geographic layout of the exhibits, would

> demonstrate the work of civilization carried out by Rome in the ancient world: casts, photographs, plans, and designs provide an exact reproduction of the monuments created by Roman genius in the most distant regions of the world, remaining today as indelible testimony of Latin greatness.[17]

The theme of the civilizing mission was further emphasized by the objects on display. Instead of artifacts that reflected indigenous or syncretic ancient cultures, the organizers chose pieces that remained relatively uniform across the provinces: aqueducts, triumphal arches, and bridges. The result was that visitors went from room to room, seeing essentially identical pieces in different national contexts, reinforcing a sense of the unity and uniformity of Roman culture as it spread inexorably through the ancient world, ultimately laying the foundation for modern civilization. For Lanciani, this arrangement demonstrated "how these countries, which were our ancient provinces, are still governed by Roman laws, and how their inhabitants walk on roads that we built, cross mountains through passes that we opened and rivers over bridges that we constructed, drink from aqueducts that we connected, and find refuge for their ships...in the ports that we founded."[18] By extension, modern Europe's debt to the Empire reinforced the claim of cultural and historical primacy made by the most direct descendant of ancient Rome—namely the Italian state, reunited after centuries of internal strife and foreign intervention. The pieces provided by foreign countries represented "an act of filial devotion to the ancient mother."[19] The theme of empire carried an additional resonance in 1911: only months away from the conquest of Libya, the legacy of Rome's *Mare*

Nostrum served as a powerful rhetorical tool for Italian aspirations for an overseas colonial empire.[20]

The other two facets of Lanciani's "triple purpose" involved the restitution of works that had been carried off from Italy since the Renaissance, and the reconstruction of damaged monuments. Given financial and logistical constraints, this could only be achieved through the use of scale models, casts, photographs and other reproductions. While some considered the use of copies to be a major shortcoming of the exhibition (especially considering the extraordinary wealth of originals displayed in the major museums), the organizers argued that this approach represented a major technical innovation. Rome's traditional museums were imposing in their pedigree and formality, and geared almost exclusively to the fine arts; by contrast, Lanciani and his colleagues claimed that their project offered a rational, scientific exposition of the Roman world, allowing visitors to examine the artifacts much more closely than would be possible with originals; scale models, identified with labels, showed fragmented monuments in their original state, often for the first time in centuries. The use of reproductions thus enabled the development of a new collection to rival more established institutions, stressing the provenance and documentary value of the objects over their aesthetic significance. For Lanciani,

> [The exhibition] must not just offer a simple collection of important, curious or beautiful objects, but should be proof of the new energies which the Italian people have decided, in recent times, to devote to the conquest and illustration of this magnificent patrimony of forms and ideas....the Exhibition is designed above all to demonstrate the vigorous energy which Italian archaeologists employed at home and abroad, wherever they were led by visions of new victories for science.[21]

In a sense, then, the Mostra Archeologica celebrated not only the legacy of Imperial Rome—and by implication, the aspirations of modern Italy—but also the emergence of Italian archaeology as a national discipline, on par with the Northern Europeans who for so long had dominated the study of antiquity. This goal was most clearly reflected by the section devoted to Greece, which displayed objects recently recovered from Italian excavations in Crete. Although some reviewers questioned "whether it was wise so to enlarge the original scope of the exhibition as to admit casts illustrative of the whole history of Greek art....the exhibition has thus lost its unity," the Greek rooms ultimately served to provide further evidence of Italy's new standing as an archaeological power.[22] No less than the exhibitions devoted to industry and commerce, the Mostra Archeologica marked Italian progress—in this case, the ability of the nation to reclaim, recover and display its ancient past, just as the excavation of the Baths of Diocletian served to erase reminders of a backwards, medieval Italy.

To continue this mission, Lanciani envisioned the exhibition as a didactic institution, "an aid and...a meeting-place for scholars of Roman *antiquities,* just as other museums served, and continue to serve, for scholars of Roman *art."*[23] He therefore called for the Mostra Archeologica to be transformed into a permanent museum, so that "the youth of Italy will find inspiration in this future Museum of Empire, with all those virtues which made Rome the dominator of the world, morally and materially."[24]

Taking a bath in *Romanità*: the Mostra Augustea della Romanità, 1937-1938

The First World War and the turmoil of the postwar years, culminating in the Fascist seizure of power, meant that Lanciani never lived to see his dream of a permanent institution realized. In 1932, however, the project was taken up by Giulio Quirino Giglioli, a leading Italian archaeologist and Fascist deputy who had served as Lanciani's secretary in 1911.[25] Giglioli proposed that the collection be reorganized and expanded for a new exhibition to coincide with the regime's celebration, in 1937, of the bimillenary of Augustus' birth. With Mussolini's imprimatur, the Mostra Augustea della Romanità opened on the emperor's birthday—September 23rd—comprising over three thousand plaster casts, scale models, photographs and maps; it was held in the renovated Palace of Exhibitions in Rome, where a massive Mussolinian epigraph inscribed over the entrance called for "the glories of the past [to] be surpassed by the glories of the future."[26]

Although Augustus was the central figure, the exhibition was envisioned as a "vivid pageant of Roman history" in which visitors could, in another phrase of the Duce's, "bathe themselves in *romanità."*[27] The collections were greatly expanded, and the installations underwent a dramatic reorganization. In lieu of the geographic layout, the Fascist-era exhibition was divided into three sections. The main floor traced the development of Roman civilization from its legendary origins all the way to the advent of Fascism, with each phase anticipating the telos of Mussolini's new Italy: the conquests of the Republic necessitated the rise of a strong authoritarian leader; the *Pax Romana* ushered in by Augustus was the necessary precondition for the birth of Christ; the Catholic Church kept the flame of *romanità* burning during the centuries of decline, until its revival under the Fascist regime. This message was brought home most forcefully in the final room, devoted to "The Immortality of the Idea of Rome and the Rebirth of Empire in Fascist Italy," inspired by the conviction that

> The Roman imperial idea was not extinguished with the fall of the Western Empire…it persevered mystically during the Middle Ages, and through it came the Renaissance and the Risorgimento in Italy.…With Fascism, with the will of the *Duce*, every ideal, every institution, every Roman deed will return to shine in the new Italy, and after the epic conflict of combatants on African soil, the Roman Empire rises up out of the ruins of a barbarian empire.[28]

The parallels between the Rome of Augustus and Mussolini's Italy were made explicit at every turn. Both the Emperor and the Duce had emerged from a situation of civil disorder to reform and renovate decaying political structures; both had sought to effect a radical moral transformation of their people, drawing inspiration from the immutable values of the *mos maiorum* (the sacred "way of the elders"). In the wake of the conquest of Ethiopia, Mussolini could claim to have emulated the *imperium* of his ancient precursor.

The two other sections of the Mostra Augustea departed from the chronological organization of the main floor. The lower level displayed public works, monumental architecture, roads and the military, echoing the 1911 Exhibition's emphasis on empire and the civilizing mission. The upper floor dealt with aspects of everyday life in ancient Rome, from religion to fashion, family life to music. Although these rooms lacked the explicit symbolism of the main floor, every facet of Roman life was depicted as an anticipation of the disciplined, corporative modernity heralded by Fascism. Room 27, for example, with its models of latrines and sewer systems, documented the Roman state's "instinctive need for cleanliness and bodily hygiene."[29] Room 61, on family life, demonstrated that "the Roman familial institution distinguished itself from that of other ancient peoples because of its healthier and more solid spirit of rectitude and abnegation…fecund virtues that prepared the Roman citizen for the trials and triumphs of public life and for his dominion over the world."[30]

In sum, the Mostra Augustea della Romanità presented a totalitarian, technological, militarized and rigidly hierarchical picture of the ancient world. The thematic organization of the rooms, while disposing with the monotony of the geographic layout, depicted Roman culture in its entirety as uniform and homogenous not only across space, but across time and in every sector of public and private life. As one of Giglioli's collaborators put it, the exhibition "does not seek to illustrate or document events or representations of a historical period, or to limit itself to one branch of human activity; rather, it embraces...every manifestation of a great civilization, the greatest in the ancient world and the foundation for the modern world, over the span of more than a millennium."[31]

Although this tone reflected a shift from the bourgeois universalism of 1911, the Mostra Augustea closely resembled its precursor in method-ological and institutional terms. As before, it was composed entirely of reproductions and models. The plaster casts, proudly executed by Ital-ian experts, gave "a useful homogeneity to the materials and allow[ed] them to be organized in a more modern fashion than would be the case with originals [and] does not present any aesthetic drawbacks, since the technology used has reached the highest level of perfection."[32] The pieces would be arranged "not with the rigid norms of museums, but integrated with texts, photo-montages, maps and diagrams, which together create sections that unite scientific rigor and the liveliness of a modern exposi-tion....In this way, not only specialists, not only those who love history and archaeology, but all Italians can easily find documentation of the glorious first Empire of our people...."[33] To this end, many of the MAR's rooms were designed by young modernist architects, in order to avoid "monotony" and "coldness."[34] In the age of mass politics, the didactic function of the exhibition took on an added dimension. It was conceived as an institution of historical, moral and political education for the masses, and it made skillful use of film and radio to encourage attendance; the regime's "after-work" organization offered package tours and discounted train fares so that Italians from every corner of the country could converge on the capital for the bimillenary celebration. Whereas the archaeologi-cal exhibition of the Liberal era had been "inadequate to the great task of documenting Roman civilization in a totalitarian manner, and limited to narrow scientific documentation," the Mostra Augustea would offer a voluminous but accessible vision of the ancient world that reflected the values and priorities of the New Italy.[35]

Like Lanciani before him, Giglioli aspired to transform the collection into a permanent museum. This wish was granted by the regime: the collections were to be expanded and recast as a permanent Exhibition of *Romanità*, as part of the Esposizione Universale di Roma in 1942. With the Second World War and the fall of the regime, however, this plan never came to fruition.

"An Open Book": the Museo della Civiltà Romana, 1952-1955

Fascism's demise, however, did not mean that Lanciani and Giglioli's goal of a permanent museum was laid to rest. In 1950, the project was revived under the aegis of FIAT, which envisioned a "grand Museum of Latin Civilization, in which Italy would be able to see its original contribution to world civilization fully synthesized, and in which the world could rediscover the origins of so many elements of its culture, and recognize its ties with Rome."[36] The Museum of Roman Civilization (as it was renamed) was inaugurated in 1952 and completed in 1955, under the direction of Antonio Maria Colini, one of Giglioli's collaborators in 1937. Although the installations were to some extent expanded and reorganized, the overall format and tone of the Museum hardly departed from the Fascist-era exhibition. A comparison of the catalogs from 1937 and 1958 demonstrates the considerable correspondence between the two exhibits. The first set of rooms, organized chronologically, offered a synthesis of Roman history from Romulus to the rise of Christianity; the second section displayed monumental architecture and public works; and the last part of the Museum dealt with everyday life in antiquity. Over the years, individual pieces have been added or removed, and modifications made to adapt the collections to their new surroundings (for example, the room devoted to the army in the Mostra Augustea was divided into four smaller rooms in the MCR), but there have been no substantial changes that would disrupt the overall structure established in 1937. There were some attempts to efface the most explicit reminders of its earlier incarnation – the historical rooms no longer culminated in Fascist Italy, and the ubiquitous quotations from Mussolini were gone – but in its form and content, the Museum preserved the fundamental characteristics of its predecessor. The objects on display (as always, consisting solely of reproductions) were more or less identical, and even the Museum's catalog was little more than a reprint of the catalog of the Mostra Augustea with the most glaring Fascist phrases excised. As the *American Journal of Archaeology* noted approvingly, "the parts having a temporary or propaganda character, according to the political climate, have disappeared; all the material has been arranged according to more logical, rigorous criteria...."[37]

For Colini, as for Lanciani and Giglioli before him, the Museum would be a "living organism," a rigorous, "scientific" institution compared to Rome's traditional art-historical museums. Like his predecessors, he saw its value primarily in didactic terms, believing that it would serve as

a precious means of instruction for young people, especially those studying the classics; it offers direct and extremely interesting comparisons between contemporary life and antiquity for every category of professional, artist, and artisan. For every kind of tourist, it is an indispensable resource for visiting the city, its famous monuments and its museums.[38]

In the wake of Fascism's demise and the total discrediting of aggressive expansionist rhetoric, Colini had to tread carefully in expounding upon the Museum's larger significance. While the 1911 exhibition had stressed the universality of the City's imperial mission, and the Mostra Augustea had depicted the Roman world as a disciplined, organic martial state, he acknowledged that "…we have to recognize that we have fairly vague ideas about ancient civilization in general, and in our case, about Roman civilization."[39] The chief value of the objects on display was therefore their ability to evoke the details of daily life in the ancient world:

> What did the ancient Romans eat? How did the wealthy and the most humble classes live? How did they travel? How were the soldiers of various specialties dressed and armed?....How did Roman women dress? How did they do their hair?[40]

Whereas claims of scientificity and didacticism had once been inextricably linked to the "national" mission of the exhibitions, they now served to distance the Museum from its association with its Fascist precursor; technology was recast as a guarantor of rigor and objectivity, free from ideological contamination. Furthermore, argued Colini, the devastation wrought by the war meant that many of the Museum's holdings were now the only extant copies of valuable artifacts. Wedding technical achievement with accessibility, the new Museum would therefore serve several interconnected functions: it would provide a rational, scientific presentation of Roman history in contrast to the city's traditional museums, which were "fundamentally concerned with artistic phenomena, and overlook the other aspects of ancient life"; it would serve as an educational institution for every type of visitor; and it would act as a scientific archive of Roman antiquities for researchers, unparalleled in volume and breadth.[41] Though the MCR has seen its collections enlarged and its building renovated over the years, it has maintained essentially the same mission and format since 1955.

What conclusions can be drawn from this narrative, and how does it relate to the problem of nationalism, historiography and the (re)construction of the past? Clearly, all three cases demonstrate the malleability and multiple meanings of the Roman past in Italy. In 1911, the Roman Empire was cast as a precursor to liberal bourgeois internationalism and as a justification for Italian colonialism. In 1937, it was depicted as a blueprint for Fascist modernity, a fully mobilized and hierarchical mass society ruled by discipline. The current Museum presents Roman history in the manner of a secondary-school textbook.

Beyond reiterating the flexibility and subjectivity of historical representation, however, this story is also useful in elucidating the relationship between the historical disciplines and the political culture of nationalism. In the wake of constructivist theories of the nation, of "imagined communities" that "invent traditions," many contemporary scholars have tended to posit the relationship between nationalism and the historical disciplines as one of ideological distortion or "using and abusing" the past: archaeology and museology are cast as objective sciences producing neutral results, which are in turn subject to manipulation, particularly on the level of interpretation and display.[42]

Some recent scholarship, however, has demonstrated the extent to which the nation not only influences, but *constitutes* the historical disciplines.[43] Certainly professional archaeology and museology—in contrast to earlier antiquarianism—emerged in the nineteenth century as an instrument of the modern nation-state.[44] The material evidence produced by excavations and put on display for a general public provides scientific legitimation to myths of national origin, not just reflecting pre-existing discourse but producing historical "facts" that are constuitive of national identity.[45] Thus archaeology must be understood not just as a science subject to manipulation, but as a form of textual production; not solely the recovery of a static, objective past but a rhetorical strategy located in the present.[46] I would therefore like to suggest that the historical disciplines should not be seen only as practices which can serve as vehicles for nationalist discourse, but as "national sciences," as profoundly national projects in themselves.

The three incarnations of the archaeological exhibition offer a compelling case in point. The "nationalization," "Fascistization," or "de-Fascistization" of Roman history cannot be attributed solely to the presence or absence of ideologically charged symbols, but more fundamentally to the physical layout of the installations themselves. As Eilean Hooper-Greenhill has argued, the taxonomy of museological artifacts – though presented as self-evident or "obvious" – both alters the significance attributed to the objects and expresses underlying social values and power relationships.[47] In this instance, the objects acquired their particular resonance from their respective taxonomic structures: the geographic layout of 1911 was essential to its celebration of progress and universalism; the historical and thematic approach in 1937 was essential to the juxtaposition of Augustan Rome and Mussolinian Italy; and, conversely, the absence of a fundamental reorganization in 1955 has meant that the present-day Museum serves as much as a monument to

Italy's inability to come to terms with the Fascist past as it does as a lesson in Roman history.

In the end, though, the continuities between the three are just as suggestive as their differences. Lanciani, Giglioli and Colini all made similar claims to scientificity, envisioning their projects in terms of a national mission and using technology and modern display techniques to mediate between Roman past and Italian present, in contrast to traditional art-historical museums; the exclusive use of reproductions in all three cases was the key aspect of this orientation. All three archaeologists shared the conviction that the exhibitions should serve a didactic function, particularly for future generations. The frequent distinction between the "scientific" representation of the past of 1911 and the present-day Museum on the one hand, and the rhetorical excesses of the Mostra Augustea on the other, therefore depends on a problematic distinction between practice, representation, and meaning.

Notes

[1] This paper is based on research at the Archivio Centrale dello Stato (ACS), the Archivio Storico Capitolino (ASC), the Istituto Nazionale di Studi Romani (ISR), and the Museo della Civiltà Romana (MCR), which also houses the archives of the Mostra Augustea della Romanità. Special acknowledgement should go to the staff of the MCR (in particular to Dr. Clotilde D'Amato) and the City of Rome's Superintendence of Antiquities and Fine Arts.

[2] Matilde Burri Rossi, *Il Museo della Civiltà Romana: itinerario ragionato per una visita al Museo* (Rome: C. Colombo, 1976), 8.

[3] *Let's Go Italy*, (Cambridge: MacMillan, 2003), 512; and *TimeOut Guide to Rome*, (London: Penguin Books, 2001), 155.

[4] *TimeOut Guide to Rome*, 155; and *Let's Go: Rome*, (New York: St. Martin's Press, 2004), 176.

[5] For an institutional history of the three exhibitions, produced by the personnel of the Museum, see Giuseppina Pisani Sartorio, ed., *Dalla mostra al museo: dalla Mostra archeologica di 1911 al Museo della Civiltà Romana* (Venice: Marsilio, 1983). For a detailed analysis of the Mostra Augustea della Romanità, and some discussion of the other cases, see Friedemann Scriba, *Augustus im Schwartzenhemd? Die Mostra Augustea della Romanità* (Frankfurt am Main: Peter Lang, 1995).

[6] Marla Stone, "A Flexible Rome: Fascism and the Cult of Romanità," in *Roman Presences: Receptions of Rome in European Culture, 1789-1945*, ed. Catherine Edwards (Cambridge: Cambridge University Press, 1999), 215. See also Mariella Cagnetta, "Il mito di Augusto e la "rivoluzione" fascista," *Quaderni di Storia* 2, no. 3 (1976).

[7] Giuseppina Pisani Sartorio, "Dalla mostra al museo," in *Dalla mostra al museo*, 15.

[8] Giuseppina Pisani Sartorio, "Il Museo della Civiltà Romana," in *Dalla mostra al museo*, 106. For a similar assessment, see Alessandro Guidi, "Nationalism without a Nation: the Italian Case," in *Nationalism and Archaeology in Europe*, ed. Margarita Díaz-Andreu and Timothy Champion (London: UCL Press, 1996), 113.

[9] The Kingdom of Italy was proclaimed in 1861, though Rome remained under Papal rule until 1870. For a general discussion of the *Cinquantenario* of 1911, see Gianna Piantoni, ed., *Roma 1911* (Rome: De Luca, 1980).

[10] Program of the Executive Committee, 6 July 1909, in ACS PCM 1910, fasc.16.

[11] Orlando to Tittoni, 21 July 1904, ACS MPI AABBA 1908-1912 Div. I, b.151, fasc.2808.

[12] Aldibrandi-MPI, 20 October 1906, ACS MPI AABBAA 1908-1912 Div. I, b.151, fasc.2808.

[13] MPI parliamentary report, 28 January, 1907, ACS MPI AABBAA 1908-1912 Div. I, b.151, fasc.2808.

[14] *Catalogo della Mostra Archeologica nelle Terme di Diocleziano*, (Bergamo: Istituto Italiano d'Arte Grafiche, 1911), 9.

[15] Ibid.

[16] "Un vernissage archeologico alle Terme," *Il Giornale d'Italia*, 21 April 1911.

[17] Comitato Esecutivo per le Feste Commemorative del 1911 in Roma, *Guida ufficiale delle esposizioni di Roma* (Rome: G. Bertero & Co., 1911), 202.

[18] *Catalogo della Mostra Archeologica nelle Terme di Diocleziano*, 9-10.

[19] Attilio Rossi, "Le Terme Diocleziane e la Mostra archeologica," *La Tribuna*, 7 March 1911.

[20] Archaeology played an important part in Italian claims to colonial territories in North Africa; see Massimiliano Munzi, *L'epica del ritorno: archeologia e politica nella Tripolitania italiana* (Rome: L'Erma di Bretschneider, 2001); and Marta Petricioli, *Archeologia e Mare Nostrum: le missioni archeologiche nella politica mediterranea dell'Italia, 1898/1943* (Roma: V. Levi, 1990).

[21] Program of the Executive Committee, 6 July 1909, in ACS PCM 1910, fasc.16.

[22] Mrs. Arthur (Eugenie) Strong, "The Exhibition Illustrative of the Provinces of the Roman Empire, at the Baths of Diocletian, Rome," *Journal of Roman Studies* 1.1 (1911), 44.

[23] Rodolfo Lanciani, "La Mostra Archeologica alle Terme Diocleziane," *Roma – Rassegna Illustrata dell'Esposizione del 1911*, 27 March 1911, 11-12. Italics in original.

[24] *Catalogo della Mostra Archeologica nelle Terme di Diocleziano*, 11.

[25] In fact, the collections of the Mostra Archeologica were reopened to the public in 1926 as a new Museum of the Roman Empire, with Giglioli as director, although this was a temporary arrangement that maintained essentially the same structure as the 1911 Exhibition.

[26] On Fascist *romanità*, see my forthcoming doctoral dissertation, *Roman Modernities: Nation, Empire and Romanità in Fascist Italy*. See also Mariella Cagnetta, *Antichisti e impero fascista* (Bari: Laterza, 1979); Luciano Canfora, *Ideologie del classicismo* (Turin: Einaudi, 1979); Andrea Giardina and André Vauchez, *Il mito di Roma da Carlo Magno a Mussolini* (Bari: Laterza, 2000); Luciano Perelli, "Sul culto fascista della romanità," *Quaderni di Storia* 3, no. 5 (1977) and Romke Visser, "Fascist Doctrine and the Cult of Romanità," *Journal of Contemporary History*, no. 27 (1992).

[27] Pamphlet *Mostra Augustea della Romanità – Bimillenary of the Birth of the Emperor Augustus*, 1937; in MCR MAR, loose files.

[28] *Mostra Augustea della Romanità: catalogo,* 1 ed. (Rome: C. Colombo, 1937), 362.

[29] Ibid., 378.

[30] Ibid., 599.

[31] Massimo Pallottino, "La Mostra Augustea della Romanità," *Capitolium* 12, no.12 (1937), 520-521.

[32] *Mostra Augustea della Romanità: catalogo,* x-xi.

[33] Ibid., xvi.

[34] On the design of the MAR's rooms, see Marco Rinaldi, "La Mostra Augustea della Romanità (1937-1938): architettura, scenografia e propaganda in alcuni progetti inediti di allestimento," *Ricerche di Storia dell'Arte,* no. 63 (1997).

[35] Pallottino, "La Mostra Augustea della Romanità," 526.

[36] Colini to dalla Torre, 7/3/50, in ASC Rip. X, 1920-1953, b.278, fasc.4. In fact, FIAT had been involved in the construction of the museum prior to the fall of the regime.

[37] B.M. Felleti Maj, *American Journal of Archaeology* 65, no.3 (1961), 327.

[38] Undated and unsigned, 1955, MCR, loose file "Museo dell'Impero – Schede ecc."

[39] Ibid.

[40] Ibid.

[41] Ibid.

[42] For this approach, see for example Paul Graves-Brown, Siân Jones, and Clive Gamble, eds, *Cultural Identity and Archaeology: the Construction of European Communities* (New York: Routledge, 1996); Philip Kohl and Clare Fawcett, eds, *Nationalism, Politics and the Practice of Archaeology* (Cambridge: Cambridge University Press, 1995); and Michael Galaty and Charles Watkinson, eds, *Archaeology under Dictatorship* (New York: Kluwer Academic/Plenum Publishers, 2004). In the Italian context, see especially Daniele Manacorda and Renato Tamassia, *Il piccone del regime* (Roma: Armando Curcio, 1985); and Luisa Quartermaine, "'Slouching Towards Rome': Mussolini's Imperial Vision," in *Urban Society in Roman Italy,* ed. T.J. Cornell and Kathryn Lomas (London: University College London Press, 1995).

[43] See for example Margarita Díaz-Andreu García and Timothy Champion, "Nationalism and Archaeology in Europe: an Introduction," in *Nationalism and Archaeology in Europe.* ed. Margarita Díaz-Andreu and Timothy Champion.

[44] For a useful history of modern archaeological theory, see Bruce Trigger, *A History of Archaeological Thought* (Cambridge: Cambridge University Press, 1989).

[45] This argument is particularly well-articulated in Nadia Abu El-Haj, *Facts on the Ground: Archaeological Practice and Territorial Self-fashioning in Israeli Society* (Chicago: University of Chicago Press, 2001).

[46] This argument owes much to Michael Shanks and Christopher Tilley, *Re-Constructing Archaeology: Theory and Practice* (New York: Routledge, 1992).

[47] Eilean Hooper-Greenhill, *Museums and the Shaping of Knowledge* (New York: Routledge, 1992), 5-6.

3

Renovating the Public Past
Nation-building, Symbolic Reparation and the Politics of Heritage in Post-Apartheid South Africa

M.K. Flynn and Tony King

Introduction

Since the end of apartheid in 1994, the new South African government has attempted, as a crucial element of its democratizing project, to implement a policy of civic nation-building which allocates, as stipulated by the 1996 Bill of Rights, "everyone" the same entitlements and obligations. This is intended as a deliberate replacement for the apartheid-era (1948-1990) construction of South African nationhood around the interests and identity of a white minority which was accompanied by the *de jure* exclusion of the black majority from even the most basic claim to citizenship. The shift from a racially exclusive to non-racially inclusive definition of South African nationhood dovetails with an official policy of national reconciliation, as articulated especially by the Truth and Reconciliation Commission (TRC).[1]

While the TRC is best known for conducting hearings on past human rights abuses and evaluating resultant amnesty applications, another important role of the Commission has been to articulate a broad vision of what national reconciliation must entail. This includes both atonement for the past and creation of a democratic public culture premised on the primacy of universal human rights. One element for reconciliation mandated by the TRC is symbolic reparation with a new emphasis on public commemoration—through memorials, monuments and museums—of the histories and experiences of all South Africans, and especially those individuals and groups historically oppressed under apartheid.

However, existing South African museums and other heritage sites have not experienced the heavy hand of government, which has strongly encouraged transformation, but without explicitly stipulating content. Where transformation and change have taken place to varying degrees, in some institutions the process has looked more like simply pasting token black history onto the old white displays, an issue compounded by a general lack of understanding of what is required for comprehensive transformation.[2] Moreover, while the state has, in the main, left the old South African heritage sector relatively untouched, it has embarked on a series of high profile developments, known as the Legacy Project, to redress the balance in presentation and create new museums and monuments reflecting a post-apartheid civic identity and nationhood that transcends ethnic divisions. The introduction of the Legacy Project has, in effect, created a two-tier heritage sector: one from the old South Africa struggling in piecemeal fashion to update itself, and one from the new South Africa commemorating its heroes and struggles. This layered approach to the presentation of public history and national identity reflects a violent and divided past, while also representing early efforts to fashion a new civic identity for all South Africans, and has been described as making South African history "a twice-told tale."[3]

This chapter concentrates on two sites that illustrate the refashioning of heritage and the public realm in the new South Africa. Both sites were central to apartheid iconography related to the Battle of Blood River of 1838. The battle's anniversary on 16 December was an apartheid-era public holiday, and after the fall of apartheid was kept as a national holiday renamed the Day of Reconciliation. The first site is the Ncome/Blood River site in KwaZulu-Natal, at the location of the battle itself where the old Afrikaner memorial is now just across the river from a new memorial and museum that pay tribute to the Zulu dead. The second, outside Pretoria, is the Voortrekker Monument, built to commemorate the Afrikaner migration of the nineteenth century into the interior, and its new rival on a neighboring hill, Freedom Park. Both Blood River and the Voortrekker Monument are central to the public narrative of white South Africa, and their fate in post-apartheid South Africa is full of significance for the democratic dispensation. Importantly, the Ncome museum and Freedom Park do not replace the old white sites. Rather, they present a deliberate point-counterpoint of the newly inclusive South Africa next to the old segregated one. As such, they are metaphors for the status of the public past in post-apartheid South Africa, where old sites, memories and identities, exist side by side with new ones.

Public history and political transition

In common with many other societies undergoing political transition, South Africa contends with monuments and public symbols of the old order sitting in varying degrees of discomfort with the new. Not only does this reflect changes to officially sanctioned and promoted memory, but, more importantly, it provides visual, material and durable reminders of, as well as symbolic reinforcement for, permanent changes to the sanctioned allocation and exercise of political power. In other words, transition in the present and the future mandates a concomitant transition of the remembered past in terms of content, presentation and interpretation.

The situation in some former Soviet republics is analogous to South Africa's and, despite the Baltic states' significance in spearheading the USSR's dissolution, their example should not be taken as necessarily indicative. Popular movements in the Baltic states from 1987 through independence in the early 1990s worked to replace the Soviet-dominated official national narrative. However, in other former Soviet republics the commemoration of the Soviet legacy is more equivocal. Certainly, not all Soviet monuments have been retired as archaic artifacts, such as those displayed with deliberate irreverence *en masse* at the Soviet Sculptures Park in Lithuania. For example, monumental statues of Lenin continue to stand in some Ukrainian cities, especially those in the east and south of the country, as they have in parts of Russia and Kazakhstan. As late as 2000, a monument to Josef Stalin, originally removed in 1956, was restored in Georgia's second city of Kutaisi.[4] Stalin, once Georgia's favorite son, may not be overwhelmingly popular, but his museum in Gori was left standing to cater to a nostalgic minority.[5]

Juxtaposition of the historically old and new and the related question of potentially dissonant commemoration are also a matter of contention in parts of Western Europe. For example, in Northern Ireland debate predictably polarized over future re-development of the site of the now empty Long Kesh prison, otherwise known as the Maze.[6] While the prison once housed both republican and unionist prisoners, its unhappy history is particularly associated with iconic moments of the republican struggle, such as the Hunger Strikes and Dirty Protest. Understandably suggestions from republican organizations for establishment of a museum or other type of official heritage site, an idea only possible to contemplate in the context of an ongoing peace-process and reconfiguration of regional politics, met with overt objection from some unionist quarters. As a result, official regeneration plans for the site, tabled early in 2005, do not recommend establishment of a museum, but instead an "International Centre for Conflict Transformation" to be explicitly developed alongside a number of other undertakings, most notably a multi-purpose sports stadium.

Meanwhile, in Spain the Socialist Party won the 2004 election, overturning the eight-year premiership of the centre-right Popular Party, whose detractors sometimes accuse it of nostalgia for the rule of General Francisco Franco. The new government has encouraged a reconfiguration of not only the politics of the present, but also the politics of the past. This is manifested by parliament, three decades after the death of Franco, requesting that the remaining symbols of his dictatorship be removed from public buildings.[7] This will be a difficult task, since in Madrid alone over 160 streets have names with Francoist connotations, and some would say it is also surprising given the negotiated agreement for a "closure of the remembered past" in the 1970s.[8] Discussions and debates about the redefinition, role, content and significance of Spanish public memory of the Francoist past have proliferated dramatically in the last few years along with the number of relevant books.[9] This has been encouraged by recent excavation of the remains of republican soldiers killed during the Civil War (1936-39) while fighting the Francoist insurgents, a project carried out and initially publicized by the Association for the Recovery of Public Memory.[10]

Changing public history in South Africa

As in Spain, Northern Ireland and the former Soviet Union, the extent of South Africa's political transformation is reflected in changes, proposed and actual, to its commemorated public history. On the eve of the first democratic elections in South Africa in 1994, the public past was so skewed towards the whites that there was not a single statue, monument or site dedicated to a black South African.[11] An indication of the size of the heritage sector under apartheid is that, from 1936 to the late 1980s, over 700 places had been declared national monuments, and over half that number had been declared so after 1969.[12] As part of the negotiated transition from apartheid, the heritage sector was left broadly untouched, and museums and sites that had been financed by the public purse under apartheid continued to be so under the new democratic dispensation. Unsurprisingly, the journalist and writer John Matshikiza wrote that after only a few years of democracy that "monuments to the power of apartheid are everywhere" and South Africa had had "an inconclusive sort of revolution."[13]

Echoing the report of the Arts and Culture Task Group (ACTG), established in 1994 to advise on the transformation of the heritage sector, the poet Mongane Wally Serote, former Deputy Minister for Arts and Culture, stated that "the African voice has been silenced and trampled on" and that it was time to redress the balance.[14] In 1996 the South African government's policy analysis of the heritage sector, contained in the *White Paper on Arts, Culture and Heritage*, clearly defined where the problems lay.[15] The heritage sector that the democratic government inherited "lacked coordination …many communities do not have access to museums, and cultural collections are often biased."[16]

This sat comfortably with the TRC's recommendation for symbolic reparation through a refashioning of the public realm to recognize the suffering caused by apartheid. It is in this capacity, therefore, as a manifestation of symbolic reparation, that the politics of heritage in post-apartheid South Africa have a greater significance than simply the practicalities of updating existent museums and replacing old monuments. Symbolic acts are significant beyond what is immediately apparent, and a case can be made for symbolic reparation as bloodless.[17] It costs less than financially compensating as many individuals as possible, and exacts no price from the former oppressors in terms of money or prison time. Individuals are not asking for amnesty in return for confessing to torture or murder. Instead, symbolic reparation refashions the public domain to include the memories of the formerly oppressed without – in South Africa's case – completely erasing those of the oppressors who, after all, continue to live in the same country as their victims.

As a result of the negotiated nature of the transition, there has been no wholesale purge of the heritage sector or closure of apartheid-era museums. The Department of Arts, Culture, Science and Technology (DACST) adopted a list of twenty four Declared Cultural Institutions (DCIs) in 1998.[18] All are museums or sites considered worthy of preservation and receive an annual subsidy from what became the Department of Arts and Culture (DAC, Arts and Culture were separated from Science and Technology in 2000), although the rationale for why these and not other sites are considered "national" is cloudy.[19] All but one are connected to or were built by the apartheid regime. The only addition to the list since 1994 is Robben Island, the notorious former prison off Cape Town. The subsidizing of apartheid-era monuments has been controversial as former DACST minister Lionel Mtshali stated that the "continued declaration of colonial buildings as national monuments by the National Monuments Council is indeed a sickening reality."[20]

In order to recognize the histories of the previously marginalized, the DACST launched the flagship Legacy Project in 1996.[21] This is a deliberate, highly visible move to build a number of new monuments and sites relevant to the new South Africa. It is reflective of inclusiveness that the policy of reconciliation suggests and is in line with the ANC's cultural policy to devote attention to the neglected and hidden histories of the majority.[22] Just as the pre-1994 heritage sector and the DCIs mentioned above reflect the old South Africa, the Legacy Project reflects the new dispensation. Keeping the heritage institutions of the old and new South Africa administratively separate may appear to contradict the idea of developing a unified nation, but it is easier to redefine an inclusive heritage if a clean slate of new resources exists.[23] In effect, two parallel heritage sectors are operating in South Africa. As the then DACST minister, Lionel Mtshali, said:

> These projects … were conceptualized to fill an important but re-grettable vacuum in the presentation of the history and heritage of this country. Our argument is that while we have no intention of removing any statues, existing monuments or heritage sym-bols, the priority should now be to redress the gaps left by colo-nialism, apartheid practices and sheer greed on the part of some of those who went before us. The time has come for these matters of heritage to be treated with the dignity that befits their stature, which is the restoration of the human self.[24]

Important sites were identified to be funded by the DAC in the same way as the DCIs, and initially the different projects were slated for deliv-ery in 1998 and 1999. The sites almost invariably draw from the history of the anti-apartheid struggle in the twentieth century, with the exception of the Anglo-Boer war site outside Vereeniging (south of Johannesburg) and the Blood River Commemoration/Ncome in KwaZulu Natal. Some have a practical use, such as the Old Fort in Johannesburg that is now part of the Constitution Hill development housing the Constitutional Court. Finance is, in the first instance, through DAC's own budget, while the Cabinet and Treasury will be involved in larger projects.[25] All these projects have either been completed, in the case of the Mandela Museum in Umtata, or are in the process of being finished. By the end of 2008 the whole of the Legacy Project should be ready and open to the public.

Blood River and Ncome (KwaZulu Natal)

From 1836 a series of Afrikaner, or Boer, migrations from the Cape into the interior, commonly called the Great Trek, brought Afrikaners into contact and conflict with a variety of African polities and states. On 15 December 1838 one *voortrekker* column in what is modern KwaZulu-Natal camped overnight on the banks of the Ncome River and drew the wagons into a circular laager or defensive position. This laager withstood a series of attacks by Zulu regiments the following day. It is said that 3,000 Zulu soldiers were killed without the loss of a single Boer life.[26] Moreover, the Boers had made a covenant promising to build a church, if God granted them victory and to some people the victory against overwhelming numbers was more than the superiority of gunpowder over spears: it was a sign of God's favor.[27] As a result, the Battle of Blood River became central in the iconography of Afrikaner nationalism. The 16 December was declared a public holiday by the Union government in 1910. Originally known as Dingaan's Day, after the Zulu king at the time of the battle, the holiday was renamed Day of the Covenant in 1952 by the National Party government to focus on the vow to God and the idea of manifest destiny. The site of the battle became a place of religious pilgrimage for many Afrikaners, something that continues to this day.[28] As one celebrant says, "the people here take this absolutely seriously. It is not just empty symbolism or the fulfillment of an annual ritual—it is the confirmation of a promise they made to God."[29] Another called it "a covenant forged in blood."[30] While pilgrimages to the site began in earnest in the 1930s, the bronze ox-wagon replica laager was not erected until 1971.[31]

Since the Blood River site is tied to white Afrikaner identity and is synonymous with the subjugation of the South African interior, its reinterpretation in a democratic South Africa is symbolic of more than just the building of a new museum. The site has obvious resonance with Zulu nationalism, as the site of a major battle. In addition, 16 December 1961 was chosen for the start of uMkhonto weSizwe's armed struggle against apartheid.[32] The day was also adopted by the ANC as Heroes' Day from 1961 until 1990, drawing a parallel between armed resistance to white domination in the 1830s and the late twentieth century.[33]

The Ncome site was declared as part of the Legacy Project and, because Ncome itself is remote, is administered by the Voortrekker Museum in Pietermaritzburg, some 100 kilometers away. Like other developments of the Legacy Project, it was paid for by the DAC and not the local provincial government, in this case that of KwaZulu-Natal. Today the Ncome site comprises a museum of Zulu militaria and culture built "in the shape of the Zulu war horn formation" offering a "positive reinterpretation of the 1838 war and Zulu culture in general"[34] (see Fig. 1, page 59, and Fig. 2, page 60).

Interestingly the Ncome museum was the first Legacy Project to be opened officially, even if at the time it had not yet been built. This took place on 16 December 1998, or, in other words, the Day of Reconciliation as Day of the Covenant had been renamed. Keeping 16 December as a public holiday in post-apartheid South Africa was a deliberate decision because it "focused on reconciliation among former enemies."[35] Importantly, the opening was also a symbol of reconciliation between the ANC and the Zulu-nationalist Inkatha Freedom Party (IFP) which had competed, often violently, for influence in KwaZulu-Natal in the run-up to the 1994 election. The opening ceremony was attended by Thabo Mbeki (then Deputy President), the IFP leader Chief Mangosuthu Buthelezi (then Home Affairs Minister and formerly Chief Minister of the homeland of

KwaZulu), King Goodwill Zwelethini and national and provincial leaders, as well as a crowd of 6000.[36] At the time, nothing had been finished
except for a single wall.[37] The Johannesburg weekly newspaper, the *Mail
& Guardian*, reported that two separate Day of Reconciliation ceremonies
would be held, a sentiment supported by the Foundation of Blood River
(the then owner of the Blood River site) that stated "two different cultures
are involved."[38] The Foundation's chair, Hennie de Wet, thought that "the
two memorials adjoining each other could be a symbol of reconciliation
and how two cultures could co-exist, as well as an added tourist attraction.
A small bridge was planned to span the drift and allow sightseers access
to both memorials."[39]

The Ncome museum itself was opened in November 1999, almost a
year after the site's opening ceremony. The museum is the only Legacy
Project initiative that portrays only one ethnic group—the Zulu—rather
than trumpeting the diversity of South Africa. As a tour guide told the
authors in April 2002, "this is not about reconciliation. It is about a war
between two nations."[40] Problematically the remoteness of the Ncome site
makes it expensive to maintain and manage. The then Deputy Director-
General of DACST, Musa Xulu, was fired in October 2000 for misconduct
connected to two tenders to build roads to the site, and the cost of flying
in seven helicopters full of VIPs to the opening of the museum was com-
mented on unfavorably by the press.[41]

The juxtaposition of Ncome/Blood River is obvious to any visitor.
The two sites are barely one hundred meters apart, and visible as though
cheek-by-jowl from the road (Fig. 1), even though some commentators
claim that the Ncome Museum is far from the scene of the battle.[42] The side
of the Ncome museum that faces the circular laager of wagons of Blood
River is pointedly lined with Zulu regimental shields (Fig. 2). The bridge
has not been built, a process "halted by acrimonious threats to blow it
up."[43]

But even Blood River is not preserved in aspic. At the Day of the
Covenant gathering in 2003 at the Blood River site, four black families
in cars followed the Boer horsemen through the crowds, declaring "we
are inquisitive," much to the consternation of more traditional members
of the audience who observed something unthinkable in the old days of
apartheid.[44] As though to underline the division between Blood River and
Ncome that day, "across the river , the ululating cries of Zulu women,
the beating of drums and the loud crunching of their dancing feet on the
ground offered a stark contrast to the religious pall in the laager. The after-
effects of history were glaring as both groups celebrated the same epochal
event yet blatantly ignored each other."[45]

The Voortrekker Monument and Freedom Park, Pretoria

In similar fashion to the Blood River Monument, the Voortrekker Monument was built as a symbol of white Afrikaner subjugation of the interior. If Blood River was about victory over the Zulus against overwhelming odds through God's favor, then the Voortrekker Monument represented the establishment of Afrikaner power in the country's capital. Construction began in 1938 and the monument opened on the Day of the Covenant, 16 December, in 1949. Significantly, the monuments drew together strands of Afrikaner identity, so much so that the white Prime Minister of neighboring Southern Rhodesia (now Zimbabwe), Godfrey Huggins, refused to send a message of congratulations because it smacked of Afrikaner republican disloyalty to the British Empire.[46]

The Voortrekker Monument was intentionally built on a tall hill overlooking central Pretoria and within line of sight of the Union Buildings.[47] The Union Buildings were (and remain) the official seat of the administrative arm of government and were completed in 1913 to commemorate the establishment of the Union of South Africa in 1910.[48] Although the Union Buildings were built (and thus named) to symbolize white reconciliation after the South African War of 1899-1902, they were nonetheless a symbol of British domination and South Africa's status within the British Empire, hence the importance to Afrikaner nationalists of the Voortrekker Monument within sight and on a taller hill[49] (see Fig. 3, page 60).

The Monument itself resembles the *Volkerschlachtdenkmal* (Battle of Nations Monument) built outside Leipzig to celebrate Napoleon's defeat in 1813 by a combined Prussian, Russian, Swedish and Austrian army, and opened in 1913 on the hundredth anniversary of the battle.[50] Drawing on the idea of manifest destiny of the Afrikaner people, the Voortrekker Monument has a symbolic altar, much like the one in the *Volkerschlachtdenkmal*. The monument's centerpiece is an opening on the dome that directs a shaft of sunlight onto the inscription "Ons vir jou Suid-Afrika" ("We for thee, South Africa") at midday on 16 December.[51]

Day of the Covenant celebrations continue to be held at the Voortrekker Monument to this day, although crowds are getting smaller. During the apartheid years, crowds of tens of thousands regularly attended Day of the Covenant ceremonies at the Monument. In 2004, only 3500 Afrikaners, some in traditional dress, gathered to celebrate the day, wave old South African and Transvaal flags, and sing *Die Stem*, the apartheid-era national anthem.[52] A Voortrekker Monument spokesperson stated that the event was cultural, not political, and an opportunity for Afrikaners to celebrate their own heritage.[53] As though to emphasize the marginalization of apartheid-era public discourse, *The Star*, Johannesburg's biggest daily newspaper, concentrated on President Mbeki's speech to the gathering at Freedom Park and his emphasis on the symbols of a new, democratic South Africa.[54]

However, it would be wrong to imagine the context of the Voortrekker not moving with the times. Perhaps because the Monument is so contentious and physically and metaphorically imposing, its activities are considered newsworthy, even though for black South Africans "the Voortrekker Monument has always been something you prefer to forget about."[55] After the 1994 elections, rumors spread that it would be demolished, or painted pink and turned into a gay nightclub. In 1995 the Afrikaans-language soft porn magazine *Loslyf* published a photo shoot of Trek leader Hendrik Potgieter's great-great granddaughter in a state of undress in front of the monument.[56] Yet, according to the Monument's CEO, Gert Opperman, it is thriving.[57] Since taking over in 1999 he has worked to demythologize the monument and turn it less into a shrine to Afrikaner nationalism and more into a museum of Afrikaner culture "that welcomes everybody," adding—contentiously—that the monument "has nothing to do with the apartheid period."[58] The displays have been updated and present the Great Trek as merely one of a number of migrations during human history, with maps of the Trek alongside maps of Jewish, Chinese and Greek diasporas. There is also signage in African languages, which is a deliberate welcome to black visitors. The Monument's demythologization has worked to the extent that DAC opinion is that Opperman has done "an admirable job" and the monument's annual public subsidy was doubled to R825,000 (US$145,000) in 2004.[59]

The Voortrekker Monument's counter-point is Freedom Park, which is being built on the neighboring hill of Salvokop. It is the biggest and most expensive part of the Legacy Project and the democratic South African government's retort to the Voortrekker Monument. According to Serote, CEO of Freedom Park, the choice of Salvokop was to make Freedom Park visible when entering Pretoria "from any angle" and, significantly, from the Voortrekker Monument.[60] From Freedom Park's own memorial the Voortrekker Monument is behind the viewer. Yonah Seleti, Freedom Park's Heritage Manager, described the tableau as looking back to the Voortrekker Monument representing the divided past, and Freedom Park with its views over the city as symbolizing the future "where all the people of the country will have a place in the sun."[61]

Freedom Park's mandate is, according to Serote, explicitly political. Its purpose is to serve as a practical example of the TRC's emphasis on symbolic reparation and the refashioning of public history. It is to be a visible symbol of a new South African nation to "emancipate the African voice."[62] The site is based around three pillars or areas. A Garden of Remembrance with indigenous plants and contributions from every province is the first, and is the only part of Freedom Park fully functioning at the time of writing. The second is a memorial "South African spiritual place" to remember anti-apartheid cadres and activists. The third pillar is a museum tracking southern African history over 3.6 billion years.[63]

An *isivivane*, or shrine, at the heart of the Garden of Remembrance is treated as "almost a holy place" in clear comparison to the quasi-religious symbolism of the Voortrekker Monument across the highway, and Mbeki and Serote performed a traditional cleansing ceremony when the site was opened in March 2004.[64] Indeed, Serote took the opportunity to stress that the Garden was "something bigger than the Voortrekker Monument since it was in memory of all the fallen heroes and heroines of South Africa whatever their race."[65] The Garden has views of the Voortrekker Monument and Union Buildings, giving rise to a triangle of significant buildings and sites all of which have claimed, and continue to do so, their primacy in the iconography of South Africa.

Conclusion

The contested nature of the politics of heritage is amply demonstrated by the point-counterpoints of Blood River/Ncome and Voortrekker Monument/Freedom Park. On 16 December every year separate celebrations are held at both sites. It is significant that, while the rhetoric at Freedom Park and, to a lesser extent, Ncome concentrates on reconciliation, democracy and freedom from oppression, the Afrikaner commemorations display nostalgia for a past that, outside the immediate environment of the single day's events, is considered by many to be bad taste in contemporary South Africa. Significantly, the two sites examined above fulfill similar purposes in redressing the public sphere. However, the moral balance of the two is different. Ncome seeks *equal* status with the Blood River monument to show the Zulu as equally deserving of commemoration as the Boers. In that sense, the juxtaposition of the Ncome museum is a way of simply balancing the scale. Freedom Park, conversely, seeks to demonstrate moral *superiority* over the Voortrekker Monument as a symbol of post-apartheid South Africa, especially considering the significance of the Voortrekker Monument in apartheid iconography. In either case, however, public history in South Africa is being deliberately refashioned not to erase the colonial past, but to remember it in its fuller context, thereby representing the history of all South Africans.

Notes

[1] The TRC ran from 1996 to 2001, and considered over 30,000 cases of gross human rights abuses during apartheid. See the following for analyses and critiques: Wilmot James and Linda van de Vijver. *After the TRC: Reflections on Truth and Reconciliation in South Africa* (Cape Town: David Philip Publishers, 2000).

[2] The authors have discussed this elsewhere. See chapter: M.K. Flynn and Tony King, "South African Identity after 1994: Museums and Public History" in *Cultures of Violence*, ed. Tobe Levin (Amsterdam: Rodopi, 2006).

[3] Kenneth Walker, "The History of South Africa: A Twice-Told Tale," *Carnegie Reporter*, Vol 2/4 (Spring 2004). http://www.carnegie.org/reporter/08/southafrica/index.html (accessed 6 November 2004).

[4] *Georgia Daily Digest*, 18 December 2000, http://www.eurasianet.org/resource/georgia/hypermail/200012/0044.html (accessed 29 January 2005).

[5] Natalia Antelava, "Stalin Still Revered in Georgia," BBC News, 21 December 2001, http://news.bbc.co.uk/1/hi/world/europe/2596671.stm (accessed 29 January 2005).

[6] Details about the government-sponsored public consultation, undertaken in 2003-4, about the site's redevelopment, along with related information, can be viewed at: http://www.newfuturemaze.com (accessed 30 January 2005).

[7] Giles Tremlett, "Call to Cleanse Spain of Franco," *The Guardian* (London), 4 November 2004, 12.

[8] Soledad Alcaide, "167 calles de Madrid conservan nombres asociados al franquismo," *El País* (Madrid), Madrid supplement, 1 December 2004, 1 and 5 and M.K. Flynn, "Constructed Identities and Iberia," *Ethnic and Racial Studies* 24/5 (2001): 703-18.

[9] For example, see: Antonio Castillo and Feliciano Montero, eds, *Franquismo y memoria popular: Escrituras, voces y representaciones* (Madrid: Siete Mares, 2003); Juan Sisinio Pérez Garzón, et al., *La Gestión de la memoria: La historia de España el servicio del poder* (Barcelona: Crítica, 2000); and Emilio Silva et al., eds, *La memoria de los olvidados: Un debate sobre el silencio de la repression franquista* (Valladolid: Ambito, 2004).

[10] See the Association's homepage: http://www.memoriahistorica.org/index.php (accessed 30 January 2005).

[11] Kenneth Walker, "The History of South Africa."

[12] Andrew Hall and Ashley Lillie, "The National Monuments Council and a Policy for Providing Protection for the Cultural and Environmental Heritage," *South African Historical Journal* 29 (1993), 112-3.

[13] John Matshikiza, "Time For a Cultural Revolution," *Mail & Guardian*, 11-17 January 2002, 22.

[14] K. Mpulwana et al., "Inclusion and the Power of Representation: South African Museums and the Cultural Politics of Social Transformation," in *Museums, Society, Inequality* ed. Richard Sandell (London: Routledge, 2002), 249. Walker, "The History of South Africa".

[15] The White Paper can be found at: http://www.dac.gov.za/legislation_policies/white_papers/white_paper_on_arts_culture_heritage.htm (accessed 12 December 2004).

[16] Ibid., ch. 5, para. 9.

[17] Desmond Tutu, *No Future Without Forgiveness* (London: Random House, 1999), 227.

[18] A full list can be found at: www.dac.gov.za/about_us/cd_heritage/declared_ cultural_institutions/declaredcultural_inst.htm (accessed 1 September 2004).

[19] Mpumlwana et al., "Inclusion and the power of representation," 248.

[20] LPHM Mtshali, "Address" in *The Reinterpretation of the Battle of Blood River/Ncome: One Day Seminar Held on 31 October 1998, University of Zululand, Kwa-Dlangezwa* ed. Department of Arts, Culture, Science and Technology, (Pretoria, DAC, 1998), 10. The authors are grateful to Henrietta Ridley for drawing attention to this publication. The National Monuments Council was renamed the South African Heritage Resources Agency (SAHRA) in 1999.

[21] DACST was split into two in 2001. Heritage became the remit of the new Department of Arts and Culture (DAC).

[22] J. E. Tunbridge and G. J. Ashworth, *Dissonant Heritage. The Management of the Past as a Resource in Conflict* (New York: John Wiley & Sons, 1996), 259.

[23] Ibid., 247.

[24] Mtshali, "Address," 9.

[25] See www.dac.gov.za/about_us/cd_heritage/legacy_project/legacy_project. htm (accessed 18 March 2003).

[26] Hermann Giliomee, *The Afrikaners* (London: Hurst, 2003), 234.

[27] The Church of the Covenant is in Pietermaritzburg.

[28] A useful potted history of Ncome/Blood River as Afrikaner symbolism is Anton Ehlers, "Apartheid Mythology and Symbolism. Desegregated and Re-invented in the Service of Nation-building in the New South Africa: the Covenant and the Battle of Blood River/Ncome," http://academic.sun.ac.za/history/dokumente/FOUNDINGMYTHSCONFERENCEREFERAATAPARTHEID_MYTHOLOGY.pdf (created 25 January 2005) (accessed 27 June 2005).

[29] "Burden of Whiteness," *Mail & Guardian*, 5 April 2004, http://www.mg.co.za/articledirect.aspx?articleid=45992&area=%2finsight%2finsight__national%2f, (accessed 23 November 2004).

[30] "Blood Feud on the Banks of the River," *Mail & Guardian*, 18 December 2003, http://www.mg.co.za/articledirect.aspx?articleid=39288&area=%2finsight%2finsight__national%2f, (accessed 20 December 2003).

[31] J. Grobler, "Afrikaner Perspectives on Blood River: A Never-Ending Debate?' in *The Reinterpretation of the Battle of Blood River/Ncome: One day seminar held on 31 October 1998, University of Zululand, Kwa-Dlangezwa,*, ed. Department of Arts, Culture, Science and Technology (Pretoria: DAC, 1998), 47; Bloedrivier Terreinmuseum, *Welkom by die Bloedrivier Terreinmuseum,* brochure, n.d.

[32] Nelson Mandela, *No Easy Walk to Freedom* (London: Heinemann, 1990), 120. *uMkhonto weSizwe* (MK for short) was the armed wing of the ANC. The name means 'Spear of the Nation'.

[33] J. Sithole, "Changing images of the Battle of Blood River/Ncome," in *The Reinterpretation of the Battle of Blood River/Ncome: One Day Seminar Held on 31 October 1998, University of Zululand, Kwa-Dlangezwa,* ed. Department of Arts, Culture, Science and Technology (Pretoria: DAC, 1998), 34-5.

[34] Voortrekker Museum, *Ncome Museum*, brochure, 2001.

[35] "Mbeki Lauds SA Reconciliation," *Mail & Guardian*, 16 December 2004, http://www.mg.co.za/Content/l3.asp?cg=BreakingNewsNational&ao=176759 (accessed 16 December 2004).

[36] Jabulani Maphalala, *Ncome Museum*, brochure, n.d.

[37] Interview, Henrietta Ridley, Acting Director, Voortrekker Museum, Pieter-maritzburg, 3 April 2002.

[38] "No Unity on Day of Reconciliation," *Mail & Guardian*, 4 December 1998, http://www.mg.co.za/articledirect.aspx?articleid=180555&area=%2farchives__ print_edition%2f (accessed 24 July 2004).

[39] Ibid.

[40] Authors' notes from visit to Ncome/Blood River, 4 April 2002.

[41] "Senior Arts & Culture Man Charged with Misconduct," http://www.anc. org.za/anc/newsbrief/2000/news1026.txt (accessed 7 December 2004); Craig Bish-op, "Deputy DG Suspended for R2m Irregularity," *Mail & Guardian*, 26 October 2000, http://www.mg.co.za/articledirect.aspx?articleid=222478&area=%2farchives __online_edition%2f (accessed 7 December 2004).

[42] Jabulani Maphalala, *Ncome Museum*.

[43] "Crossing the Divide," *Mail & Guardian*, 28 September 2001, http:// www.mg.co.za/articledirect.aspx?articleid=217957&area=%2farchives__print_ edition%2f, (accessed 24 July 2004).

[44] "Blood Feud on the Banks of the River".

[45] Ibid.

[46] Anthony King, "Identity & Decolonisation: The Policy of Partnership in Southern Rhodesia, 1945-62," (DPhil thesis: Oxford University, 2001), 134.

[47] See fig. 3. The Union Buildings are clearly visible in the top-right corner of the picture, with the centre of Pretoria between them and the Voortrekker Monu-ment. See also Elizabeth Delmont, "The Voortrekker Monument: Monolith to Myth," *South African Historical Journal* 29 (1993), 80.

[48] Pretoria is the administrative capital, Cape Town the seat of Parliament, and Bloemfontein is the judicial capital.

[49] The war is also commonly known as the Boer War or the Anglo-Boer War.

[50] Delmont, "The Voortrekker Monument: Monolith to Myth," 81.

[51] Riana Heymans, *The Voortrekker Monument* (Pretoria: Board of Control of the Voortrekker Monuments, 1986), 4.

[52] "Mbeki Lauds SA Reconciliation," *Mail & Guardian*, 16 December 2004, http://www.mg.co.za/Content/l3.asp?cg=BreakingNews-National&ao=176759 (ac-cessed 16 December 2004).

[53] Hanti Otto, "Die Stem at the Centre of Cultural Celebration," *Pretoria News*, 17 December 2004, http://www.pretorianews.co.za/index.php?fSectionId=665&fA rticleId=2348538 (accessed 18 December 2004).

[54] Karima Brown, "From Despair to a Nation Filled with Hope," *The Star*, 17 December 2004, http://www.thestar.co.za/index.php?fSectionId=129&fArticleId=2 348383 (accessed 28 December 2004).

[55] John Matshikiza, "An Epitaph of Smoke and Mirrors," *Mail & Guardian*, 21 June 2002, http://www.mg.co.za/articledirect.aspx?area=mg_flat&articleid=144251. (accessed 24 July 2004).

[56] Annie Coombes, *History After Apartheid: Visual Culture and Public Memory in*

a Democratic South Africa (London: Duke UP, 2003), 40.

[57] "Voortrekker Monument Changes in the New SA," *Mail & Guardian*, 7 May 2003, http://www.mg.co.za/articledirect.aspx?articleid=19833&area=%2fbreaking_ news%2fbreaking_news__national%2f (accessed 24 July 2004).

[58] Ibid.

[59] Ibid.

[60] Mongane Wally Serote, Talk given at the Arts and Culture Commission, "Ten Years of Freedom" Conference, South Africa House, London, 25 October 2003.

[61] Nordic Africa Institute, "Yonah Seleti on Freedom Park," *News from the Nordic Africa Institute* 2 (May 2005): 23.

[62] Serote, see n. 62.

[63] Ibid.

[64] Charles Phahlane, "Sowing the Seeds of Remembrance," *The Star* (Johannesburg), 10 March 2004, www.star.co.za/index.php?fSectionId=327&fArticleId=3 70255 (accessed 23 November 2004).

[65] Ibid.

Figure 1. The Ncome/Blood River site. The representation of the ox-wagon laager is visible on the right. The adobe-colored Ncome Museum is in the centre (Photo: authors' own, 4 April 2002).

Figure 2. The side of the Ncome Museum that faces the Blood River site (Photo: authors' own, 4 April 2002).

Figure 3. The Voortrekker Monument. The Union Buildings are at top right across the city. Salvokop is on the right above the highway (Photo: www.voortrekkermon.org.za/images/Monument_foto_2.jpg (accessed 12 December 2004).

4

"Greek" Objects on Turkish Soil
A Link between the Inalienability of "Cultural Property" and Notions of Place in the Context of Turkish Claims for Repatriation

Eisuke Tanaka

Introduction

Recently, issues surrounding "cultural property" have attracted consider-able interest at a global level, becoming the focus of much national and international scholarly and legislative activity. One of the issues that has emerged is that of the repatriation of cultural property. Certain nation-states and groups are taking legal actions for the restitution of histori-cal, archaeological, and ethnographic materials displayed at Euro-Ameri-can museums. This is partly because of the rise of indigenous movement worldwide.[1] In addition, some existing nation-states have laid claim to objects that they claim had been illegally taken out of the country in the past. A famous example of this is the dispute about the Parthenon or Elgin Marbles between the British Museum and the Greek state.[2]

Turkey is one of the countries where such issues attract public atten-tion. The Turkish government has attempted to regulate movements of cultural property across the state boundary since the establishment of the Republic of Turkey in 1923. Since the 1980s, it has begun to claim the re-turn of archaeological and historical objects whose place of origin is Tur-key but which are now outside the country, particularly those that were il-licitly taken abroad for sale and have found their way into Euro-American museums. A huge amount of archaeological material has been taken from Anatolia, which constitutes most of the territory of this country, mainly by European countries in the nineteenth century, and more recently by the looting of archaeological sites for the international art market.

In general, archaeological or historical material objects play an im-portant role in constructing national or ethnic identity in the sense that they are considered to present and preserve a particular past of a nation or an ethnicity in a very concrete form. Through the notion of cultural property, the existence of a nation or ethnic group is objectified both spa-tially and temporally. In this respect, ethnicity or nationhood is implicated in the identification of archaeological or historical artifacts as "cultural property," although the exact meanings of the objects vary depending on the political interests of the groups that claim their ownership. Objects considered "cultural" are thus discursively linked with national or ethnic identity. It is in this context that ownership of cultural property and the possession of culture becomes important to the extent that it appears now to be internationally acknowledged as a right of nations and also of "ethnic" and indigenous groups.[3]

However, it is important to note that the antiquities that the Turkish state now claims to repatriate include some that are not straightforwardly identifiable as "Turkish," notably classical Greek objects. In modern Greek nationalist discourse, these are associated with "Greekness" as opposed to "the Orient" or, more precisely, "Turkishness."[4] The association of classical Greek antiquity and modern Greek nationhood is based on the idealization of ancient Greece by eighteenth and nineteenth century western Europeans, which was imported and adopted by Greek nationalists to claim the European identity of the modern Greek nation.[5]

In arguing its claims to antiquities marked as "Greek," but found in Anatolia, the modern Turkish state presents them as evidence of the existence of various civilizations on Anatolian soil in the past several millennia. At the same time, the Turkish state has also attempted to claim Anatolia as the "Turkish" homeland, both spatially as well as temporally, since its establishment in 1923.[6] In this respect, Turkish claims for the restitution of certain antiquities, notably classical antiquities, does not appear to be a straightforward case of the link between the ownership of "cultural property" and the construction of national identity through continuity with the past.

In order to analyze Turkish claims to classical antiquities and the ownership of cultural property that was illegally taken from the national territory, this paper focuses on the link between the ownership of cultural property and the notion of place. First of all, it briefly reviews definitions of cultural property and the nature of ownership of objects considered "cultural property." Secondly, in order to consider the socio-cultural background of Turkish claims to the ownership of classical antiquities, it looks at Turkish efforts to connect the modern Turkish nation with Anatolia. Finally, based on interviews and library research on the case of the Zeus Altar of Pergamon, I will show that Turkish ownership of classical antiquities is claimed through linking the modern Turkish nation with Anatolia as its Homeland. I will suggest that the notion of place of origin works to override the idea of ethnicity in claiming ownership of objects considered cultural property.

What is cultural property?

With a growing interest in the protection of sites and objects of historical importance, many scholars have studied the role of cultural property or heritage in constructing the past and history. Both "property" and "heritage" are used to represent phenomena related to the appropriation of culture and history in the name of "identity."[7] These terms are often used without any clear distinction. However, some further points on the usage of these terms can be made.

The term "cultural property" has been commonly used to refer to objects and sites of historical importance by international organizations such as UNESCO.[8] In one of the definitions often cited in the literature, "cultural property"

> represents in tangible form some of the evidence of man's origins and development, his traditions, artistic and scientific achievements and generally the milieu of which he is a part. The fact that this material has the ability to communicate, either directly or by association, an aspect of reality which transcends time or space gives it special significance and is therefore something to be sought after and protected.[9]

Moreover, in Article I of UNESCO's 1970 Convention, which dealt with the illicit traffic of antiquities, "cultural property" is defined as "property which, on religious or secular grounds, is specifically designated by each State as being of importance for archaeology, prehistory, history, literature, art or science."[10]

On the other hand, in terms of the relationship between objects and ideas about the past, it seems that the term "heritage" is used more often. The meaning of "heritage" was originally 'the collective generalization derived from the idea of an individual's inheritance from a deceased ancestor.'[11] However, it has broadened to denote all cultural phenomena in relation to activities surrounding artifacts, buildings, sites, and landscapes transmitted from the past.[12]

These definitions indicate that the identification of objects as "cultural property" is dependent upon nation-states claiming ownership of these objects.[13] Issues of "cultural property" thus have a very strong link with the ideas of nation and ethnicity, which emerged in the West and have spread across the world in the past two centuries. Regarded as the "cultural property or heritage" of a specific group of people, particular objects are implicated in the constitution of "local" differences between nations and ethnic groups. In this sense, the idea of "cultural property" works to generate a sense of the nation as a temporally continuous and spatially bounded entity.[14] Accordingly, discussions concerning cultural property seem to concentrate on the political aspects of the idea of heritage, particularly on how cultural property monumentalizes the past in the interests of nationalism. Cultural property has often been regarded as the best way of signifying the nation.[15] Once objects are considered "cultural property," they function to present national traits in a concrete form. By constructing the "national" past through the protection of national heritage, the state thus objectifies its nation.

In other words, objects considered "cultural property" work to combine national history with a certain site or an object, through which the nation, as Foster puts it, "can [...] be presented as a thing to see or place to (re)discover."[16] Moreover, the process of identifying objects as "heritage" involves "the extraction of history from everyday life" and "[its] restaging or display in certain sanctioned sites, events, images and conceptions" that are given historical significance.[17] A particular interpretation of the past selected from multiple alternative ideas, is fixed through the idea of heritage as if it had a static and timeless existence.[18]

The materiality of objects considered "cultural" plays an important role in providing a concrete image of a particular past, the history of the nation or an ethnic group, and thereby proving their existence and presence. This is one of the central aspects of the relationship between nationalism and the idea of the past. An aspect of this reification of the nation is that the nation can "own" cultural objects. Richard Handler discusses how "ownership" of cultural objects is conceptualized in relation to the notion of the individual, to which great value is attached in the modern Western tradition.[19] He makes the point that the nation is seen as "a property owning "collective individual.""[20] This implies that the nation or ethnic group is always concerned with having a culture, and the culture that such a group claims to possess is "preserved and embodied in material artifacts, such as buildings, works of art, ceremonial things, and antiques."[21] Thus, the nation or ethnic group must claim and specify its ownership of cultural property as "both representative and constitutive of cultural identity."[22]

In addition, David Lowenthal points out that in many societies memory is considered the source of self-identity construction, as "to know what we were confirms what we are."[23] Past experiences are not simply preserved in the process of remembering. Rather, they are manipulated and adapted in order to explain the present situation and to make the link between the past and the present continuous and coherent.[24] In a similar way, the "individual" is held to be continuous across time, i.e. to have a unified personal "history." The temporal continuity of the "individual" is another aspect linking the individualized idea of the nation and culture as "heritage."[25]

Given that the concept of the nation was born in the West, Handler's linking of the concept of the nation with Western individualism explains some important aspects of the logic that legitimizes the nation's ownership of cultural property. Restitution of the objects considered "cultural property" thus stems from the idea that "being [the nation or ethnic group] depends on having [cultural property]."[26] However, it is important to examine further the idea that the cultural is conceptualized as something that can be inherited or owned, i.e. as "heritage" or "property." What is it that the nation or ethnic group "owns" as "heritage" or "property"?

Owning objects considered "cultural" and the idea of place

In the discussions concerning objects identified with "culture," ownership is often at stake. In the case of stolen and illegally exported cultural property, great importance is placed on its restitution to the rightful owner, usually identified with a nation or ethnic group, both by international organizations like UNESCO and by nation-states.

Linked with the construction of collective identity, "cultural property" is considered to be integral to, or inseparable from, a nation or an ethnic group. From this point of view, removal of cultural property from a nation or an ethnic group is regarded as theft, but a particular kind of theft in the sense that it is "an attack on the integrity and coherence of that group or nation's identity," as James Leach notes.[27] Anthropologists working on issues surrounding cultural property[28] compare this view to Annette Weiner's notion of "inalienable possessions."[29]

Weiner discusses particular kinds of objects whose value is generated not through mechanisms of exchange, but through resistance against such mechanisms. She argues that the primary value of inalienable possessions is generated through the notion of the past in the sense that these objects have the power "to define who one is in an historical sense."[30] They work as an agency to bring the past into the present, through which the histories or titles of previous owners or past events, including mythological ones, become part of the identity of their current owner. The owner is not just the individual, but also the collective, i.e. the family or the descent group, that inherited the objects defined as inalienable.[31] Thus, inalienable possessions make "the past a powerful resource for the present and the future"[32] to the extent that "a loss is not merely the loss of something in a social sense, or even in an economic sense, but a loss may indicate a perceived weakness in a group's identity and therefore in its power to sustain itself for future generations."[33]

In a similar way, objects considered "cultural property" acquire a particular symbolic value for their rightful owner, the nation or ethnic group. Those who claim ownership of cultural property must verify their link or continuity with the originators of the objects. In debates over the Parthenon/Elgin Marbles for example, the Greek state has stressed the continuity between ancient Greeks and the Modern Greek nation, which is central to Greek national identity.[34] There is an assumption that contemporary people should inherit the items of historical and cultural value from their "ancestors" who produced them, even though that genealogical link may be imagined rather than real.[35]

However, disputes surrounding repatriation of cultural property suggest that this inalienable nature of the ownership of cultural objects also has a strong connection with the idea of place as well as with the idea of the past.[36] In practice, claims of repatriation of cultural property are often based on the assumption that an object's place of origin is self-evident (see the Parthenon/Elgin Marbles debates). The idea of repatriation also assumes the existence of place of origin as a natural entity: that things have a well-defined singular place of origin as such. In other words, the idea of place of origin already reifies "place" as an essential reality. This is why it is essential for groups claiming repatriation to clarify where the objects in question come from. Groups claiming the return of "their" cultural property are required to demonstrate the link between the objects at stake and themselves through the notion of place of origin.

Finally, what is problematized in repatriation disputes is the fact that the objects in question are outside their place of origin. The link between cultural property and place accords with the idea that the nation is thought to be bounded spatially as well as temporally. Thus, the idea of place works to provide authenticity for the items transmitted from the past and considered "cultural property," and such objects conversely may also help to authenticate the idea of place and of the nation as a temporal entity.

The idea of place thus plays an important role in claiming restitution of objects considered "cultural property." A sense of ownership of "cultural property" by a nation or an ethnic group is generated through the notion of place of origin as well as the idea of nationhood and ethnicity. In Turkey's case, the role of place is essential, partly because objects claimed by the Turkish state for repatriation include those that are not straightforwardly considered "Turkish," notably classical antiquities.

The emergence of Anatolianism: Linking the Turkish nation with Anatolia

The idea of Anatolia as the "Turkish Homeland" emerged following a series of events between the late nineteenth and early twentieth centuries, especially in the process of the founding of the Republic of Turkey when Anatolia became the territorial basis of the new Turkish nation state.[37] Kemal Atatürk, who became the leading figure of the republic, attempted to produce a homogeneous "Turkish" space in Anatolia. Erasure of the previously cosmopolitan atmosphere of Ottoman Anatolia entailed massive population exchanges with neighboring countries such as Greece.[38]

In addition to the physical removal of most of the non-Muslim communities, formulating a national history thesis was also considered important. By the 1930s, Atatürk's government had founded institutions to study history, folklore and archaeology. Given that a nation's legitimacy is based on its primordiality and rooted-ness to its national territory, linking the Turkish nation with Anatolia entailed constructing associations between the Turkish nation and the various past Anatolian civilizations. For example, the Turkish History Foundation (*Türk Tarih Kurumu*) was established in 1931 for the purpose of studying the history of the Turkish nation and Anatolia.[39] Archaeological excavations of Sumerian and Hittite sites, organized by the Turkish History Foundation and Ankara and Istanbul universities, began in this period, and worked to demonstrate the new historical theory.[40] It is worth noting that the history thesis formulated by the Kemalist government in the 1930s stressed racial elements and linked the Turks with Central Asia, which it considered to be their place of origin. Using physical anthropological studies, this historical thesis claimed that Turkish people had continually migrated from Central Asia to Anatolia since the Neolithic period. It thereby constructed a racial connection between Hittites and Sumerians and the modern Turkish nation.[41] In other words, by claiming that the Hittites were from the Turkish race, it attempted to legitimize the existence of the Turkish nation on Anatolian soil throughout history. For Atatürk's government, providing evidence of a link between the Turkish nation and the distant past was a way of claiming the legitimacy of the Turkish nation-state in Anatolia against Greek and Armenian territorial claims over Anatolia.[42] Archaeological and physical anthropological studies were important as they were considered to provide material evidence for such claims.[43]

From the late 1940s, this race-centered discourse of Turkish nationhood gradually lost its importance. Concerned with the relationship between the modern Turkish nation and the pre-Islamic past of Anatolia, it was replaced by a discourse that stressed a cultural link with past Anatolian civilizations while not necessarily abandoning Central Asia as the place of origin of the Turkish nation. Humanist writings founded on this culture-based idea, which has been called Anatolianism, began to appear in the 1940s.[44] Halikarnas Balıkçısı, Azra Erhat, and Sabahattin Eyüboğlu were the most influential figures among these humanist writers called "Anatolianists (*Anadolucular*)."[45] Taking Anatolia as the "cradle of civilizations," they link the modern Turkish nation with the whole combination of cultural heritage of Anatolian past civilizations.[46] Their idea is indicated in Sabattin Eyuboğlu's writing as follows:

> This land belongs to us [Turks] because it is our homeland, not because we conquered it.... It is we who conquered, and it is we, too, who were conquered.... We realized that we molded this land and that it molded us, too. For that reason, whatever is found in this country, whether it was made in the oldest time or in the most recent, is our genuine property. Our history is the history of Anatolia.[47]

Ayşegül Baykan and Roland Robertson point out that the political aim of such writings was resistance against the Greek appropriation of Anatolia.[48] In fact, while the official discourse about Turkish national history formulated in the 1930s emphasized a racial link with the ancient Anatolian peoples before classical antiquity, Anatolianist writings attempted to relate the modern Turkish nation with classical antiquity as well as with the Hittites. They stressed that some of the Gods and Goddesses in Greek mythology, and well-known figures in classical Greek literature, such as Homer and Herodotus, had Anatolian origins.[49] Thus, Anatolianists tried to make the point that it was in Anatolia, not (mainland) Greece, that so-called "Western Civilization" was born.[50]

Moreover, the idea of cultural continuity seems to have become one of the strong currents in Turkish historiography. A number of publications on national and local history have been published from this Anatolia-centered point of view.[51] Ekrem Akurgal, a well-known archaeologist in Turkey, wrote this in an article for a national newspaper in 1977:

> Without doubt, Hittites were not Turks. However, ... the present-day Turkish nation is a blend of ancient Anatolians with Turks. In other words, Turks in Turkey are Anatolians in their spirit and blood.[52]

By taking Turkish national culture as an amalgam of various past civilizations that had flourished on its soil, modern Turkish national identity is linked with Anatolia and its cultural diversity. Paradoxically, in such attempts to create a continuity between the Turkish national identity and the cultural diversity of Anatolia, Anatolia emerges as a distinct singular locality. In this process, the Turkish nation is essentially linked with cultural objects including those are not straightforwardly identifiable as "Turkish." It is in this context that a sense of Turkish ownership of classical antiquities found in Anatolia is generated.

The Zeus Altar of Pergamon

In the literature on illicit trade of cultural property and Turkish archaeology, Turkey is often referred to as one of the countries which are facing large scale smuggling of antiquities and which are making explicit and forceful attempts to retrieve antiquities that have been taken abroad.[53] Turkey affirms its ownership of all the cultural materials found in the national territory. State legislation on the protection of antiquities began in the late Ottoman period, and state ownership of antiquities discovered within the state territory has been the leitmotif of the legislation on antiquities to the present.[54]

Particularly since the 1980s, the Turkish state has begun to claim the return of antiquities illicitly taken abroad for sale, including those that have found their way into museums, and it has succeeded in the repatriation in some cases. One such example is the restitution of a group of antiquities called the "Lydian Hoard" from the Metropolitan Museum of Art, New York in 1993. This is a very famous case in that a body of looted antiquities held by an internationally renowned museum was returned to the country of origin after a court battle.[55] There are also several cases in which the Turkish state is officially demanding the repatriation of archaeological and historical objects that were taken abroad from Anatolia.[56] The Zeus Altar of Pergamon, which is currently exhibited in the Pergamon Museum in Berlin, is one of the well-known examples.

The Zeus Altar was built on the Acropolis of Pergamon (present-day Bergama, western Turkey) during the reign of King Eumenes II (197-159 BCE), and so is often associated with "Greekness." In the late nineteenth century, a German civil engineer, Carl Humann, who was visiting Bergama, discovered its frieze depicting Gigantomachy. He later excavated the site and sent the altar to Berlin, where it was reconstructed at the gallery of the Pergamon Museum in the early twentieth century[57] (see Fig. 4, page 77).

In the early 1990s, approximately a hundred years after this German excavation, the local authority of Bergama and its inhabitants started a campaign for the repatriation of the Zeus Altar.[58] Sefa Taşkın, who was the mayor of Bergama at the time, initiated the campaign in order to fulfill one of the promises he made during the mayoral elections in 1989. During his campaign, a huge number of signatures supporting the repatriation of the Altar from all over the country were collected.[59] In addition, Taşkın and town councilors of Bergama twice visited the Pergamon Museum in Berlin, in order to appeal for the return of the Zeus Altar.

Taşkın's campaign was not always viewed positively in the Turkish mass media. Can Bilsel notes that articles about his campaign, which appeared in the Turkish daily press in the early 1990s, 'rang[ed] in tone from mourning the stolen altar to accusing Mayor Taşkın of being crazy in thinking that Germans might give the altar back at all.'[60] However, the case gained substantial popularity in the country, and Taşkın's first visit to Berlin for the repatriation campaign in 1990 was reported on the front page of *Milliyet*, one of the popular Turkish national newspapers[61] (see Fig. 5, page 78).

Moreover, in the early 1990s, Turkish national newspapers often asked Taşkın to comment on the issues concerning antiquities illegally taken from Turkey. For example, when the "Lydian Hoard" was returned from the Metropolitan Museum of Art in 1993, a Turkish national newspaper asked him for his views on the repatriation.[62] Following his campaign, the Turkish state set up a section in the Ministry of Culture to deal with the restitution of the Zeus Altar.[63]

During the repatriation campaign, Taşkın emphasized that Bergama was the Zeus Altar's place of origin. While he claimed that its acquisition by the Germans was illegal, he first and foremost attempted to problematized the fact that the Zeus Altar was in Berlin, and outside Bergama. For him, all the archaeological and historical remains found in Bergama are inseparable components of the town.[64] He thus referred to the altar's exhibition in Berlin as "*Sürgündeki Zeus* (Zeus in Exile)."[65] In addition, at a press conference during his first visit to Berlin for his campaign, he said 'While the Zeus Altar has been in Berlin for one hundred years, it was in Bergama over a period of two thousand years. It is part of the city of Bergama.'[66] He also adopted a Turkish proverb "*Taş yerinde ağırdır* (a stone is heavy in its place)" as a slogan for his campaign, by which he meant that historic monuments must stay in their place of origin. Similar slogans were made for other repatriation campaigns led by the Turkish state. For the campaign of the repatriation of the Lydian Hoard, Özgen Acar, a Turkish journalist who has written a number of articles on cultural heritage issues in Turkey for a Turkish national newspaper, came up with "*Tarih yerinde güzel* (history is better appreciated in its place of origin)." A similar slogan was made for the Elmalı Coins by the Ministry of Culture: "*Kültür*

Varlıkları Ait Oldukları Yerinde Güzeldir (Cultural treasures are better understood in the place they belong to)." In this way, the Zeus Altar and Bergama are closely linked with each other, and through this the Altar acquires a particular value for those who claim its repatriation.

In addition to drawing an essential link between Bergama and the Altar, the discourse of the repatriation campaign for the Zeus Altar indicates that those who claim repatriation stress a link between Bergama's past and the contemporary inhabitants of the town: Turks. From Taşkın's point of view, the culture of present-day Bergama is "the accumulation of all previous cultures which flourished in Bergama in the past."[67]

Evidently, this is based on an Anatolianist relating of the Turkish nation with Anatolia and its past civilizations. In fact, Taşkın uses Halikarnas Balıkçısı's works in his book on the people in northwest Anatolia before classical antiquity.[68] Arguing that Turks who came to Anatolia gradually assimilated with the locals who had lived there for thousands of years, he attempts to make an essential link between Turks and Bergama in terms of a cultural continuity of sorts. In this context, all the archaeological and historical remains of different periods found in Bergama become the cultural property of the modern inhabitants of the town. Thus, in the repatriation discourse, the Zeus Altar, regarded as part of Bergama's "cultural property," becomes inseparable not only from the town, but also from the identity of the people living there.

Through the idea of "place of origin," Bergama appears as a distinct spatial as well as temporal entity beyond a physical environment and is linked with the identity of the locals. Analyzing the way in which western Apache people relate themselves with particular places and trails, Keith Basso makes the point that selfhood is intertwined with locality. Engaging with place, which involves spatial and temporal notions such as belonging to a community and connectedness to the past, is viewed as a way of making the self.[69] This works in turn to construct place as a moral reality rather than as a physical setting.[70] In the case of the repatriation of the Zeus Altar, this fusion of selfhood and locality seems to generate an inalienable value for the Altar based in locality and ownership. Through the idea of "place of origin," those who claim the Altar's repatriation construct continuity with those who created it. Such continuity is generally claimed through the idea of ethnicity. In this context, the notion of ethnicity seems to become less important for the ownership of "cultural property." Thus, the notion of place of origin is used to override the notion of ethnicity.

However, it should be noted that the notion of place of origin works to reproduce the "nation-state" rather than "locality." By the middle of the 1990s, the Turkish state set up a section in the Ministry of Culture to deal with the restitution of the Zeus Altar and started talking with Germany. At this point, however, Taşkın stopped his activities. He said that his role as the mayor of Bergama finished because all historical monuments in Turkey belong to the state.[71] The negotiation with Germany is, he said, the government's job. The idea of cultural property is thus mobilized to define Bergama as the Zeus Altar's place of origin in the framework of the Turkish nation-state.

Conclusion

A nation-state's legitimacy is based on its primordiality and rooted-ness to the national territory, and objects considered "cultural property" work to reify the nation as a temporal and spatial entity. Ownership of "cultural property" is inalienable, unlike the case of conventional forms of property, and for the nation or ethnic group, objects considered cultural property are inseparable from their identity. In this context, the movements of "cultural property" across national borders without state authorization can be cast as illegal, and claims for the restitution of such objects outside their country of origin emerge.

Analyzing Turkish discourse on the repatriation of the Zeus Altar, this paper has attempted to illustrate how a sense of ownership of objects considered "cultural property," in particular those not usually considered to be "Turkish," is generated in Turkey. As shown above, Anatolia as their place of origin plays a central role in Turkish claims of ownership, suggesting that ethnicity is not the only dimension drawn upon in discourses of cultural property.

The repatriation campaign for the Zeus Altar indicates that Turkish claims for the ownership of cultural property are based on the nationalist ideology that links the modern Turkish nation with Anatolia as its Homeland. In the process of building the modern Turkish nation-state, various efforts were made for the "Turkification" of Anatolia, both spatially as well as temporally. Formulating a Turkish national history on Anatolian soil, in which the Turkish nation was related to past Anatolian civilizations (notably pre-Islamic ones) and their material culture, was essential.

In this context, Turkish claims for repatriation of the Zeus Altar emerged. What is problematized most is that the Altar is outside Bergama, its place of origin. Through the notion of place of origin, the Altar becomes inseparable from Bergama. It is part of Bergama's cultural property, and as such, the altar is also linked with the identity of the locals living in the town. Thus, the notion of place of origin works to combine Turks in Bergama and the Zeus Altar. A sense of inalienable ownership of objects considered "cultural property," if not identifiable as "Turkish," is thereby generated. Using the idea of place of origin, the people who claim repatriation construct an essential link with the producers of the objects in question.

Notes

The research was supported by the Mastushita International Foundation Research Grant, the William Wyse Fieldwork Fund, the Richards Fund, and Hughes Hall, Cambridge. A version of this paper was also presented in the writing-up seminar at the Department of Social Anthropology, Cambridge in March 2005. I am particularly indebt to my supervisor Paola Filippucci for her support during the research as well as in the preparation of this paper. I am also grateful to Marilyn Strathern, who chaired the writing-up seminar, the participants of the seminar, and Gwyn Williams, who carefully read the draft. Finally, I would like to thank Claire Norton for her interest, encouragement and patience.

[1] An example is the Native American Graves Protection and Repatriation Act (NAGPRA) that was passed in the United States in 1990. See Angella J. Neller, "From Utilitarian to Sacred: the Transformation of a Traditional Hawaiian Object," in *Pacific Art: Persistence, Change and Meaning* ed. A. Herle (London: Crawford House Publishers, 2001).

[2] The Greek state has formally requested the return of the marbles from Britain since 1983. See Jeanette Greenfield, *The Return of Cultural Treasures* (Cambridge: Cambridge University Press, 1996).

[3] UNESCO has adopted several international conventions concerning cultural property such as the Convention for the Protection of Cultural Property in the Event of Armed Conflict (adopted in 1954); the Convention on the Means of Prohibiting and Preventing the Illicit Import, Export and Transfer of Ownership of Cultural Property (adopted in 1970); and the Convention concerning the Protection of the World Cultural and Natural Heritage (adopted in 1972). See UNESCO's official website (http://www.unesco.org/)

[4] Michael Herzfeld, *Ours Once More: Folklore, Ideology, and the Making of Modern Greece* (Austin: University of Texas Press, 1982), 7 and 20.

[5] Michael Herzfeld, *A Place in History: Social and Monumental Time in a Cretan Town* (Princeton: Princeton University Press, 1991), 11.

[6] Çağlar Keyder, "Whither the Project of Modernity?: Turkey in the 1990s," in *Rethinking Modernity and National Identity in Turkey* ed. S. Bozdoğan, and R. Kasaba, (Seattle: University of Washington Press, 1997), 44.

[7] See David Lowenthal, *The Heritage Crusade and the Spoils of History* (Cambridge: Cambridge University Press, 1997); John E Tunbridge and Gregory Ashworth, *Dissonant Heritage: The Management of the Past as a Resource in Conflict* (Chichester: Wiley, 1996); Kevin Walsh, *The Representation of the Past: Museum and Heritage in the Post-Modern World* (London: Routledge, 1992); and Patrick Wright, *On Living in an Old Country: the National Past in Contemporary Britain* (London: Verso, 1985).

[8] James Leach, "Owning Creativity: Cultural Property and the Efficacy of Custom on the Rai Coast of Papua New Guinea," *Journal of Material Culture* 8 (2003): 123-143.

[9] Geoffrey Lewis, "The Return of Cultural Property," *Journal of the Royal Society of Arts* 128 (1981): 435-440, 436 quoted in Greenfield, *The Return of Cultural Treasures*, 253.

[10] Ibid., 253.

[11] Tunbridge and Ashworth, *Dissonant Heritage*, 1.

[12] Ibid.

[13] Greenfield, *The Return of Cultural Treasures*, 253-4.

[14] Benedict Anderson, *Imagined Communities: Reflections on the Origin and Spread of Nationalism* revised edition (London and New York: Verso, 1991).

[15] Walsh, *The Representation of the Past*, 70.

[16] Robert Foster, "Making National Cultures in the Global Ecumene," *Annual Review of Anthropology* 20 (1991): 235-60, 249.

[17] Wright, *On Living in an Old Country*, 69.

[18] Barbara Bender, "Theorising Landscapes, and the Prehistoric Landscapes of Stonehenge," *Man* 27 (1992): 735-755, 735-6; Foster, "Making National Cultures in the Global Ecumene," 244.

[19] Richard Handler, *Nationalism and the Politics of Culture in Quebec* (Madison: The University of Wisconsin Press, 1988); and "Who Owns the Past?: History, Cultural Property, and the Logic of Possessive Individualism," in *The Politics of Culture* ed. B. Williams (Washington and London: Smithsonian Institution Press, 1991).

[20] Handler, "Nationalism and the Politics of Culture in Quebec," 141.

[21] Handler, "Who Owns the Past?" 154.

[22] Ibid.

[23] David Lowenthal, *The Past is a Foreign Country* (Cambridge: Cambridge University Press, 1985), 197.

[24] Ibid., 210.

[25] See also Richard Handler, 1994. "Is "Identity" a Useful Cross-Cultural Concept?" In *Commemorations: the Politics of National Identity* ed. J.R. Gillis (Princeton: Princeton University Press, 1994).

[26] Handler, "Who Own the Past?" 68.

[27] Leach, "Owning Creativity," 124-5.

[28] See Leach, "Owning Creativity"; and Eleana Yalouri, *The Acropolis: Global Fame, Local Claim* (Oxford and New York: Berg, 2001).

[29] Annette Weiner, "Inalienable Wealth," *American Ethnologist* 12/2 (1985): 210-227; and *Inalienable Possessions: the Paradox of Keeping While Giving* (Berkeley: University of California Press, 1992).

[30] Weiner, "Inalienable Wealth," 210.

[31] Ibid.

[32] Ibid., 224.

[33] Ibid., 212.

[34] Greenfield, *The Return of Cultural Treasures*, 72. See also Yalouri, *The Acropolis*, 82-3.

[35] See Anderson, *Imagined Communities*.

[36] In fact, words such as "return," "restitution," and "repatriation" themselves imply the move of objects from one place to another.

[37] Yael Navaro-Yashin, *Faces of the State: Secularism and Public Life in Turkey* (Princeton and Oxford: Princeton University Press, 2002), 46-7.

[38] After the Lausanne Treaty signed in 1923, Greek speaking Orthodox

Christians in Turkey, except for the inhabitants of Istanbul, and most of the Muslims in Greece (excluding those in western Thrace) were forcibly exchanged by the Turkish and Greek states. Dimitri Pentzopoulos, *The Balkan Exchange of Minorities and Its Impact upon Greece* (Paris and the Hague: Mouton & Co, 1962), 52; see also Renée Hirschon, *Heirs of the Greek Catastrophe: The Social Life of Asia Minor Refugees in Piraeus* (Oxford: Clarendon Press, 1989); and *Crossing the Aegean: An Appraisal of the 1923 Compulsory Population Exchange Between Greece and Turkey* (New York and Oxford: Berghahn, 2003).

[39] İlber Ortaylı, *Gelenekten Geleceğe* revised edition (İstanbul: Ufuk Kitapları, 2001[1982]), 109-12.

[40] Türk Tarihi Kurumu. *Birinci Türk Tarihi Kongresi* (Ankara: Türk Tarihi Kurumu, 1932).

[41] See Âfet İnan, "Tarihten Evel ve Tarih Fecrinde," in *Birinci Türk Tarihi Kongresi* ed. Türk Tarihi Kurumu (Ankara: Türk Tarihi Kurumu, 1932).

[42] Ayşe Özdemir, "'Hayalı Geçmiş': Arkeoloji ve Milliyetçilik 1923-1945 Türkiye Deneyimi," in *Arkeoloji: Niye? Nasıl? Ne İçin?* ed. O. Erdur, and G. Duru (İstanbul: Ege Yayınlarıö 2003), 14.

[43] Ibid.

[44] Mehmet Yashin, "Introducing Step-Mothertongue," In *Step-Mothertongue From Nationalism to Multiculturalism: Literature of Cyprus, Greece, and Turkey,* ed. M. Yashin (London: Middlesex University Press, 2000), 21; see also Can Bilsel "Zeus in Exile: Archaeological Restitution as Politics of Memory," *Working Paper Series* #13 Princeton University Center for Arts and Cultural Policy Studies (2000): 1-21, 9-10.

[45] See Bilsel, "Zeus in Exile," 9.

[46] Kaya Akyıldız and Barış Karacasu, "Mavi Anadolu: Edebi Kanon ve Milli Kültürün Yapılandırılışında Kemalism ile bir Ortaklık Denemesi," *Toplum ve Bilim* 81 (1999): 26-43, 30.

[47] Sabahattin Eyuboğlu, "Bizim Anadolu," in *Mavi ve Kara* ed. S. Eyuboğlu (İstanbul: Türkiye İş Bankası Kültür Yayınları, 1999), 9. Translated by the author.

[48] Ayşegül Baykan and Roland Robertson, "Spatializing Turkey," in *Identity, Culture and Globalization,* ed. E. Ben-Rafael and Y. Sternberg (Leiden: International Institute of Sociology and Brill Academic Press, 2002).

[49] See Halikarnas Balıkçısı, *Altıncı Kıta Akdeniz* (İstanbul: Bilgi Yayınları, 1982); Azra Erhat, *Mavi Anadolu* (İstanbul : İnkılâp Kitabevi, 1997).

[50] Akyıldız and Karacasu, "Mavi Anadolu," 41.

[51] See İskender Ohri, *Anadolu'nun Öyküsü* (İstanbul: Bilgi Yayınları, 1987); and Ekrem Akurgal, *Türkiye'nin Kültür Sorunları* (İstanbul: Bilgi Yayınevi, 1998).

[52] Akurgal, "Türkiye'nin Kültür Sorunları," 113. Translated by the author.

[53] See Janet Blake "The Protection of Turkey's Underwater Archaeological Heritage: Legislative and Other Approaches," *International Journal of Cultural Property* 2 (1994): 273-293; Neil Brodie, Jenny Doole, Colin Renfrew, *Trade in Illicit Antiquities: the Destruction of the World's Archaeological Heritage* (Cambridge: McDonald Institute for Archaeological Research, 2001); and Mehmet Özdoğan, "Ideology and Archaeology in Turkey," in *Archaeology under Fire: Nationalism, Politics and Heritage in the Eastern Mediterranean and Middle East,* ed. L. Meskell (London and New York: Routledge, 1997).

[54] In the current legislation framework under Law No.2863 on the Protection of Cultural and Natural Property (Kültür ve Tabiat Varlıklarını Koruma Kanunu No. 2863), "movable and immovable cultural and natural property that needs to be conserved and is found or is to be found on property belonging to the state, public institutions or private institutions and individuals is considered state property" (Article 5, *No. 2863 Kültür ve Tabiat Varlıklarını Koruma Kanunu* 21 July 1983 quoted by Blake, "The Protection of Turkey's Underwater Archaeological Heritage," 277).

[55] Colin Renfrew, *Loot, Legitimacy and Ownership: The Ethical Crisis in Archaelogy,* Duckworth Debates in Archaeology. (London: Duckworth, 2000), 42-3. These Lydian antiquities were looted from the Uşak region in northwest Turkey in the 1960s and purchased by the Metropolitan Museum a few years after the looting. The Turkish government took legal action against the museum for the first time in 1987.

[56] See Anıtlar ve Müzeler Genel Müdürlüğü, *Yıtık Miras'ın Dönüş Öyküsü* (İstanbul: Yapı Kredi Kültür Sanat Yayıncılık, 2003).

[57] Ibid., 42; and Staatliche Museen zu Berlin, *The Pergamon Altar* (Berlin: Staatliche Museen zu Berlin, 1993). According to a German account, Humann sent the materials to Berlin after the excavation with an official permit from the Ottoman Empire was begun in 1878 (Staatliche Museen zu Berlin). In the Turkish discourse by contrast, he secretly sent some of the frieze sculptures of the Altar to Germany when he found the sculptures, which was before he started excavation with Ottoman state authorization (Anıtlar ve Müzeler genel Müdürlüğü, *Yıtık Miras'ın Dönüş Öyküsü,* 44)

[58] Bilsel, "Zeus in Exile," 6.

[59] Ibid. According to Bilsel, 15 million signatures were collected throughout the campaign.

[60] Ibid., 7.

[61] Önder Özçorlu, "Doğu Berlin'de Türk Eylemi," *Milliyet,* 8 July 1990, 1, 9.

[62] *Cumhuriyet,* "Sıra Zeus Sunağında," 25 September 1993, 6.

[63] Anıtlar ve Müzeler Genel Müdürlüğü, *Yitik Miras'ın Dönüş Öyküsü,* 46-8.

[64] Sefa Taşkın, *Ege Rüzgarları: Sürgündeki Zeus, Pergamon Hümanızması, ve İzmirli kör ozan Homeros* (İstanbul: Sel Yayıncılık, 1997). This is a collection of essays about the history of the Zeus Altar in Bergama and illegitimacy of its exhibition in Berlin

[65] Ibid., 11-74.

[66] Handan Şenköken, "Zeus Sunağı, Bergama'ya ait," *Cumhuriyet* 8 July 1990, 16.

[67] Taşkın, *Ege Rüzgarları,* 44 translated and quoted by Bilsel, "Zeus in Exile," 6.

[68] Sefa Taşkın, *Mysia ve Işık İnsanları: Anadolu'nun Gizli Tarihi* (İstanbul: Sel Yayıncılık, 1997).

[69] Keith H. Basso, "Wisdom Sits in Places: Notes on a Western Apache Landscape," in *Senses of Place,* eds S. Feld and K. H. Basso (Santa Fe: School of American Research Press, 1996), 85-6.

[70] Ibid., 86.

[71] I interviewed Taşkın in March 2004.

Figure 4. The Foundations of the Zeus Altar in Present-Day Bergama (Photo by E. Tanaka).

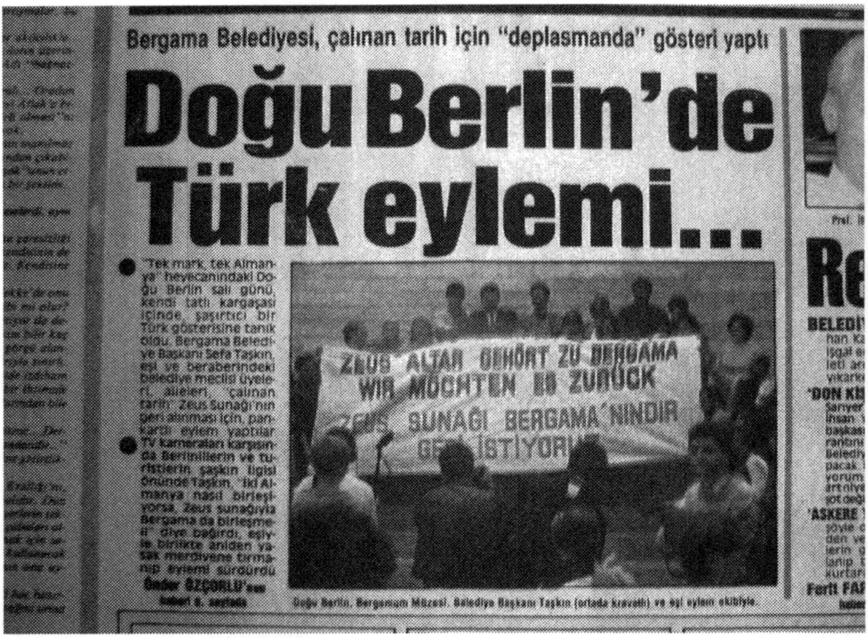

Bergama Belediyesi, çalınan tarih için "deplasmanda" gösteri yaptı

Doğu Berlin'de Türk eylemi...

● "Tek mark, tek Almanya" heyecanındaki Doğu Berlin salı günü, kendi tatlı kargaşası içinde şaşırtıcı bir Türk gösterisine tanık oldu. Bergama Belediye Başkanı Sefa Taşkın, eşi ve beraberindeki belediye meclisi üyeleri, aileleri, "çalınan tarih" Zeus Sunağı'nın geri alınması için pankartlı eylem yaptılar.

● TV kameraları karşısında Berlinlilerin ve turistlerin şaşkın ilgisi önünde Taşkın, "İki Almanya nasıl birleşiyorsa, Zeus sunağıyla Bergama da birleşmeli" diye bağırdı, eşiyle birlikte aniden yasak merdivene tırmanıp eylemi sürdürdü.

Önder ÖZÇORLU'nun haberi 8. sayfada

Doğu Berlin, Bergamum Müzesi. Belediye Başkanı Taşkın (ortada kravatlı) ve eşi eylem ekibiyle.

Figure 5. Article about Taşkın's visit to Berlin in the Turkish Newspaper *Milliyet*, 8 July 1990 (Photo by E. Tanaka).

MYTHS OF DESCENT, RACE AND CONTEMPORARY POLITICS

5

The End of *"Jugoslovenstvo"*
New Myths of Ethnic Descent Among the Southern Slavs

Ulf Brunnbauer

Introduction

In March, 2003, the president of the "Scientific Society for the Study of the Origins of the Croats," Ivan Biondić, gave an interview to the Croatian weekly *Hrvatsko slovo*, in which he pointed out that seventy one per cent of Croats whose DNA had been examined belonged to a "non-Slavonic genetic type." In their DNA, Croats had much more in common with Germans than with Slavs. He concluded, "it is evident that genetics buried the Yugoslav idea."[1] The Croats, however, are not the only people previously considered to be Southern Slavs, whose DNA presumably proves non-Slavonic origins. In 2001, Macedonian websites reported a human-genetic study which had collected evidence that the Macedonians had genes similar to other autochthonous Mediterranean peoples. A year later, the Macedonian news agency *MakNews* reported on a Macedonian-British team of researchers who tried to prove that contemporary Macedonians' DNA was similar to Philip's II, the ruler of ancient Macedonia.

These examples are characteristic of the reconfiguration of the mytho-poetic foundations of the Yugoslav (literally "southern Slavic") nations since the end of socialism and of Yugoslavia. These new myths claim that the southern Slavic peoples of former Yugoslavia are either autochthonous Slavs, are autochthonous non-Slavs, or are non-Slavs who have migrated from elsewhere. After Yugoslavia with its uniting myth of common Slavic origins had gone, nationalistic intellectuals in countries like Croatia, Macedonia or Bosnia-Herzegovina opposed the idea of Slavic descent and presented their nation as a non-Slavic one. By doing so they wanted either to lay claim to a different people's patrimony or to emphasize the essential difference of their own nation to its Slavic neighbours. Another way of increasing the differences with one's neighbours and of buttressing the claims of one's own nation for singularity was to construct a myth of autochthonous and continuous presence in the Balkans. While it is commonly assumed that the Slavs came to the Balkans in the sixth and seventh centuries, authors in Slovenia and Serbia claimed that their people, as Slavs, had lived in the Balkans for much longer. A rough classification of the myths under consideration is depicted in the table on page 96 (Fig. 6).

In this paper, I will present and analyse the myths of both non-Slavic and autochthonous origins, which have gained popularity in former Yugoslavia during the last two decades. I will consider all former Yugoslav republics with the exception of Montenegro. The aim of this paper is not to prove that the discussed myths of descent are wrong, in the sense of contradicting historical 'facts,' because this, firstly, is a futile endeavour and, secondly, would presuppose that we are able to find the 'historical truth,' which I consider a very problematic presupposition. I am instead interested in the relation of the contents of these myths to the ideological and political currents in these countries as well as to perceived threats to the particular nation.

Myths of ethnic descent

In his essay on the significance of myths of ethnic descent, Anthony Smith points out that "no aspirant ethnic group can be without its myth of descent, if it is to secure any recognition from competitors.... The roots of its unique identity *must* reside in its origins and genealogy."[2] Since nations in the Balkans conceptualise themselves as ethnic communities, the idea of common origins that link all members together is of particular importance. Myths of descent render the nation a community of fate and construct a meaningful link between its past, present and future. They usually also emphasize ideological and cultural continuity making the contemporary nation heirs to a proud historical tradition. The ethnic ancestors are often presented in a way to serve as models of behaviour for today's national citizens. That is why myths of origin contribute importantly to the image the nation has, and wants to project, of itself.[3]

Myths of ethnic descent also give an answer to the crucial question of who belongs to the nation. George Schöpflin states that "[m]yth is, then, a key element in the creation of closures and in the constitution of collectives."[4] All those sharing the same ancestry belong to the nation. However, the same people can be the object of diverging myths of ethnic descent and therefore find themselves addressed by different nation-building projects. To give an example from the Balkans: according to the dominant myth of descent in Bulgaria, the Macedonians are part of the Bulgarian nation because they allegedly are of Bulgarian ethnicity. The Macedonians, though, have their own myths of origin, which make a clear distinction between themselves and the Bulgarians, but also include other people living abroad who maybe do not share this vision. In situations of cultural proximity, myths of descent must often compensate for the difficulty in finding meaningful 'primordial' features to pin down ethnic specificity. This is evidently the case among the southern Slavs, who share many of the features so dear to ethnic engineers—be it language, religion, customs, folklore, or cuisine. Similar processes have been identified in the Ukrainian and Belo-Russian nation building processes, where nation-builders also emphasized the need to find different origins to those of the Russians.[5]

Myth-making as the creation of ethnic boundaries is closely related to ethno-political contestation. Myths of descent are therefore highly dependent on the political contexts in which they emerge. Not only do they have to make sense to contemporaries, but their success is also related to whether political and social forces make use of these myths as legitimisation for their policies. Lucian Boia, in his analysis of historical myths in Romania, pointed to the fact that each political regime and each political current that struggles for dominance promotes its own version of the mytho-poetical foundations of the nation.[6] Political elites look for myths because these can render the seemingly chaotic historical experience meaningful and provide answers to the longing for moral orientation. Political forces also use myths to sell their perception of the nation's past and present and their visions of the future to the public. The political conditionality of myths of descent becomes especially evident in times of crisis. The cases from the former Yugoslavia discussed below may serve as illustrations of Anthony Smith's assumption that "historically and sociologically, these myths emerge into the political daylight at certain junctures; these are usually periods of profound culture clash, and accelerated economic and social change. Very often, too, there is a definite threat, political or military, from outside to the viability of the community."[7]

During the last two decades mytho-poetic production was very dynamic in the former Yugoslavia. In the late 1980s, nationalist movements, whose myths of the nation challenged the Yugoslav founding myth of 'brotherhood and unity' and its emphasis on a common southern Slavic heritage, gained strength. At the same time, Communism as the dominant ideology withered away, leaving an ideological vacuum. The Yugoslav wars in the 1990s further stimulated the creation of new nationalistic myths. Economic devastation and social deprivation, which affected large parts of the population of former Yugoslavia, had the same effect. The public longed for all sorts of esoteric ideas which seemed to give meaning to their incomprehensible experiences and reduced the complexity of the world. Many people were also glad to hear that, at least in the past, their nation had been glorious and this also gave them hope that a 'golden age' might come again. The mushrooming new media, after public opinion had been pluralized, were also often keen to promote all kinds of 'new' theories.

Slovenia

Since the late 1980s, one myth of ethnic descent has been inspiring the imagination of many Slovenians, though not of scholars: the ancient Venetians as the ancestors of the Slovenians.[8] The Venetians were located by ancient authors in the northern Adriatic region, and although we know little about their language, Slovenian authors promoting this myth proclaim that they spoke a Slavonic idiom. So, the Slovenians become heirs to an ancient people and are not only autochthonous, but also a sort of original Slav.

This myth, which is based on the erroneous identification of the Adriatic Venetians with the Slavonic 'Veneti' who had lived at the mouth of the river Vistula, first emerged in 16th century Slovenian Protestant writing. During the 19th century, the myth gained a political edge, as it served Slovenian nationalists to fend off German and Italian claims on the territories populated by Slovenians. The Venetian theory should substantiate the Slovenian claim for territory and make them a people with a history, something denied by many Germans and Italians who described the Slovenians as a simple peasant folk without a history of their own.[9] The prominent Slovenian politician Henrik Tuma (1858–1938), for example, not only equated Slovenians and Venetians, but declared the Slovenians to be the oldest people of Europe.[10]

In communist Yugoslavia, such thoughts could not be promoted in public for a long time. These ideas, though, survived in the Slovenian diaspora and in the second half of the 1980s, when the Yugoslav idea became increasingly hollow and a Slovenian independence movement emerged, they returned to Slovenia. This was mainly due to the activities of the priest Ivan Tomažič, who lived in Vienna and took care of Slovenian students there. In 1989 he edited the book "The Venetians – our Ancestors," which attracted much attention, mainly because one of its contributors was the prominent Slovenian writer Matej Bor.[11] The book consists of three parts: a historical section, written by the economist Jožef Šavli, a linguistic one by Matej Bor, and a review chapter by Ivan Tomažič. The authors claim that the ancestors of the Slovenians were the ancient Venetians, who "were of original Slavic ethnicity" and inhabited much of Europe in pre-Christian times. The Slovenians are therefore heirs to a "continuity of three thousand years."[12] One of their main arguments is linguistic similarity which serves as evidence for the presence of Venetians and Slovenians in various parts of Europe. All place names including the syllable *"holm"* (hill) allegedly refer to a former Venetian-Slovenian presence, such as Stockholm, Chelmsford (England) and Colmar (France). A Venetian presence in the Middle East is also likely, as indicated by the name Suez in Egypt, which the authors say derives from the Slovenian *svez* (link). The book sold pretty well and letters to newspaper editors expressed their support for the Venetian myth.

During the 1990s, Ivan Tomažić continued to publish widely on the Venetian theory, and in 2001, the Slovenian World Congress organised the first Slovenian conference on the Venetians, at which domestic and foreign participants elaborated further the myth of Venetian descent.[13] This myth made the Slovenians not only one of the oldest peoples in Europe, but also a genuinely European people because the Venetians contributed to the ethno-genesis of many other European peoples.

Croatia

Croatian nationalists are faced with a perennial problem: how to make their ethnic nation unique despite the fact that it both shares its language with the Serbs, Bosnians and Montenegrins and that strong currents of nationalist thought in Croatia in the nineteenth century proclaimed the Croats to be part of one southern Slavic nation (Illyrianism and, later, Yugoslavism). Hence Croat nationalists often turn to the ethno-genesis of the Croats in order to determine their essential difference from the other south Slavs and above all from the Serbs. Since even the origins of the ethnonym *Hrvati* (Croats) is unclear, and due to the almost complete lack of first-hand information on the Croats at the time when they came to the Balkans, the question of the ethnic origins of the Croats is liable to speculation. Professional historians also devote considerable attention to this topic.[14] In the early 1990s, when the problems of ethnic descent attracted particular attention in a galvanised atmosphere of high-rising nationalist spirit and propaganda, there was even formed a "Scientific Association for the Study of the Origins of the Croats" in Zagreb.

Since the late 1980s, two alternative versions of ethnic descent have inspired Croatian nationalists.[15] Both theories deny that the Croats are Slavs. One argues that the Croats descend from the autochthonous pre-Slavic population of the Croatian lands, the other concedes that the Croats have come from somewhere else, but not as Slavs. The most popular version of the latter theory is that the Croats are of Iranian descent, although there are also other theories (such as them being of Gothic or Sarmatian descent). In contrast to Slovenia, these myths of descent can be linked to academic research, which either points to the contribution of the pre-Slavic inhabitants in the Croatian lands to the culture of the Croats or refers to a potential Iranian background of the immigrating Croats.[16]

One of the most prolific authors of the 'autochthonity' school is the former lawyer and pseudo-historian Ivan Mužić, who in 1989 published a book on "The Origins of the Croats. The Autochthonity of the Croatian Ethno-Genesis in the Area of the Roman Province of Dalmatia."[17] In his book the author piles up quotations from historical sources which allegedly confirm that the ancient population of Dalmatia was not displaced by migrants in the late ancient or early medieval period. Croatian national history therefore reaches beyond the arrival of the Slavs in the Balkans. Mužić also sees a contribution of the Goths to Croatian ethnicity, reinventing an idea which in 1935 had been expressed by Kerubin Šegović in the Nazi-German journal *"Nordische Welt."*[18] This theory was further elaborated in the 1990s by Robert Tafra, who published materials on the Gothic presence in Croatia and their role in the Croatian ethno-genesis.[19] More recently, the myth of autochthonous origins of the Croats was put forward by Stjepan Pantelić in his dissertation on the "Original Homeland of the Croats."[20] This author found a very imaginative solution to the contradiction between the account of the Byzantine emperor Konstantin Porphyrogennetos (905–959), who wrote about the immigration of the Croats from beyond the Danube, and the claim to ethnic continuity since ancient times: the immigration described by Konstantin Porphyrogennetos was actually the return of the Croats to their "original homeland" in Dalmatia and Pannonia, from where they had been expelled by the Romans![21]

More popular than the myth of autochthonous existence, though, is the myth of the Iranian descent. The main argument for this theory is the very name *Hrvati*, which by many authors is identified as a Persian word. This idea first emerged in the late eighteenth century and was also backed by prominent scholars of the inter-war period, who believed in an Iranian contribution to the ethno-genesis of the Croats.[22] During the Yugoslav period, the Iranian theory could not be openly expressed in Yugoslav Croatia, but once the Yugoslav federation was dissolved, it re-emerged. Mijo Ćurić, for example, in 1991 identified the Iranian *Harauvati* as the ancestors of the Croats, who had come to the Balkans with the army of Dareius and remained there. As evidence, he points to the Croatian chess-board like flag, which was also in use in ancient Persia, to dualist beliefs in ancient Persia and in medieval Croatia, and to the presence of many Persian nouns in place names in Croatia, such as *Ragusa* (Dubrovnik), the name of which, the author claims, derives from the Iranian town of *Raga*.[23]

In 1994 the newly founded "Scientific Association for the Study of the Origins of the Croats" edited a lavish volume on the Iranian origins of the Croats.[24] In the preface, the editors thank President Tudjman's office, the Municipal Council of Zagreb, and the Iranian Embassy for their support.[25] The central argument of this publication also revolves around the name of the Croats: *Hrvati* refers to Persian languages and is reflected in many place names in the Middle East. Two contributors even emphasize that the Croatian language contains many loanwords from Persian. For example the name of the island of *Krk* is said to come from the island of *Karkh* in the Persian Gulf.[26] Aside from linguistic parallels, the volume identifies Iranian cultural legacies in the Croat culture. Most importantly, the Iranian descent makes the Croats genetically different from all Slavs. Whereas the Croats are heirs to a great ancient civilization, the origins of the Serbs are located in Black Africa, which is proven by place names such as *Serba* in Eritrea and Burkina Faso. The African legacy of the Serbs is allegedly also evident in their practising of female circumcision, their orgiastic obsession with sex, their disorganised way of life, their intolerance and their warmongering.[27]

The climax of the propagation of the myth of Iranian descent was reached in 1998, when the "Scientific Association for the Study of the Origins of the Croats" together with the Cultural Centre of the Islamic Republic of Iran organised the conference "Old-Iranian Origins of the Croats" in Zagreb, opened by the Iranian ambassador to Zagreb. Contributors to the conference proceedings claimed that, during socialism, adherents of the Iranian theory had been brutally suppressed or even killed and the Croats had been forcefully "Slavicized."[28]

Serbia

Compared to Croatian nationalism, myths of ethnic descent play a minor role with the mytho-poetic foundations of the Serbian nation. The Kosovo myth and the myths of victimisation and divine selection, revolving around it, are much more important.[29] But the 1990s were a time of such profound political, social, intellectual and moral crises in Serbia that the most obscure ideas found a receptive audience.[30] The prominent Serbian Byzantinist Radivoj Radić wrote, in his rejection of the new myths of origin, that "the theories of the pseudo-historians were regarded by a part of the Serbian population as a weak consolation for the pity, which was brought upon us, a last resort in the convulsion of collapsed national self-esteem."[31] Even some intellectuals and students proved not to be immune to theories which rendered the Serbs the oldest people in the world.[32]

To my knowledge, the first contemporary articulation of the theory that the Serbs were the oldest people came from the Serbian émigré Olga Luković-Pjanović. She published, in Serbia in 1990, two volumes on "The Serbs... the Oldest People", which appeared in 2,500 copies.[33] The author believes that the Serbs are the original Slavs, who around 5,000 BCE came from their ancestral homelands in northern India to Europe. She wants to prove the "uninterrupted continuity with respect to language, tradition and spiritual wealth from the era of the Veda up to nowadays Serbs."[34] She claims that during certain periods, the Serbian orbit reached from the British islands and Scandinavia to Siberia and northern Africa. Moreover, that the Celts are also of Serbian descent is easily proven by the name of their priests: "Druid" consists of the Serbian words *"drugi"* and *"vid."*[35] The Serbs have therefore not only an old, but also a brilliant cultural tradition: they invented, for example, the Cyrillic alphabet.[36]

After this book, a couple of other authors advocated similar views, such as in the lavishly designed two-volume collection *"Catena mundi."*[37] This collection of almost 1,800 pages elaborates all essential Serb national myths and claims for example that a succession of ancient peoples, such as the Illyrians, Thracians and Venetians, were all Serbs. The original homeland of the Serbs is said to be in Mesopotamia and Persia, from where they migrated in pre-Christian times to the Balkans.[38] This "truth" was allegedly for a long time suppressed by, at first, German and, later, Communist influence.

Bosnia-Herzegovina

Given the conditions in Bosnia-Herzegovina in the 1990s, when the Bosnian Muslims became victims of Serb and later also Croat aggression, it is not surprising that new historical myths easily gained popularity among them. In contrast to Slovenia and Serbia, in Bosnia professional historians also produced new myths of descent. This was due to the fact that Bosnian nation-building was a recent phenomenon which began when the Yugoslav Communists decided to turn the Muslims of Bosnia into a nation in the 1960s, and culminated during the Bosnian war (1992–95), when an all-Bosnian convention accepted the name *Bošnjak* as the ethnonym of the Bosnian Muslims. Historians felt responsible for furnishing the *Bošnjak* nation with a proud national history.[39] For that purpose, they had to overcome the great obstacle of dating the emergence of the Bosnians beyond the arrival of Islam in the Bosnian lands (fifteenth century). The extension of the national pedigree was also supposed to bolster the Bosnian claims to their territory which was under obvious threat.

As a new paradigm in nationalist Bosnian history, the idea of a Bosnian nation before the coming of the Ottomans emerged. This theory, paradigmatically elaborated by the legal historian Mustafa Imamović, refers to a separate Bosnian tribe of the Slavs, when they came to the Balkans.[40] The medieval Bosnian state and its allegedly heretical Bosnian church are seen as expressions of Bosnian singularity. Hence, Bosnian national history was said to begin in the early medieval period, as do the national narratives of the other Slavic nations in the Balkans.

However, there was an even more radical new myth of descent which claimed that the Bosnians were an autochthonous people. This idea was advocated by Enver Imamović, professor of history at the University of Sarajevo, and prolific author.[41] In two books, he presented 'proof' that the Bosnians were autochthonous and descended from the ancient Illyro-Romanian population of Bosnia.[42] "The fact that the Bosnian-Herzegovinian Muslims are an autochthonous Balkan-European people, who have been living in this region for more than 4,000 years, as long as they can be traced back archaeologically, is generally not any more contested by scholars."[43] According to this author, the Bosnians safeguarded their individuality which made them very different from the Serbs and Croats, even though the ancient Bosnians accepted a Slavic tongue. The autochthonous element made itself felt in the medieval Bosnian state, in the Bosnian church and in the superior Bosnian civilization which was a "unique ethnic and cultural oasis." The arrival of the Slavs, by contrast, marked a cultural regress, as "villas" were replaced by nomadic "huts." Only the Bosnians have a legitimate claim to the ancient and medieval tradition of Bosnia and its "cultural, national, political and historical" legacies.[44] It is therefore preposterous, according to this author, to attribute a constitutive role to the Serbs and Croats in Bosnia-Herzegovina, as had been done by the Dayton Agreement in 1995 which ended the war. In Enver Imamović's vision of the history of Bosnia there is no place for a Bosnian-Herzegovinian political nation, because he defines the Bosnian nation in strictly ethnic terms.

In 1998, Enver Imamović repeated his vision of the Bosnians as an autochthonous people. This time he also referred to bones found in medieval Bosnian graves, which were significantly different from Serb and Croat remains.[45] He also slightly modified the boundaries of the envisioned Bosnian nation: he claimed that Serbs and Croats, after coming to Bosnia, succeeded in converting native Bosnians to Orthodoxy and Catholicism respectively. This implies that many of the presumably Serbs and Croats in Bosnia are actually Bosnians.[46] Hence the vision of a multireligious, though mono-ethnic Bosnian nation. The prominent Bosnian historian (and former minister of education) Dubravko Lovrenović called

Imamović's ideas "ethnic apartheid"—a concept of the history of Bosnia which hardly helped to build a viable future for the common state.[47]

Macedonia

The Macedonian case shares an important similarity with the Bosnian one: the redefinition of the mytho-poetical foundations of the Macedonian nation was carried out also by academic historians. The reason for this similarity is the likewise recent character of the Macedonian nation-building, which started in earnest only after the establishment of a Macedonian republic within Tito's Yugoslavia in 1944. Historians were among the main actors in the process of creating and disseminating the Macedonian national identity. The explicit rationale of the dominant historical institution in Macedonia, the "Institute for National History" in Skopje (established in 1948), was, and still is, to write the history of the Macedonian people. This, of course, included the search for the origins of the Macedonians. Macedonian historians never emancipated themselves from the nation-building effort and most of them still regard their profession a patriotic endeavour to bolster Macedonian national identity.

The Macedonian case also proves the unwillingness of nations to accept their modern character, but rather to look for their origins in the far past. Such a process becomes even more evident if a nation defines itself in ethnic terms, which the Macedonian one does. Furthermore, the myths of descent in Macedonia are highly dependent on the external political context because they seek to create legitimacy vis-à-vis hostile neighbours. The first of such neighbours was Bulgaria, who traditionally had considered the Slavic population of Macedonia part of her own fold. Thus, Macedonian historians did their best to disconnect Macedonian from Bulgarian history. In the 1950s, when Bulgaria launched a ferocious campaign to deny the existence of a Macedonian nation, historians in Skopje responded by dating the origins of the Macedonian people to the Middle Ages. The ethno-genesis of a separate Macedonian branch of Slavs was said to have taken place immediately after they had come to the Balkans.[48]

The master narrative changed after 1991, when Macedonia became independent and Bulgaria was replaced by Greece as the significant other. While Bulgaria was the first state to recognise an independent Macedonia, Greece managed to bully the European Community and the United Nations into postponing recognition of Macedonia for more than two years. Greece felt offended by the name "Macedonia," as there is a province of the same name in Greece; by the chosen flag of the Republic of Macedonia, which displayed an ancient Macedonian symbol found in Greece, and by the constitution of the new state, which included a clause on the protection of "Macedonian national minorities" abroad—the existence of which in Greece Greek governments have always been denying. Greece accused her northern neighbour of irredentist aims and declared an economic boycott.

The symbolic bone of contention was the right to claim the heritage of the ancient Macedonians, which is embodied in the name 'Macedonia.' Greece claimed exclusive ownership rights, something the Macedonians opposed. Hence, Macedonian historians set out to prove that the ancient Macedonians were a completely different people from the ancient Greeks and that they contributed to the ethno-genesis of the contemporary Macedonians.[49] The Macedonian Academy of Science commissioned a book which said that those ancient Macedonians "who had remained in their native homesteads gradually became assimilated by particular Slavonic tribes, in the process transmitting to the Slavs certain of their own customs, the Christian faith, culture and also the name of their fatherland, Macedonia."[50] The same line of thinking is evident in the first volume of the major project of contemporary Macedonian historiography "The History of the Macedonian People." Its authors amass evidence that the ancient Macedonian state was not a Hellenic affair because the ancient Macedonians belonged to another ethnic group. Then they continue in saying that the ancient Macedonians successfully resisted Hellenization and Romanization and instead "preserved their ethnic characteristics, their language, their religious beliefs and their customs." In the end, they mixed with the "Macedonian Slavs."[51] Ancient Macedonian history thus became part of Macedonian national history.

Only a few professional historians in Macedonia claim that today's Macedonians are direct descendants of those led by Philip II and Alexander the Great. Instead they prefer to construct a cultural continuity and aim to link the name and the territory of Macedonia, and thus the people who live there today, with the grandeur of ancient Macedonia. The most important tradition which the ancient Macedonians have left in this region and handed down to the contemporary Macedonian nation is said to be state-craft. The writer, legal expert and prominent politician Vasil Tupurkovski, who in the 1990s wrote a number of very successful books on the ancient Macedonians, attributed all cultural and political values which he wanted the modern Macedonian state to embody, to Alexander the Great: he allegedly believed in the feasibility of universal peace and built an empire based on the principles of national, religious and racial tolerance.[52]

However, at the fringes of professional historiography, and beyond, there are people who claim a direct ethnic continuity between the ancient and the modern Macedonians, a notion apparently very popular among the population. The most prolific author in this respect is the historian Aleksandar Donski who, in his book "The Descendants of Alexander the Great of Macedon" — translated into English thanks to the Macedonian diaspora in Australia — claims that their is no ethnic difference between the Macedonians of Alexander's and of our times. He quotes "anthropological evidence" that shows how little Macedonians and Slavs have in common: there is allegedly not one Macedonian folk song which includes the noun "Slav," and customs, folk poetry and language clearly indicate the ancient Macedonian descent of the Macedonians.[53] In an earlier book he had elaborated on the "ethno-genetic differences between Macedonians and Bulgarians."[54] Recent genetic 'research' in Macedonia, which aims to prove the link between ancient and today's Macedonians, lends further 'scientific' credentials to this myth of ethnic descent.

Conclusion

The myths discussed above share some commonalties. First, they enjoy a certain amount of popularity in the public realm, which is why in some cases prominent historians have set out to prove their absurdity. But even if they are marginal they are important — and not just entertaining — because they represent the demarcating lines of what is thought and articulated on national history in the public sphere. Under certain conditions, these myths may become the dominant popular version of the past, especially if they are supported by academic historians, such as in Macedonia and Bosnia and to a certain extent in Croatia.

Second, the authors of these myths — whether academic historians or para-historians — employ blatant dilettantism. Their accounts are results of wishful thinking and of very eclectic — to be kind — methods: they draw on evidence from various disciplines without being a specialist in any of them. Their most popular method is the 'linguistic' one, which means establishing relationship between languages simply by identifying phonetic similarities, however superficial and in neglect of all principles of linguistic development. This refers mainly to place names, but also to personal names and other terms. Another popular method is human anthropology, alluding to phenotypic, cranial and genetic similarities as scientific proof. Such reasoning illustrates the shared conviction of these authors that there are unchanging ethnic and cultural essentials which link people over thousands of years. Finally, in using historical evidence, they exploit the often contradictory ethnic terminology in ancient sources and freely equate ancient peoples with their own nation. They often reiterate accounts of the origins of their nations by eighteenth and nineteenth century romantic historians who had a patriotic, and not a scholarly, agenda. The myth-makers also never miss the opportunity to proclaim their views as the only objective ones and to accuse established historians of ideological distortions. Mainstream historical knowledge is said to be imposed by hostile forces, especially the Communists and Tito, who erroneously portrayed the peoples of Yugoslavia as southern Slavs with common origins, who therefore should live in one state.

These myths illustrate the ideological disorientation in the former Yugoslavia as well as the popularity of all sorts of esoteric ideas. The creation of new, or the re-invention of old, myths of ethnic descent proves that, after the dissolution of Yugoslavia, its nations define themselves only by ethnic terms, and if an attractive idea of ethnic descent is lacking a suitable one is created. Nationalist elites as well as ordinary people have a strong feeling that the future of their nation must be grounded in its ethnic history. Hence the perceived need to recreate the mytho-poetical foundations of the nation. The danger of political action being informed by such myths, which are ethnically exclusive, expansionist and aggressive, is evident. On a more general level, the examples from the former Yugoslavia illustrate the potential dangers that can arise when history is evoked in the search for "origins": such activity can result in the production of myths that can bind communities together, but at the same time put them in opposition to others.

Notes

[1] Ivan Biondić, "Biogenetika je pokopala južnoslavenstvo" (Interview), *Hrvatsko slovo*, No. 411, March 7 2003, http://www.hkz.hr/Hrvatsko_slovo/2003/411/t16.htm.

[2] Anthony Smith, *Myths and Memories of the Nation* (Oxford: Oxford University Press, 1999), 60–1. Italics in original.

[3] See George Schöpflin,"The Functions of Myth and a Taxonomy of Myths," in *Myths and Nationhood*, ed. Geoffrey Hosking and George Schöpflin. (London: Routledge, 1997), 20.

[4] Ibid.

[5] Andrew Wilson, "National history and national identity in Ukraine and Belarus," in *Nation-building in the Post-Soviet Borderlands. The Politics of National Identities*, ed. Graham Smith et al. (Cambridge: Cambridge University Press, 1998), 28–30.

[6] Lucian Boia, *History and Myth in Romanian Consciousness* (Budapest: Central European University Press, 2001).

[7] Smith, *Myths and Memories of the Nation*, 83.

[8] Michael Weithmann, "Ein neuer Mythos am Alpenrand," *Münchner Zeitschrift für Balkankunde* 6 (1990): 175–187; Antonia Bernard, "La Théorie des Vénètes en

Slovénie. Problème d'histoire, d'historiographie ou d'idéologie," *Revue des études slaves* 70, no.1 (1998): 113–123; Peter Štih, "Avtohtonistične in podobne teorije pri Slovencih in na Slovenskom," in *Karantanien – Ostarrichi. 1001 Mythos*, ed. Andreas Moritsch. (Klagenfurt/Celovec: Hermagoras, 1997), 25–49.

[9] Andreas Moritsch, "Aber schön wäre es schon, wenn es so gewesen wäre....," in Moritsch, *Karantanien – Ostarrichi. 1001 Mythos*, 17.

[10] Štih, "Avtohtonistične in podobne teorije," 30–1.

[11] The book originally appeared in German in 1988, and was later published also in Italian (1991), English (1996) and Russian (2002) translations. Matej Bor had been president of the Slovenian Writers' Union (1959–61), president of the Yugoslav and the Slovenian PEN Centre, and was a member of the Slovenian Academy of Sciences and Arts.

[12] Ivan Tomažič, Jožef Šavli and Matej Bor, *Unsere Vorfahren – die Veneter* (Wien: Ed. Veneti, 1988), 5–6, 12.

[13] Anton Perdih, and Jože Rant, eds, *Zbornik prve mednarodne konference Veneti v etnogenezi srednjeevropskega prebivalstva* (Ljubljana: Jutro, 2002).

[14] Neven Budak, ed., *Etnogeneza Hrvata* (Zagreb: Matica Hrvatska, 1995).

[15] Radoslav Katičić, "Pitanje o podrijetlu hrvata u hrvatskome intelektualnom diskurzu danas," *Historijski zbornik* 52 (1999): 117–120.

[16] For the continuity theory see: Mate Suić, "Pristupna razmatranja uz problem etnogeneze hrvata," in Budak, *Etnogeneza Hrvata*, 13–27; Nenad Cambi, "Kontinuitet ili diskontinuitet: kasna antika – rani srednji vijek?" *Historijski zbornik* 52 (1999): 107–116; for the Iranian theory see: Vladimir Košćak, "Iranska teorija o podrijetlu hrvata," in Budak, *Etnogeneza Hrvata*, 110–16.

[17] Ivan Mužić, *Podrijetlo Hrvata. Autohtonost u hrvatskoj etnogenezi na tlu rimske provincije Dalmacije* (Zagreb: Matica Hrvatska, 1989).

[18] Robert Tafra, ed., *Hrvati i Goti* (Split: Iberia, 1996), 5.

[19] Ibid.

[20] Stjepan Pantelić, *Die Urheimat der Kroaten in Pannonien und Dalmatien* (Frankfurt am Main: Peter Lang, 1997).

[21] Ibid., 126–7.

[22] Košćak, "Iranska teorija o podrijetlu hrvata," 110–11.

[23] Mijo Ćurić, *Staroiransko podrijetlo Hravata* (Zagreb: [M. Ćurić], 1991).

[24] Znanstveno društvo za proučavanje podrijetla Hrvata, ed., *Tko su i odakle Hrvati. Revizija etnogeneze* (Zagreb: Znanstveno društvo za proučavanje podrijetla Hrvata, 1994).

[25] The Croatian President Tudjman was, at least, sympathetic to the Persian theory. In his office he kept an archaeological artefact from Persia, showing a chess-board like flag engraved in stone, which had been donated to him by the Islamic Republic of Iran.

[26] Znanstveno društvo za proučavanje podrijetla Hrvata, *Tko su i odakle Hrvati*, 45.

[27] Ibid., 91–3.

[28] Zlatko Tomičić, and Andrija-Željko Lovrić, eds *Staroiransko podrijetlo Hrvata* (Zagreb: Kulturni centar pri Veleposlanstvu I. R. Iran, 1999).

[29] See Branimir Anzulovic, *Heavenly Serbia. From Myth to Genocide* (New York, London: New York University Press, 1999).

[30] Olivera Milosavljević, *U tradiciji nacionalizma ili stereotipi srpskih intelektuala-ca XX veka o „nama" i „drugima"* (Belgrade: Helsinški odbor, 2002).

[31] Radivoj Radić, *Srbi pre Adama i posle njega* (Belgrade: Stubovi kulture, 2003), 173.

[32] Ibid., 11.

[33] Olga Luković-Pjanović, *Srbi... narod najstariji*, 2 vols (Belgrade: Miroslav, 1990). Both volumes were republished in 1993–4.

[34] Ibid., 11.

[35] Ibid., 346.

[36] Ibid., vol. 2, 255–7.

[37] Predrag Dragić Kijuk, ed., *Catena Mundi. Srpska hronika na svetskim verigama*, 2 vols (Belgrade, Kraljevo: Književne novine, 1992).

[38] Ibid., vol. 2, 888–913.

[39] Christian Promitzer, "Whose is Bosnia? Post-communist Historiographies in Bosnia and Herzegovina," in *Historiography in Southeast Europe after Socialism*, ed. Ulf Brunnbauer (Münster: Lit-Verlag, 2004), 74–80.

[40] Mustafa Imamović, *Historija Bošnjaka* (Sarajevo: Bošnjačka zajednica kulture Preporod, 1997).

[41] See Jon Kværne, "Da li je Bosni i Hercegovini potrebno stvaranje novih pov-ijesnih mitova?," in *Historijski mitovi na Balkanu*, ed. Husnija Kamberović (Sarajevo: Institut za istoriju, 2004), 85–107.

[42] Enver Imamović, *Korijeni Bosne i bosanstva* (Sarajevo: Međunarodni centar za mir, 1995); Enver Imamović, *Porijeklo i pripadnost stanovništva Bosne i Hercegovine* (Sarajevo: Art 7, 1998).

[43] Imamović, *Korijeni Bosne i bosanstva*, 129.

[44] Ibid., 37, 293.

[45] Imamović, *Porijeklo i pripadnost stanovništva Bosne i Hercegovine*, 45.

[46] Ibid., 112–13.

[47] Dubravko Lovrenović, "Snažna ambicija slabog znanja," *Dani*, No. 173, September 22 2000.

[48] Stefan Troebst, *Die bulgarisch-jugoslawische Kontroverse um Makedonien* (Munich: Oldenbourg-Verlag, 1983).

[49] Lidija Slavaeva, *Etnogeneza na makedonskiot narod – kontinuitet i tradicija* (Skopje, 1992); Nade Proeva, *Studii za antičkite Makedonci* (Skopje, Ohrid: Macedonia Prima, 1997).

[50] Council for Research into South-eastern Europe, ed., *Macedonia and its Relations with Greece* (Skopje: Macedonian Academy of Sciences and Arts, 1993), 16.

[51] Branko Panov, ed., *Istorija na makedonskiot narod*, vol. 1.: *Makedonija od prais-toriskoto vreme do potpaġanjeto pod turska vlast (1371 godina)* (Skopje: Institut za na-cionalna istorija, 2000), 41–2, 234, 297.

[52] Vasil Tupurkovski, *Istorija na Makedonija. Od drevnina do smrtta na Aleksandar Makedonski* (Skopje: Titan, 1993), 436–7.

[53] Alexander Donski, *The Descendants of Alexander the Great of Macedon. The Arguments and Evidence That Today's Macedonians are Descendants of the Ancient Mac-edonians* (Sydney: Grigor Prlichev, 2004).

[54] Alexandar Donski, *Etnogenetskite razliki pomeġu Makedoncite i Bugarite* (Štip, 2000).

| | Autochthonous | | Non-Slavic Migratory Origins |
	as Slavs	*as other people*	
Slovenians	Venetians		
Croats		Illyrians, Romans	Iranians (Goths, Sarmatians, etc.)
Serbs	Serbs (original Slavs)		
Bosnians		Illyrians	
Macedonians		ancient Macedonians	

Figure 6. Classification of Myths of Origin Among the Southern Slavs of Former Yugoslavia

6

Nationalism, Historiography, and the (Re)Construction of the Rwandan Past

Tom Turner

The genocide of 1994 resulted from a conflict of 'dual nationalisms,' one in which Hutu were autochthonous and Tutsi were foreigners, and another in which all Rwandans were one.[1] Since 1994, when the Tutsi-dominated Rwandan Patriotic Front took power, a considerable effort has been made to impose a common version of history as a basis of national unity.

Many of the facts are clear. Virtually all Rwandans speak the same language, Kinyarwanda. All were subjects of the same *mwami* (king). The monarchy that was overthrown during decolonisation was a Tutsi monarchy, headed by a member of the Nyiginya clan. The Tutsi, from whom the monarch and his major lieutenants were drawn, were a minority of the population (14 percent, as compared to 85 percent Hutu and 1 percent Twa or "pygmies", according to outdated figures). Stereotypically, Tutsi were wealthy cattle raisers and Hutu were poor cultivators, but in fact most Tutsi were neither noble nor rich.[2]

The genocide was prepared by virulent anti-Tutsi propaganda, based on a racist version of history.[3] It cannot be surprising that the post-genocide regime has taken care to control the media and the writing of history in order to avoid a repeat of 1994's tragic events. I shall examine Rwandan history, in terms of past and present political influences on historiography and in terms of disputed points, before closing with the effort to impose a common vision.

Politics and historiography in Rwanda

Since the genocide, no Rwandan has produced a comprehensive history of his country (with the partial exception of Muzungu), and no school textbooks have been produced, but President Paul Kagame provided the outline of such a history.[4] In a speech to the Nigerian War College in 2002 (as summarised by his office) he,

accused colonialists of dividing the people of the Great Lakes region in order to further their interests. They did this through the
creation of racial theories, myths, artificial borders, and other divisive practices... When the colonialists arrived in Rwanda they
found an organised state, with well-established institutions that
dated back to the 15th Century.[5]

According to Kagame, "people lived in harmony with each other in
the same villages and sharing the same culture and language..." The colonisers practised divide and rule, disrupting the societies of the Great Lakes
region, "making them extremely hierarchical and effectively destroying
all social cohesion." The president also criticised post-colonial regimes,
which had "failed to eradicate the negative ideologies inherited from our
colonisers..."[6]

President Kagame's speech was the latest in a series of efforts to redefine Rwanda's history, in line with political interests. Pre-colonial Rwanda,
in common with many other African states, comprised a central core under tight control surrounded by peripheral areas where central control
was loose and episodic.[7] At the centre, keepers of tradition conserved an
official version of the history of the kingdom and adapted it to changing
circumstances. In various regions, alternative versions were preserved, often varying considerably from the central version.

Rwanda was colonised politically by Germany, which lost its colony to
Belgium during the First World War. Ideologically, Rwanda was colonised
by the White Fathers, a missionary order of French origin. The White Fathers were searching for an African Constantine or Clovis and eventually
succeeded in gaining the dedication of the kingdom of Rwanda to Christ
the King.

The three components of Rwandan society—Tutsi, Hutu, and Twa—
existed prior to colonisation. What was new was the identification of these
categories as "races". That began with the German, Captain Bethe, in
1898.[8] Within a few years the Tutsi "race" had been linked to the "Hamites" previously identified in East Africa by the British explorer J. H.
Speke.[9] Implementing the racist idea that the Tutsi were "born to rule,"
the Belgians eliminated Hutu chiefs and provided western-style training
mainly to Tutsi boys.

Both administrators and missionaries collected various versions of
Rwandan history, but tended to value the version of the central court more
than regional variants. They synthesised this material and, crucially, they
interpreted it in terms of two macro-themes not present in the pre-colonial
versions, namely race and migration.

When Belgian administrators arrived in 1916, Father Léon Classe provided a document entitled *L'organisation politique du Ruanda au début de l'occupation belge*. [10]This served as a guide to the administrators as they took charge of Belgium's new possession. The major theme of Classe's synthesis was that Rwanda's political regime "can be assimilated rather exactly to the feudal regime of the Middle Ages" in Europe.[11]

The colonial synthesis of history incorporated key contributions from White Fathers Albert Pagès and Louis de Lacger, Rwandan priest Alexis Kagame, and Belgian anthropologist Jacques Maquet. Pagès legitimated the concept of Rwanda as *Royaume hamite* (Hamitic kingdom).[12] He saw the Tutsi not only as coming from Ethiopia, but as carriers of a monophysite Christian tradition.

Canon de Lacger confirmed the identification of the Tutsi ruling group as foreigners, describing Rwanda as occupying (with Burundi) the "Abyssinia of the Great Lakes."[13] He took his native France as a model of the "natural" development of a state. Although Rwanda lacks an "inevitable" shape like the French hexagon, the growth process was natural, "a rising curve, continuous and regular." [14] Much as France had grown outward from the Ile de France, Rwanda had expanded from its core, over a period of five centuries.

The Abbé Kagame produced a series of works presenting the history of Rwanda and its monarchy. He made concerted efforts to push back the founding of the kingdom. As David Newbury suggests, Kagame was a "trick cyclist", postulating a fixed cycle of royal names, and filling in the gaps with newly created kings to whom a cycle of attributes (e.g. war leader) could be assigned. [15]During the 1930s, when Belgium was supervising the transfer of Rwandans to the present Democratic Republic of Congo, Kagame produced a version of history that pushed nineteenth century Rwandan incursions into Congo far into the past. This would provide ideological justification for post-independence irredentism. Kagame described Rwandan institutions in terms of a "code", consequently fixing a static vision of them.[16]

At the end of the colonial era, the Belgian anthropologist Jacques Maquet made another influential contribution to Rwandan historiography.[17] He gave a new lease of life to racial stereotypes of Rwandans: the tall Tutsi, stocky Hutu, and diminutive Twa. More important, Maquet adopted a functionalist perspective, according to which all the elements of the Rwandan social system interacted harmoniously in the ethnographic present. Pre-colonial Rwanda "enjoyed harmony, so the story went, because its chief social institution—*ubuhake* cattle clientship—had facilitated social mobility across fluid occupational categories."[18]

This vision of pre-colonial harmony was the fruit of research collaboration between Maquet and Kagame so one should not be surprised that

Maquet confirmed many of Kagame's arguments, and in particular his static view of Rwandan society. Maquet's view, oriented toward the Tutsi aristocracy, was derived from Tutsi aristocratic informants. He declined to work with Hutu informants because "the more competent people on political organisation were the Tutsi" and his "aim was not to assess the opinions and knowledge of the Rwandan population on their past political organisation but to discover as accurately as possible what that organisation was."[19]

Use of the ethnographic present seems to have blinded Maquet to changes in Rwandan society and in particular to the centralisation carried out under *mwami* Rwabugiri in the second half of the nineteenth century. Pottier notes that while the categories Tutsi, Hutu and Twa had existed earlier, "Rwabugiri's administration not only rigidified social distinctions in ethnic terms, but also engendered a process of ethnic self-consciousness among groups of Tutsi in Nduga, central Rwanda."[20] Thus, the Europeans did not so much divide the Rwandans as add the ideological themes of race and migration to an existing system of stratification. They simplified Rwandan stratification by eliminating Hutu chiefs, seen as anomalous, and crystallised it by distributing identity cards bearing the label "Tutsi", "Hutu" or "Twa".

During decolonisation, the Rwandan electorate faced a choice between two forms of nationalism, a monarchist version addressed to all Rwandans and a Hutu ethnonationalist version. The monarchist Union Nationale Rwandaise (Rwandan National Union, UNAR) had emerged from an organization called the Association des Eleveurs du Ruanda-Urundi (Association of Cattle Raisers of Ruanda-Urundi), created in 1957 with the support of the *mwami* and the Tutsi clergy.[21]

UNAR was Janus-faced. Its call for immediate independence drew the support of the Lumumbist wing of the Congolese National Movement (MNC-L). Other monarchists were backward looking. Citing Kagame, they 'proved' that the Hutu could not be the brothers of the Tutsi, since the Hutu had been present when the Tutsi arrived and had been conquered by the latter.[22]

On the Hutu side the terms of the debate had been set by the so-called Bahutu Manifesto of 1957, later adopted by Parmehutu (Parti du Mouvement de l'Emancipation Hutu - Party of the Movement for Hutu Emancipation). The Manifesto cast the decolonisation struggle in terms of Tutsi dominance versus Hutu emancipation. Tutsi dominance was described through metaphors borrowed from the colonisers: for example the Tutsi were described as "Hamites" and "feudalists."[23]

Rwandan historian Déo Byanafashe argues that the "politicisation of the Hutu-Tutsi frustration" dates from the Bahutu Manifesto.[24] However, this document, which is actually entitled *Note on the Social Aspect of the Native Racial Problem in Ruanda*, was a reply to the "Mise au point" (setting the record straight) issued by the Tutsi-dominated Conseil Supérieur du Pays (Higher Council of the Country). The Bahutu Manifesto later became the "gospel of the 'revolutionaries'" according to Byanafashe, who argues that the manifesto politicised what was until then only a "social" problem of discrimination.[25] In my view the "Mise au point," produced by a council chaired by the *mwami*, was already in the political domain.

The manifesto contrasted the appeal to unity that could serve to "veil" continued Tutsi domination to a perceived necessity to maintain ethnic identity, as reflected in the identity cards. The Hutu authors claimed that to suppress the reference to ethnicity would make it impossible to track the progress in promoting the social standing of their community. (Such ethnic marking would facilitate ethnic violence, including the genocide of 1994.)

During the turbulent period 1959-1962, Rwanda was the theater of a "social revolution" led by the Hutu counter-elite and supported by the Belgians, which led to independence.[26] The governments first of Grégoire Kayibanda (1962-1973), then of Juvénal Habyarimana (1973-1994), promoted a Hutu ethno-nationalist version of history. Rwandan writer Benjamin Sehene describes the period of the Hutu republics as one of "growing amnesia, dominated by the law of silence, of the unspoken, of memories collectively repressed."[27]

Yet despite the hegemonic discourse, important historical writing did take place. The Maquet vision of pre-colonial harmony was discredited by new research. *Ubuhake*, (service in exchange for cows — the basis of Tutsi-Hutu relations according to Maquet) was shown to be only one form of clientship. Control over land was much more important, and as Pottier summarizes, "the vast majority of the population, Hutu and Tutsi, had had virtually no control over their land and labour power."[28]

Rwandan historian Ferdinand Nahimana wrote a doctoral dissertation in which he demonstrated that some Hutu kingdoms were annexed during the colonial era.[29] (Years later, Nahimana became director of the extremist radio RTML. He was convicted of genocide by the international tribunal in 2003.)

In 1987, historian Emmanuel Ntezimana attacked the orthodoxy of the day, arguing that the three old hereditary social categories — Tutsi, Hutu and Twa — were not different ethnic groups. He denounced "the absurdity of certain debates on the part of supposedly well-read people who aim to take exclusive ownership of earlier civilizations." [30] His opinions were rebutted by the magazine *Kangura*, which preferred the orthodoxy according to which the Twa had arrived first, followed by the Hutu, and last of

all the Tutsi. The nomadic Twa could not have created "social organisation." The Hutu, who cleared the land, were the true founders of Rwanda.
"Who has the right to change the history of the country?" the magazine
demanded.[31]

The Rwandan Patriotic Front (RPF) invaded Rwanda from Uganda
in 1990, beginning a four-year civil war that culminated in the genocide.
Pottier denounces "knowledge construction by the Rwandan Patriotic
Front."[32] Based on the interpretation of Maquet—one of the few English-
language works available to the exiles—the RPF began promoting the image of a prosperous, harmonious pre-colonial Rwanda.

An important step in consolidating the new RPF orthodoxy took place
between May 1998 and March 1999, in the office of then President Pasteur
Bizimungu (a Hutu). In the report on the series of "reflection meetings",
"The Unity of Rwandans" figures as chapter one, followed by chapters on
democracy, justice, the economy, and security. In chapter one, some of the
main points later presented by President Kagame are set forth:

> Before colonizers arrived in Rwanda, Rwanda was a Country
> which had developed its governing structures, all its citizens feel-
> ing that they were together, that it was their Country which they
> were protecting together and expanding when it was necessary
> (sence [sic] of national identity).... The meeting found out that
> in the history of anti-colonial Rwanda, there had never been war
> between Hutus and Tutsi, or between Tutsis and Twas or between
> Twas and Hutus, as nowadays there are journalists who say that
> the war between Tutsis and Hutus has been existing for too many
> years. Wars which took place in Rwanda were aimed at fighting
> enemies or expanding its borders.[33]

The assembled politicians, military leaders, and academics apparently
reached a consensus on "national unity" as well as democracy and justice.
This consensus forms the basis of the new, semi-official history of Rwanda. It has been complemented by recent scholarship, notably the work of
David Schoenbrun, demonstrating the presence in the Great Lakes region
of Cushitic cattle-raisers and Bantu agriculturalists, for several millennia.
[34] This is seen as decisive refutation of the claim that the Tutsi arrived
recently. Other recent scholarship, notably by Jan Vansina and Catharine
Newbury is ignored or resisted. I turn next to Vansina for a list of challenges to the new orthodoxy.

Vansina's challenge

In the terminal colonial period, the Institut de Recherche Scientifique en Afrique Centrale (IRSAC) launched a massive research project to collect regional versions of Rwandan history. Jan Vansina published a preliminary synthesis in 1962, then returned four decades later with a comprehensive interpretation. In *Le Rwanda ancien* he called into question many points in both the colonial orthodoxy as adapted by the Hutu regimes, and in the RPF's revised history.[35] I will comment on some of the most important of these interpretations of Rwandan history to 1900, juxtaposing them to Fr. Kagame's colonial orthodoxy as summarized by Fr. Muzungu. Then I will refer to other problems concerning colonial history.

   1.   "There never were any massive immigrations of Twa hunter-gatherers, of Hutu cultivators and of Tutsi pastoralists, since these social categories developed little by little, on the spot, to classify people already there." [36]

The trope of the three migrations lies at the heart of the colonial orthodoxy as crystallised in the writings of de Lacger, Kagame and others, and conserved in the post-colonial orthodoxy of the Hutu republics. The website of the banned political party Mouvement Démocratique Républicain (MDR) presents such a history.[37] The MDR's persistence in disseminating this version presumably was one of the factors leading to its being banned on the eve of the presidential elections of 2003.

Muzungu summarises recent archaeological findings, from which he concludes that nothing indicates that "our present populations" had an "external" origin. However he immediately qualifies this sweeping assertion by writing that it was in "a second phase of peopling of the Rwandan territory that migratory movements would bring in populations of diverse origins, and in different periods."[38] He cites the Nyiginya, Rwanda's ruling clan, among immigrant populations from Uganda.[39]

Muzungu (born 1932) is attempting to cleanse Kagame's version of Rwandan history by stripping it of Tutsi-Hutu conflict. In contrast, younger Rwandan scholars reject the orthodox version with its recent Tutsi migration. They cite the work of archaeologists and the historical linguistics of Schoenbrun in support of an alternative version. However, they appear reluctant to abandon the notion of successive waves of migration. Kanimba Misago cites Schoenbrun to make the Bantu wave of migration reach the Great Lakes region later than the Cushitic cattle-raisers. [40] Vansina's assertion that the social categories Tutsi, Hutu, and Twa "were elaborated little by little..." has neither been accepted nor challenged. The connection of Hutu with migrating Bantu cultivators and Tutsi with Cushitic pastoralists is assumed.

2.   "No one fell from heaven and there never was a historic person-age named Gihanga (the creator), founder of an immense kingdom." [41]

Prior to the European reworking of Rwandan history in terms of three waves of migration, the founding of Rwanda was explained by a myth according to which Sabizeze, founder of the Nyiginya line, was born in heaven and his body pulled miraculously from a jar of milk. His father Nkuba (thunder) did not want to recognise the child. So Sabizeze left heaven to live here on earth. He brought with him his sister Nyampundu ("cries of joy"), his brother Mututsi, and a couple of "faithful Twa servants," cows, goats, and chickens. Kagame and his disciple have no trouble recognizing this as a myth of origins, deriving Nyiginya power from heaven.[42] Muzungu, anxious to avoid reviving Hutu-Tutsi conflict, shies away from the implication that the Tutsi as a group "fell from heaven" to become rulers over the Hutu.

To Kagame and Muzungu, Gihanga was the title of a real person, or a title born by a series of persons. He established four successive royal residences, "two in the present Congo-Kinshasa and two others in Rwanda."[43] One of the sons of Gihanga supposedly inherited the kingdom of Rwanda, another Ndorwa (in the north, now divided by the Ugandan border), and a third Bugesera (in the south, now divided between Rwanda and Burundi). Two other sons founded the dynasties of Bunyabungo (the present Bushi, in Congo) and Bushubi. Recent research suggests that belief in Gihanga remains strong, particularly among older Rwandans.[44]

3.   "The Nyiginya kingdom is much more recent than one had thought; it dates only from the middle or end of the 17th century... Modern Rwandan culture is not the inheritor of an atavistic gift for organisation or for centralisation." [45]

Rwandans like to think that their state is very old. Rather than compare the chronologies of Vansina, Kagame, and Léon Delmas, Muzungu simply opts for his compatriot Kagame.[46]

Kagame and other colonial history makers did their work well. Most secondary and tertiary sources refer to five centuries of history. The Bahutu Manifesto opted for nine centuries — apparently accepting Kagame's date of 1091 for Gihanga — as though recent oppression were greater for being older.

4.   "Neither the first king nor his immediate successors conquered all of Rwanda and the history of the Nyiginya kingdom is not synonymous with that of Rwanda."[47]

Both Vansina and Muzungu devote several chapters to Nyiginya annexation of rival states, a process that began in the seventeenth century according to Vansina and in the fourteenth century according to Muzungu and Kagame. As regards the "conquest of the North-West," Muzungu describes supposed conquests extending to the shores of Lake Kivu, carried out by Yuhi II Gahima, 12th king, 1411-1477. Gahima allegedly committed the error of leaving in place the rulers of the principalities of the "Kiga" (mountain people), requiring only that they pay taxes to the centre. Muzungu remarks mildly that "the book of Ferdinand Nahimana, *Rwanda: Emergence d'un Etat* is a useful reference to the study of the particularities of the region," although the author did not take into account Gahima's policy.[48] Nahimana in fact went much further, maintaining that several states of the northwest did not pass under control of the central administration until the early twentieth century, with German and Belgian aid.[49]

6.   "The kingdom did not possess an impersonal administration, homogeneous and centralised." [50] Conquests and internal changes did not proceed from a plan, carefully worked out by the king and his advisors.

Contemporary Rwandans tend to see the highly centralised state that emerged from colonial reform as having existed in that form for many centuries. The Mortehan reform of the late 1920s (named for the Belgian resident who undertook it) instituted a French-style structure in which each province had the same relationship to the centre and to its subdivisions. Such a reform was impossible until colonial forces and those of their ally or subordinate the *mwami* had conquered the various independent or semi-independent microstates of western Rwanda. It is ironic that President Kagame and his followers criticise the colonialists for having introduced division into Rwanda, since the colonialists transformed an idiosyncratic system of administration into a much more standardised one.

8.   "Abundance and order" did not characterise the old Rwanda. It is false to think that everyone was happy in his place in the social hierarchy and lived in peace under a wise king. [51]

Abundance and wellbeing are central to the argument of the current authorities. One of my students referred in an essay to a "land of milk and honey." Colonialism was not designed to advance the welfare of Rwandans, but its legacy cannot be assessed on the basis of stereotypes such as these. As regards order, Vansina presents a convincing picture of nineteenth century Rwanda as prey to disorder and to growing tension between Tutsi and Hutu. Most of the errors he identifies, including this one, involve projecting the present into the past and regarding that past through rose colored glasses.

Similar problems arise concerning the colonial period: the first six decades of the twentieth century. My Rwandan students are virtually unanimous in asserting that Africa was divided at the Berlin Conference of 1884-85. They seem not to know that the conference set groundrules for the division of Africa, but did not for the most part rule on territorial claims.

This is strange, since one of their professors—Célestin Kalimba—wrote an article for a history department seminar setting out the various negotiations on Rwanda's frontiers that continued until 1910.[52] For nationalist purposes, it is important to be able to claim that Rwanda lost one-third of its territory at Berlin, and that the partition took no acount of political or ethnic realities on the ground. There are several problems here. First, the Rwandan state of 1885 comprised a core under direct rule as well as fringe areas where the *mwami* was prestigious, but did not rule. Moreover, it is an error to generalize about Rwanda's borders. Shyaka defines borders as "places where [various] social environments meet." He argues that the borders of Rwanda were located where the Rwandan space "met the Mushi in the West, the Murundi in the South, the Munyankole in the North and the Munyambo in the East."[53] This seems accurate as regards the south, where Rwanda and Burundi were engaged in a long-term, zero-sum conflict. However, in the southwest, small states lay between Rwanda and Bushi. In the north, there apparently was a transition zone between Nkole and Rwanda.

The assertion that the partition took no account of politico-ethnic realities is invalid. Under the rules laid down at Berlin, colonial dominions were delimited by negotiation between or among colonial powers, in which politico-ethnic realities were taken into account. In the north, Germans and British argued about whether Bufumbira was part of Rwanda. In the east, Rwanda lost its province of Gisaka to the British who were going to build their Cape to Cairo railroad across it. It was restored to Belgian-ruled Ruanda-Urundi precisely because of politico-ethnic realities.[54]

Controlling the past

In the aftermath of the genocide, observers noted two diametrically opposed versions of pre-colonial history. For Hutu, it was a period of feudal oppression. For Tutsi in contrast, it was a lost Eden.[55] Both versions are oversimplifications, dating from the colonial era. Since then, one of the communities has lost its ability to propagate its vision of the past, whereas the other has taken its place in the driver's seat.

The idea that political power includes the capability of writing or rewriting history is nothing new. Orwell expressed it through a chilling slogan, "Who controls the past controls the future; who controls the present controls the past."[56] Since 1994, the RPF has enjoyed a decade of political dominance, during which time it has moved slowly to impose its version of the past, presumably so as to "control the future."

The RPF approach is indirect but typically Rwandan. The authorities have made known what the appropriate history is through mechanisms such as President Bizimungu's "reflection meetings" and President Kagame's speech in Nigeria. They have made it clear that "divisionist" speech will not be tolerated, through the measures taken against the MDR party and against the country's main human rights organization, LIPRODHOR (Ligue rwandaise pour la promotion et la défense des droits de l'homme—Rwandan League for Promotion and Defence of Human Rights).[57] Given an outline of a non-divisive history, and examples of the dangers of non-cooperation, it seems likely that some of the country's intellectuals will cooperate in filling in the outline of Rwanda's new history. Those who disagree probably will "keep silent to live another day."[58]

The new history outline is being put to use. In solidarity camps (*ingando*), incoming university students, Hutu ex-combatants and other sensitive categories of the population are instructed on Rwandan history among other topics.[59] A public institution, the Forum for Concertation of Political Formations, provides training courses for political party leaders and staff. The curriculum for the first course includes major types of political regime and structure and functioning of a political party. More surprising, except in the context of post-genocide Rwanda, is the sixth theme, "Process of Constitution and Consolidation of the Rwandan state" with two sub-topics: "Analysis of the Interpretations of the History of the Peopling of Rwanda," and "Process of Constitution of the State and of Systems of Government in Rwanda." Suggested speakers on the sixth theme include Prof. Kanimba Misago (Archaeology), Prof. Gamaliel Mbonimana (History) and Brigadier-General Frank Rusagara.[60] One hopes that the authors of the outline recognize the gap between peopling (thousands of years ago) and state formation (during the past few centuries). Presumably party leaders and cadres will emerge with a clear idea of what to say and what to avoid saying, about the history of their country.

It would be unjust to lay all the blame for the failure to produce an up-to-date national history on the shoulders of the central government. Part of the problem derives from the composition of the post-genocide history department at the National University. The history department has had to work with whatever historians were available, whether Anglophone or Francophone, whether specialising in pre-colonial, colonial or post-colonial history. Inevitably, there were gaps.

The department held a seminar on Rwandan history in December 1998. Twenty-two papers were received and published in mimeographed form without revision. These papers constitute a useful baseline for the state of knowledge and understanding of Rwanda's past as of that date.[61] However, the quality is very uneven. Some authors are writing on topics they have mastered, for example Paul Rutayisire on "Rwandan Catholicism on trial". [62] Others reproduce dubious arguments from earlier writings, such as the presentation of the mythical Gihanga as fact.

Participants in the seminar expressed the wish that a journal of Rwandan history be published. Instead, much of the discussion of Rwanda's history has taken place in the meetings and publications of the University's Center for Conflict Management (CCM).

Rwanda remains overwhelmingly dependent upon foreign aid, but care is taken to ensure that aid in the area of history and social science does not dilute the ability to "control the past." Two examples may suffice. The US Agency for International Development (USAID) assisted the National University of Rwanda through a sub-contractor, the University of Maryland (UMD). Maryland implemented projects in several areas, including computer technology, distance learning, and the CCM. Late in 2003, at the end of the grant period, the CCM and UMD co-sponsored a seminar on the legacy of the genocide. During the seminar, foreign researchers whose papers went against the accepted view of the past were criticised by Rwandan colleagues, some even being accused of genocide denial. Their offence may have been to give a voice to silenced sectors within Rwandan society. The papers of the meeting have yet to be published.

A multidisciplinary team from the University of California, Berkeley, received financing from the US Institute of Peace for a project on writing a new history curriculum for Rwanda's schools.[63] Implementation included organisation of a seminar in Kigali, with Rwandan and American participants. The seminar allegedly was told by a representative of the Ministry of Education, "Foreigners will not write the curriculum."[64]

The desire to retain control over debate on key issues—the genocide above all—and developing the curriculum is understandable. The usefulness of nationalism in justifying such control is evident. What is unclear is the extent to which the monopolization of public discourse will lead to acceptance of the ideas being promulgated or even to another bout of "amnesia" of the sort identified by Sehene. [65]

Notes

[1] John F. Clark, "Rwanda: Tragic Land of Dual Nationalisms," in *After Independence*, ed. L. Barrington (Ann Arbor: University of Michigan Press, forthcoming).

[2] A. Mugesera, "Prépondérance de l'idéologie sur l'économie dans la crise identitaire au Rwanda (1957-1962)," in *Rwanda: Identité et citoyenneté*, ed. F. Rutembesa, J. Semujanga, et al., (Butare: Editions de l'UNR, 2003), 112-113, citing P. Leurquin, *Le niveau de vie des populations rurales du Ruanda-Urundi* (Louvain: Publications de l'Université Lovanium de Léopoldville, 1960), 203-295.

[3] Jean-Pierre Chrétien, J. F. Dupaquier, et al., *Rwanda: Les médias du génocide* (Paris: Karthala, 1995).

[4] Bernardin Muzungu, *Histoire du Rwanda pré-colonial* (Paris : Harmattan, 2003).

[5] Government of Rwanda, *Kagame Traces the Roots of Conflict in the Great Lakes* (Kigali, 2002) www.gov/rw/government/091702.html (accessed 15 July 2005).

[6] Government of Rwanda, *Kagame Traces*.

[7] Jeffrey Herbst, *States and Power in Africa* (Princeton: Princeton University Press, 2000); Benedict Anderson, *Imagined Communities: Reflections on the Origins and Spread of Nationalism* (New York: Verso, 1991); Catharine Newbury *The Cohesion of Oppression. Clientship and Ethnicity in Rwanda, 1860-1960* (New York: Columbia University Press, 1988); Ferdinand Nahimana, *Le Rwanda: Emergence d'un Etat* (Paris: Harmattan, 1993).

[8] Jan Vansina, *Le Rwanda ancien. Le royaume nyiginya* (Paris: Karthala, 2001), 242.

[9] John Hanning Speke, *The Discovery of the Source of the Nile* (New York: Dover, 1996/1868), chapter IX. "History of the Wahuma."

[10] Léon Classe, *L'organisation politique du Rwanda au début de l'occupation belge (1916). Note redigée par le R.P. Classe des Pères Blancs, Mission de Kabgayi, à la demande de l'Administration belge*. 28 August 1916. Manuscript, collection R. Lemarchand; Jean Rumiya, *Le Rwanda sous le régime du mandat belge (1916-1931)* (Paris: Harmattan, 1992), 134.

[11] Classe, *L'organisation politique*.

[12] Albert Pagès, *Un royaume hamite au centre de l'Afrique* (Brussels: Institut royal colonial belge, 1933).

[13] Louis de Lacger, *Ruanda* (Namur: Grands Lacs, 1939), 114.

[14] Lacger, *Ruanda*, 113-114.

[15] Alexis Kagame *Un abrégé de l'ethnohistoire du Rwanda* (Butare: Editions Universitaires du Rwanda, 1972); David Newbury, "Trick Cyclists? Recontextualizing Rwandan Dynastic Chronology," *History in Africa* 21 (1994): 191-217.

[16] Alexis Kagame, *Le Code des institutions politiques du Rwanda pré-colonial* (Brussels: Institut royal colonial belge, 1952); Claudine Vidal, *Sociologie des passions: Rwanda, Côte d'Ivoire* (Paris : Karthala, 1991), 45-61.

[17] Jacques Maquet, *Le système de relations sociales dans le Ruanda ancien* (Tervuren: Musée royal de l'Afrique centrale, 1954); *The Premise of Inequality* (London: Oxford University Press, 1961).

[18] Johan Pottier, *Re-Imagining Rwanda: Conflict, Survival, and Disinformation in the Late Twentieth Century* (Cambridge: Cambridge University Press, 2002).

[19] Maquet, *Premise* 3, cited by Pottier, *Re-Imagining*, 111.

[20] Pottier, *Re-Imagining*, 114.

[21] Déo Byanafashe, "Politisation des antagonismes et des attentes au Rwanda (1957-1961)," in *Rwanda: Identité et citoyenneté* ed. F. Rutembesa, J. Semujanga and A. Shyaka. (Butare: Université Nationale du Rwanda, 2003), 104, note 17, citing Filip Reyntjens, *Pouvoir et Droit au Rwanda: Droit public et évolution politique, 1916-1973* (Tervuren : Musée royal de l'Afrique centrale, 1985), 250.

[22] C. M. Overdulve, *Rwanda: un peuple avec une histoire* (Paris : Harmattan, 2003), 116-118.

[23] For the text of the "Note" or "Manifeste" see Overdulve, *Rwanda: un peuple*, 98-111.

[24] Byanafashe, "Politisation," 99-101.

[25] Byanafashe, "Politisation," 101.

[26] J. P. Harroy, *Rwanda: de la féodalité à la démocratie 1955-62* (Brussels: Hayez, 1984).

[27] Benjamin Sehene, "Rwanda's collective amnesia," *UNESCO Courier* (1999) No. 12.

[28] Pottier, *Re-Imagining* 13, citing Catharine Newbury, *Cohesion*, 13.

[29] Nahimana, *Le Rwanda*.

[30] E. Ntezimana, "Histoire, culture et conscience nationale: le cas du Rwanda des origines à 1900," *Etudes rwandaises*, no. 4, (July 1987): 488-489, cited in Chrétien, *Médias*, 84-85.

[31] *Kangura*, no. 4, (November 1990): 21, cited in Chrétien, *Medias*, 109.

[32] Pottier, *Re-Imagining*, chapter 5.

[33] Rwanda, Office of the President, *Report on the Reflection Meetings Held in the Office of the President of the Republic from May 1998 to March 1999 (Detailed Document)* (Kigali: August 1999), 18.

[34] David Schoenbrun, *A Green Place, A Good Place: Agrarian Change, Gender, and Social Identity in the Great Lakes Region to the 15th Century* (Portsmouth, New Hampshire: Heinemann, 1998).

[35] Jan Vansina, "L'Evolution du royaume rwanda des origines à 1900," *Académie royale des Sciences d'Outre-Mer* 52, no.3 (1962); Vansina, *Rwanda ancien*.

[36] Vansina, *Rwanda ancient*, 249.

[37] Mouvement Démocratique Républicain, *MDR, les grandes lignes de l'histoire du Rwanda*. www.mdrw.org/histoirerwa.htm (accessed 15 July 2005).

[38] Muzungu, *Histoire*, 296.

[39] Ibid., 296-298.

[40] C. Kanimba Misago, "Peuplement ancien du Rwanda: à la lumiére de récentes recherches," in *Rwanda: Identité et citoyenneté* ed. F. Rutembesa, J. Semujanga, et al. (Butare: Université Nationale du Rwada, 2003), 70.

[41] Vansina, *Rwanda ancient*, 249.

[42] Muzungu, *Histoire*, 73-74.

[43] Ibid., 76-79.

[44] E. Ntangana, "Le discours sur le peuplement au Rwanda à travers les perceptions de la population rwandaise," *Peuplement du Rwanda, enjeux et perspectives. Cahiers du Centre de Gestion des Conflits* no. 5 (2002): 114.

[45] Vansina, *Rwanda ancient*, 249.

[46] Muzungu, *Histoire*, 12-13, citing Léon Delmas. *Généalogie de la noblesse (les Batutsi) du Ruanda* (Kabgayi: n.p., 1950).

[47] Vansina, *Rwanda ancient*, 249.

[48] Muzungu, *Histoire*, 126-127, citing Nahimana, *Rwanda*.

[49] Nahimana, *Rwanda*, 289-314.

[50] Vansina, *Rwanda ancient*, 249.

[51] Vansina, *Rwanda ancient*, 249.

[52] P. Célestin Kalimba, "Le Rwanda: les frontières," in *Les Défis de l'Historiographie rwandaise* ed. Déogratias Byanafashe (Butare: Université Nationale du Rwanda, 2004), 150-159; Sybil E. Crowe, *The Berlin West African Conference* (Westport, Connecticut: Greenwood, 1970); and Simon Katzenellenbogen, "It didn't Happen at Berlin: Politics, Economics and Ignorance in the Setting of Africa's Colonial Boundaries," in *African Boundaries: Barriers, Conduits and Opportunities* ed. P. Nugent and

A. I. Asiwaju, (New York: Pinter-Cassel, 1996), 21-34.

[53] Anastase Shyaka, "La genèse des conflits dans les pays d'Afrique des grands lacs: Rwanda, Burundi, RDC et Ouganda," in *Peuplement du Rwanda: Enjeux et perspectives* (Cahiers du Centre de Gestion des Conflits) No. 5 (2002): 135, citing P. C. Kalimba, "Les frontières du Rwanda," 1999 (published as Kalimba, "Le Rwanda: les frontières" in Byanfashe, *Les défis*, see note 49).

[54] Rumiya, *Rwanda sous le régime*, 87-129; W. R. Louis, *Ruanda-Urundi, 1884-1919* (Westport, Connecticut: Greenwood, 1979).

[55] C. Braeckman *Terreur africaine. Burundi, Rwanda, Zaïre: les racines de la violence* (Paris: Fayard, 1996).

[56] George Orwell, *1984* (New York: Harcourt, Brace & World, 1949).

[57] B. Uzaramba, "Affaire Liprodhor, Les accusés rétorquent," *Amani* 54-55 (2004): 16-17.

[58] D. M. Gasana, "Keeping silent to live another day," *Rwanda Newsline* 15-22 September 2004, 8

[59] Fatuma Ndangiza, "Sensibilisation communautaire comme stratégie de construction de paix: Cas des 'Ingando' au Rwanda," in *Afrique des Grands Lacs: Sécurité et Paix Durable* ed. Anastase Shyaka and Faustin Rutembesa, Cahiers du Centre de Gestion des Conflits no. 9 (Butare: Université Nationale du Rwanda, 2004), 208-223.

[60] Forum de Concertation des formations politiques, *Thèmes du programme de formation politique* (unpublished document, Kigali, 2004).

[61] Département d'Histoire, Université Nationale du Rwanda, *Rapport de Synthèse. Séminaire sur l'Histoire du Rwanda* (stenciled document, Butare, 1998), published as Byanafashe, *Les défis*, 2004, see note 49.

[62] P. Rutayisire, *La christianisation du Rwanda (1900-1945)* (Fribourg: Université de Fribourg, 1987).

[63] S. Freedman, H. M. Weinstein, et al., "Education for Reconciliation in Rwanda: Creating a History Curriculum after Genocide," (unpublished document, n.d.).

[64] Personal communication.

[65] Sehene, *Collective Amnesia*, see note 27.

NATIONALIST ART AND PERFORMANCE

7

Mapping the Nation through Performance in Yemen
Sanaa as 'the Capital of the Present, the History, and the Unity'

Ulrike Stohrer

Music and dance are often regarded as the universal human language, immediately understandable by people all over the world without any translator. They are claimed to be primordial means of expression of authenticity independent of historical and cultural settings. Thus they are used again and again as means for governmental representation and political education.[1] This chapter examines how in a nationalist context an image of the past and present of a country is constructed by folkloristic performances.

Throughout its history, Yemen has been divided into several regions differing from each other politically, socially, and denominationally. In the twentieth century, two states and two different societies have been established on Yemenite soil. In the northern part, after the fall of the Ottoman Empire in 1918, the Zaidite (Shiite) Imamat took control and isolated Yemen from the outside world. In 1962 the Imam was overthrown by a revolution and the Yemen Arab Republic was established, which opened the country to the western world, while remaining a society with strong ties to tradition. The southern part, which had been part of the British Empire since the nineteenth century, was liberated from British colonial rule in 1967 and established itself as a socialist vassal state of the USSR. These two Yemen states were antagonistic towards each other throughout the Cold War. Nevertheless, a strong feeling of commonality existed in their populations and several attempts were made to unite the country. Finally, on May 22, 1990, the unification of North and South Yemen took place. Since that date national integration has been an important goal of government domestic policy. The ministry of culture and tourism is extensively involved in this process of establishing a homogenous national culture and creating one single national identity. Its efforts were intensified after the inner Yemenite war of 1994, which was a fundamental threat to the integrity of the state and made obvious that integration had not yet been successfully realized.[2]

Thus the ministry has taken measures to raise the national consciousness of the population as well as to demonstrate Yemenite unity to the outside world. Apart from promoting modernization, democratisation and integration, the "preservation" (*hifth*) of tradition (*turath*) as one of the constituents of the new identity is an important part of its activities. The performances of the National Orchestra and the National Folklore Ensemble are one of the strongest instruments to achieve this task. Even before the unification of the two Yemenite states, national folklore ensembles existed in both parts. For the correct understanding of the following it is important to note, that *both* the National Folklore Ensemble of North Yemen as well as that of South Yemen were established in cooperation with Soviet advisors and built on Soviet models. The present National Folklore Ensemble was formed by the fusion of these two ensembles. Many of its members, including its present director, were trained as choreographers, dancers and musicians in the former Soviet Union or in the German Democratic Republic.

Performances of the National Folklore Ensemble regularly take place at governmental ceremonies on national holidays such as the anniversary of the revolution (September 26, 1962 in North Yemen, October 14, 1967 in South Yemen) or the Day of Unification (May 22, 1990). Usually at these occasions stage plays are presented in the "cultural centre" (*markaz al-thaqafah*) in Sanaa in the presence of the president, numerous members of the government and foreign diplomats. These plays are often of allegorical content glorifying the given occasion and praising the government's efforts to improve the democratisation and modernization of the country.[3] Several folkloristic performances such as songs and dances from different regions of the country are integrated into these plays. The performances of the National Folklore Ensemble are also broadcasted on television.

In this chapter I will focus on one specific performance, which was presented on May 22, 2000 in Sanaa celebrating the tenth anniversary of the unification. This performance differs significantly from the above mentioned theatre plays. Thus it reveals essential features as well as present tendencies of governmental strategies to create a homogenized image of the present and past of Yemen. First I will give a short description of the performance, than I will analyse its choreographic, musical, and spatial characteristics, and finally I will point out the inherent gaps and inconsistencies of the image presented by this performance.

In this celebration the folkloristic dances were not embedded in a drama. They were not performed on a theatre stage, but in the open air in different urban squares. These were the famous Bab al-Yaman, the southern gate of the old city of Sanaa, and the Monument of the Unknown Soldier at Maidan al-Sab'in. Both places are important national symbols for Yemen.

The performers were 1000 students of the military academy, assisted by the members of the National Folklore Ensemble. The presentation consisted of two parts, each lasting about forty five minutes. The performances of the two parts were identical, distinguished only by place and set. Both parts were broadcast on television (see Fig. 7, page 124).[4]

The first part of the presentation was located at Bab al-Yaman, the gate of the old city of Sanaa. The performance started with a trumpet's signal, and the participants marched out of the gate of the old city. While marching they were chanting a chorus, which praised Yemenite Unity. A man carrying the Yemenite flag and two drummers led them. Reaching the square outside the gate, the participants divided into five groups each representing one region of the country: the mountains, the desert, Wadi Hadhramawt, the south coast and the west coast (Tihamah). The groups were distinguished by costumes of different colours and styles. Within a group all members were dressed in the same costumes. The costumes represented not every day clothes, but historical uniforms of soldiers. Therefore the performers were armed with traditional weapons such as daggers, swords and shields, spears or guns.

The five groups now took turns at performing a dance representing their region. Each took about five minutes. While one group was performing at the foreground, the other groups were standing at the back and the two sides of the square performing all together synchronously some steps on the spot and chanting. When one group had finished, the dancers returned to the gate, leaving the place to a new group that moved forwards, thus suggesting that the gate poured out more crowds of people.

Most of the performed dances—though of different musical accompaniment, tempo and dynamic—were based on the same basic step composed of two steps forwards and one hop. They were performed mostly within the choreographic pattern of a line or a circle. Sometimes the dancers joined their hands, a symbol of unity and brotherhood.

At the end of the first part of the presentation, the participants left the Bab al-Yaman and marched along the walls of the old city to the Maidan al-Sab'in, where the second part took place. This march was choreographed in the basic dance step too. Additionally the performers were chanting a chorus and weaving their daggers above their heads. The camera followed this march from the side and from the air showing the walking crowd and the silhouette of the city in such a way that the city seemed to be part of the crowd and moving as well (see Fig. 8, page 124).

The Maidan al-Sab'in was formerly the airport of Sanaa. Now it serves as a parade ground for military and government ceremonies. There is a tribune, from which the president and his guests of honour watched the performance. Opposite the parade ground, facing the tribune, the

Monument of the Unknown Soldier is situated. This monument is composed of imitations of six columns of the Sabean Bar'an temple in Marib standing on an arch. Like Bab al-Yaman, these columns are a national symbol too. Bab al-Yaman was also represented in the second part of the performance by a papier-mâché model placed in front of the monument. The performance at the Maidan al-Sab'in was the same as the one described above.

The performance ended with the appearance of a ship, from which twenty women (members of the National Folklore Ensemble) descended to dance around the square. They spun around their own axes and around each other while holding garlands of flowers in their hands. Twenty men joined them and they started dancing together in the same way, accompanied by a chorus telling about love and happiness (see Fig. 9, page 125).

Interpretation

When analysing this celebration, it is important to take into account the use of space as a symbolic transmitter of political messages and the construction of an image of the nation. In the presentation described above, the city of Sanaa plays an important role. Again and again during the performance, the camera gives a general view, simultaneously overlooking the performers, the gate and the old city. Yet the market area (*suq*) of the old city and the gate do not only form the scenery and stage; the silhouette of old Sanaa is a real actor within the performance, and sometimes seems to move together with the performers.

The meaning of this presentation is mainly constructed by means of the camera lens. The spectator's gaze on the performance is an artificial one. The camera is looking down on the performance from an elevated position, and most of the choreographic patterns can be recognized only from the air, not from stage level. No citizen of Sanaa is able to see his city from this perspective in daily live. Furthermore, to create this picture it was necessary to clear traffic and people from the street and the square outside Bab al-Yaman as well as the *suq* area behind the gate. This caused a major disruption to one of the most important traffic junctions of the capital. Also, the open square with four streets leading off was closed and given a new direction by the way the performers used the space. The performance as well as the camera lens was centred towards the gate, thus turning the city into a theatre stage according to European models. This perspective is alien to the traditional performance praxis in Yemen, where the spectators surround the performers at all sides.

The whole scene focused on Sanaa. Apart from the capital, no other city or region of the country was represented in the set. Only the costumes of the performers were reminiscent of some other regions. Although the silhouette of Sanaa dominated the visual appearance of the presentation, the urban culture of the capital—singing and dancing with lute accompaniment—was not represented in the performance. Therefore, this presentation draws a distorted picture: the urban silhouette is confronted with performances of mostly rural musical genres. Thus urban and rural cultures were visually and acoustically combined and at the same time levelled down by eliminating essential elements.

The performances did not present the dances in their traditional shape. Each regional style has been modified musically, choreographically and contextually to blend in with the others and merge into one homogenized "national style". The orchestration as well has been significantly altered. Traditional instruments that in their usual praxis belong to different musical genres and are therefore kept separated from each other were in this performance combined. Furthermore, elements of the European symphony orchestra such as violins or trumpets were added to the traditional Yemenite instruments. Finally, an anthem-like chorus chanted by all performers in unison, underscored the whole performance.

Thus the performed dances did not so much show the cultural diversity of the country, but rather reduced the characteristics of the different regions to their common grounds. The step-step-hop-base of most of the performed dances served as their smallest common denominator. Additionally, the steady accompaniment by orchestra and chorus constituted a uniform sound space, within which all the different performances were embedded. In this way the cultural differences among the various regions were levelled and their points in common were accentuated. This homogenized "national style" articulates the "one single Yemenite identity", that the government aims to establish. The ministry of culture points out:

> Our artistic heritage, though numerous in its forms from region to region and from town to town, merges and unites within the frame of the one single Yemenite identity. It expresses the unity of the Yemenite folklore arts as a vital expression of the unity of the Yemenite people and the Yemenite land.[5]

This performance represents the image that the ministry of culture wants to draw of contemporary as well as historical Yemen. It is not a presentation of folk customs in their traditional setting, but constitutes an artificial, imagined space that simultaneously symbolizes historical roots, modernization, democratisation, and unification. At the same time, however, some inconsistencies inherent in this concept become obvious, since that concept does not correspond with the real historical and present situation in Yemen.

The dancers, who represent the people of Yemen, are acting collectively and synchronously. There is no individual movement and character within this performance and no mark of any social status distinction among the protagonists. The whole group appears and acts as one single body, thus demonstrating its claimed unity and brotherhood. Yet, only one half of the population is represented. Although the ministry of culture always promotes the participation of women in cultural performances, this presentation was performed only by men. The twenty women appearing at the end of the performance seem not to be an integral part of it, but a somewhat artificial attempt to integrate women in a male dominated performance.[6] The women's costumes as well as their dancing is neither traditional nor a representation of modern Yemenite women. It is strongly influenced by Russian folklore.

The rhetoric of the ministry of culture calls Sanaa "the capital of the present, the history and the unity"[7] This title suggests that Sanaa was the capital during the whole history of Yemen and therefore stands for the primordiality and continuity of Yemenite nationalism. The unique architecture of the old city of Sanaa, which is on the UNESCO list of World Heritage, is certainly a source of national pride and identification. In fact, however, Sanaa has not always been the capital of the state, although it looks back to a long continuity of dwelling since antiquity. Sanaa played a determining role for the highlands, but not for the south coast and Wadi Hadhramawt, where other social, political, and cultural centres existed. Yemen was never such a united country as today. Throughout the history of Yemen there always existed several little states side by side. Further, there were long phases of foreign rule over some areas (the northern part belonged to the Ottoman Empire from 1539 to 1630 and from 1849 to 1918. Aden and surrounding areas were part of the British Empire from 1839 to 1967.)

Some symbols used in this celebration are ambivalent and may be interpreted differently. The gate of the old city of Sanaa, Bab al-Yaman, in its present shape is not an authentic Yemenite building. It was erected in 1885/86 by the Ottoman government as a huge stone monument in a pseudo antique style, replacing the former Yemenite mud-and-wood construction. Thus one could see Bab al-Yaman as a symbol of foreign rule rather than as a sign of Yemenite sovereignty. The performers' costumes represent the time before the revolution, an era which has in government rhetoric a negative image as a time of backwardness that was overthrown by the revolution. The historicizing costumes contrast with the modernized choreography and orchestration of the dances.

For an entire understanding of this presentation it is not sufficient to analyse only its visible and audible elements. As significant as what is represented by the performance is what is absent from it.

Yemenite nationalism as presented in this performance has a pure secular basis. Islam and the expression of religious faith is not central to it. An Islamic symbol such as the Great Mosque of Sanaa—one of the oldest in the Islamic world—is tacitly present as a part of the old city, but the camera does not emphasize it with a close-up. Also the chorus does not use religious formulas. Performative genres associated with the religious elite, such as the religious *nashshad* hymns or the Sanaani profane songs with lute accompaniment, although one of the oldest and most sophisticated musical traditions of the Arab culture, are not performed. The ministry of culture regards the Islamic era and the religious elite of the population as symbols of backwardness, feudalism, and "middle age particularism", standing as a negative antithesis to modernization, democratisation, and unity. Therefore they are eliminated from this performance, which is clearly directed towards the present and future.[8]

The performers' march from Bab al-Yaman to Maidan al-Sab'in does not only connect the two parts of the performance. Over and above that it connects the historical area of the city with its modern quarters and thus symbolizes the "continuity between past and present" as well as the "unity of our country, with which together we continue the march of unification"[9] The second part of the celebration takes place between the president's palace and the most modern and westernised quarter of Sanaa where the foreign embassies are located and international companies have their branches. The Maidan al-Sab'in was originally laid out as the airport of Sanaa and thus is itself a symbol of modernity. At the same time, however, the columns at the Monument for the Unknown Soldier point back to the age of antiquity, which serves as the very "root" of Yemenite nationalism and as a source of legitimacy for the government. The columns are part of the moon temple of Marib, the capital of the antique kingdom of Saba/Sheba (tenth to the fourth century BCE). This era symbolizes in government rhetoric the mythical foundation of the Yemenite state since this reign—one of six pre-Islamic reigns on Yemenite territory along the Incense Road—united wide parts of Yemen for some decades under its rule. Also the legendary Queen of Sheba who is an important national (and religious) figure is here implicitly associated with the performance, although she is not explicitly named. Thus the Monument of the Unknown Soldier may be seen as an arch of a bridge. It symbolically spans time and space, linking the present time with the age of antiquity and the root of Yemenite nationalism. In this way the ministry of culture is constructing a unified past for a country which has been unified only in recent times.

The symbolic visualization of Sanaa as "the capital of the present, the history and the unity" draws an imagined map of Sanaa, which represents a map of whole of Yemen. Sanaa itself becomes a metaphor for the Yemenite state. This metaphor draws an image of the state that does not show its several components as "unity in diversity". Contradicting history, social situation, and traditional performance praxis it presents a centralistic rather than a federal model. This corresponds with the governmental praxis to spread elements of the urban Sanaani architecture together with administrative institutions all over the country in spite of different climatic conditions and regional architectural traditions.[10] It also contradicts at the same time many current development projects in Yemen, which aim at administrative de-centralization.

The celebration of the tenth anniversary of Yemenite unity is strongly shaped by socialist ideology. This is due to the fact that the leading functionaries of the Department of Folk and Arts of the Ministry of Culture have a socialist background. Identifying the nation with the pagan era of antiquity instead of Christian or Islamic eras is a common feature of socialist cultural policy, and many Arab countries such as Tunisia, Egypt, Lebanon, Syria or Iraq follow this model. So the gap of nearly 1500 years between the rise of Islam and the revolution of 1962/67 in the image of Yemenite history presented by this performance can also be found in folk dance presentations and festivals for example in Lebanon, Syria and Iraq[11].

Yet, the government of Yemen as a whole is not socialist. It also comprises strong tribal and Islamic elements, which are also part of the national identity expressed otherwise by the government and also by the president. Thus the performance examined here does not only contradict reality, it does not even represent a coherent image of the government. Therefore it has also failed to achieve acceptance by parts of the Yemenite population. It can be regarded as another example of the many post-socialist countries, which are trying to find their own national identity by using the old socialist instruments.[12] Inverting Stalin's dictum that the cultural policy of the USSR had to be "national in form, socialist in content", we may say that the present cultural policy of Yemen is socialist in form and nationalist in content.

Notes
    [1] For examples see Anthony Shay, *Choreographic Politics. State Folk Dance Companies, Representation and Power* (Middletown, Connecticut: Wesleyan University Press, 2002).
    [2] See Jamal al-Suwaidi, ed., *The Yemeni War of 1994: Causes and Consequences* The Emirates Center for Strategic Studies and Research (Abu Dhabi, London: Saqi Books, 1995).
    [3] For detailed descriptions of such plays see Philip D. Schuyler, "The Sheba

River Dam. The Reconstruction of Architecture, History and Music in a Yemeni Operetta" *Revista de Musicologia* 16, no.3 (1993): 45-51 and Ulrike Stohrer, "Bar'a – Tanz, nonverbale Kommunikation und Identitaet im jemenitischen Hochland" (Ph.D. diss., University of Frankfurt, Main, 2003), 186-227.

[4] This article is based on a video kindly given to me by the Yemenite broadcast company.

[5] Ministry of Culture and Tourism of the Republic of Yemen, "Introduction," *A'ras Yamaniyah* July 8 1996, 1.

[6] This may be only a problem of organization since there are no women in the Yemenite army to be detailed for this activity in the same way and in such numbers as the male performers. Most of the female members of the National Folklore Ensemble are not Yemenites, but come from Korea, India, or Eastern Europe.

[7] Ministry of Culture and Tourism of the Republic of Yemen, "Introduction," *A'ras Yamaniyah* July 8 1996, 1

[8] In other performances the Islamic tradition is explicitly expressed in negative terms. See Schuyler, "The Sheba River Dam," 48-49.

[9] Ministry of Culture and Tourism of the Republic of Yemen, "'irs al-a'ras," *al-mahrajan al-awwal lil-a'ras al-yamaniyah,* July 7-17 1996, 7.

[10] See Werner Lingenau, and Wolfram Schneider, "Qamerias im ganzen Land. Zur Bedeutung traditioneller Architektur in der Arabischen Republik Jemen," *Jemen Report. Mitteilungen der Deutsch-Jemenitischen Gesellschaft* e.V., 1 (1989): 26-36.

[11] Cf. Christopher Stones, "The Ba'albakk Festival and the Rabbanis: Folklore, Ancient History, Musical Theater and Nationalism in Lebanon," *Arab Studies Journal* 11/12, nos 1/2 (2003/2004): 10-39 and see Amatzia Baram, *Culture, History, and Ideology in the Formation of Ba'thist Iraq, 1968-1989* (London: Macmillan, 1991), 140-142. In Ba'thist Iraq selected parts of the Islamic Middle Ages were also part of the national historiography as Saddam Hussein identified himself equally with the Babylonian King Nebuchadnezzar II (605-562 BCE) and the Islamic Caliph Harun al-Rashid (786-809 CE).

[12] For further examples see Shay, *Choreographic Politics*.

Figure 7. Silhouette of Bab al-Yaman and City with Performers

Figure 8. Maidan al-Sab'in and Spectators

Figure 9. Women from the National Folklore Ensemble Dancing with Garlands

8
The Decline of State Art in Post-Socialist Uzbekistan (1991-2004)

Kochi Okada

The meaning of the term decline depends on the specific context in which it is used: in relation to state art in the Russian Federation and former Soviet republics, the 'decline' has different causes and effects. In the case of Russia, which represents former mainstream Soviet art, the decline of state art means art functioning without state sponsorship based on Marxist-Leninist theory.[1] Whereas in the case of a former Soviet republic, the decline of state art means art functioning without state sponsorship focused on supporting the production and consumption of national arts.[2] This may explain why the effects of the decline of state art in Russia would differ from those in a former Soviet republic. Thus, in Russia the decline in state art brought down communist ideology, whereas in Uzbekistan the decline reduced the production of all state-sponsored arts. Furthermore, the separation of the republics from the Soviet Union inevitably introduces a new perception of national history in the national arts.

In order to examine the decline of state patronage and its affects on artistic practice in independent Uzbekistan (1991-2004), I am going to use as a case study the state's commissioning of a series of paintings for the Museum of History of Uzbekistan.[3] As a result of the relative lack of knowledge in the West of Uzbeki art and history the first section of this chapter will provide some background information on Uzbekistan and the history of Uzbeki fine arts in different historical periods. I will then discuss the history and development of the Museum of the History of Uzbekistan before looking in more depth at the museum's commissioning of a series of specific paintings.

Uzbekistan: cultural background

To Western cultural scholars Uzbekistan presents a special case among the former Soviet Central Asian nations because of its long history of statehood and illustrious urban culture. Unlike the other four neighboring countries in Central Asia (Kazakhstan, Kyrgyzstan, Turkmenistan and Tajikistan), Uzbekistan has a long history of statehood stretching back to the medieval period. Moreover, Russian Tsarist imperial expansion in the second half of the nineteenth century in the region did not completely conquer the three feudal states which were precursors to modern Uzbekistan. One of these states, the Kokhan Khanate, was merged into the Russian Turkestan General Governorship. The other two, the Bukharan Emirate and the Khivan Khanate, became protectorates of the Russian Tsarist Empire and even outlived it after the 1917 Russian Revolution. These protectorates were dismantled with the emergence of the Soviet Union in 1922. Nonetheless, Uzbekistan acquired characteristics of statehood with its modern frontiers, capital and institutions as early as 1938. Tashkent, the capital of Uzbekistan, was the fourth largest Soviet city after Moscow, Leningrad and Kiev and the most populous city in Central Asia with over 3,000,000 residents. Unlike neighboring capitals, which were more recently established as Russian military outposts or railway links, Tashkent has existed as a settlement for over two millennia.

Despite such a long history of statehood and an illustrious urban tradition, Western scholarship neglected Uzbeki cultural studies during the Soviet period. Soviet culture, then represented by an institutionalized Russian Soviet high culture was opposed to traditional, often religiously-oriented, popular culture. This view led to the assumption that with the establishment of the Soviet Union there was a violent replacement of one culture by the other.[4] Yet the value of this conclusion was questioned with the emergence of Uzbekistan as an independent state after 1991, when there was an introduction of new state symbols such as the anthem, flag, coat of arms and new national holidays.[5] The capacity to invent new symbolism for the independent state was a result of the Soviet high culture in Uzbekistan: the skills to rapidly create visual nationalistic symbols were learned under the Soviet system.

From then on many researchers focused on institutionalized culture, believing that the new state held a strong monopoly on cultural production. However, there was no questioning of whether the ideological framework, and its effect on the arts, had changed between the Soviet and the independence periods. Taking a closer look in particular at cultural institutions and the arts could provide a clearer view of the ideological frameworks of the different historical periods.

Arts and the state commissioning system in Uzbekistan

It is important to stress that Russian or Western style painting in Uzbekistan has always been based on state patronage functioning through a commissioning system. Providing a clear visualization of a state's political agenda, painting has become an important tool for any ideology. Being politically relevant helped Uzbekistan's painting to remain useful, whichever state came next: Tsarist, Soviet and latterly the independent nation state. Each historical period brought new dimensions to the portrayal of the state's agenda: art of the Tsarist period emphasized the importance of enlightening the backward colony; that of the Soviet era glorified the achievements of the Uzbek Soviet Socialist Republic under the communist state; and that of the independent period used art in the service of the new regime. Two issues come to the forefront in the study of Uzbeki painting. The first issue is that Uzbeki painting provided a better-visualized statement of a historical concept of the state than any literary sources could. The second is that Uzbeki painting openly emphasized the subordination of history to a particular ideological framework.

The birth of Western-style painting in Uzbekistan was due to Russian colonization which started in Central Asia in 1865. The first paintings were commissioned to portray the military and economic expansion of the Russian Tsarist Empire. Paintings showing Russian military achievements in Central Asia were brought to an international audience through exhibitions in Vienna, Paris and London in the 1870s. Russian economic advancement led to the display of paintings of the Uzbekistan landscape in the Russian pavilion in the Paris World Fair of 1900. The high status of commissions and the known authorship of these paintings by the military genre painter Vereshchagin (1824-1904) and the impressionist Korovin (1861-1939) established standards for painting in Uzbekistan.[6] Painting depicting scenes from Uzbekistan was intended to promote a positive image of Russian imperial policy, especially its political and educational aspects, to a broad spectrum of the public in the West, rather than for the satisfaction of private collectors or the decoration of private homes.

The Soviet period followed the tradition established by the Tsarists. However, in the Soviet period further developments led to the emergence of painting by Uzbeki artists and not just paintings depicting scenes of Uzbekistan. These painting were not aimed at the West, but were for local audiences. Furthermore, during this period state patronage in the Soviet Union began to be channeled through an arts institution: The Union of Artists of the USSR.[7] This institution, with its headquarters in Moscow, was a highly centralized, bureaucratized and politicized institution. It was responsible for bestowing all state commissions, the delivery of those commissions and the political correctness of the artists and their products. In 1938 in the newly created Soviet Republic of Uzbekistan, a local branch of the Union of Artists of the USSR was established which was called the Union of Artists of the Uzbek Soviet Socialist Republic. All artistic production and consumption was within an ideological framework based on the theory of Socialist Realism under a one-party state patronage system. The theory of Socialist Realism was based on the literary sources of Russian writer Maxim Gorky, and was implemented by administrator Andrei Zhdanov under Stalin's rule. Yet, there was a difference between the Russian and Uzbeki Unions of Artists. In Uzbekistan, the main goal of the Union was to develop the local artistic educational system and to educate Uzbeki artists to represent the Socialist Republic of Uzbekistan, and only after that to join a Russian attempt to promote the achievements of the Soviet state as a whole.[8]

The difference between mainstream Russian Soviet art and art from the Soviet republics further increased after the 1970s. Uzbekistan, by that time, had at last Uzbeki artists who had been educated in the local arts education institutions. These artists were not openly opposed to the central power of the Kremlin. Unlike some Russian artists who were known for their subversive resistance to the state, these Uzbeki artists worked together with, and for, the state. Uzbekis worked only within the state's commissioning system.[9] By working in the historical genre, they were capable of creating a visual history of their nation even before the emergence of the independent nation-state. The importance of their endeavor became obvious only after the dissolution of the Soviet Union in 1991. It made clear that Soviet state patronage together with its commissioning system had fuelled nationalistic imaginations instead of strengthening communist indoctrination.[10]

Once Uzbekistan gained independence, although the state patronage system was maintained, the commissioning system was changed. A 1997 decree by Uzbeki President Islam Karimov replaced the Union of Artists of the Uzbek Soviet Socialist Republic with the Academy of Fine Arts of Uzbekistan.[11] The new institution ended the previous state system of commissions because the newly independent state was financially incapable of continuing to fund fine arts on the same scale as had been the case under the Soviet Union. Instead, commissions depended on the president's immediate circle of appointed advisers rather than the arts institution.

The president's advisers took over control of ideological production. The advisers hired, in a seemingly random way, specialists from various socio-political disciplines to promote the new state ideology. The new ideological goal was to replace communism with the ideology of *mustakilik* (independence). However, what this term actually implied was unclear.

With time the word 'independence' became associated with the state, and *mustakilik* was gradually interpreted to mean a 'revival of the greatness of the independent state of Uzbekistan.' However, the content of the new ideology was and is rather vague and open to manipulation. Instead of supporting the emerging state itself, those many concepts based on 'independence' only reinforced the present regime of President Karimov.[12] In the period after Uzbekistan became independent, state patronage placed Uzbeki art in a hopeless situation. Art could not exist without state patronage, but the acceptance of state commissions meant that art would have to submit to the complete servitude of the new regime.

The Museum of the History of Uzbekistan: background

One aspect of the new ideology was the revival of a greater past, which meant a rejection of the immediate past: that associated with the Russian-connected, Tsarist and Soviet periods. It began with the replacement of the old Soviet monuments and institutions by new ones which were packaged as a part of the new ideological discourse. The epitome of these new state institutions is the Museum of the History of Uzbekistan. Its task was to obliterate the Russian past of Uzbekistan as well as to destroy the influence of Marxism-Leninism. To achieve this goal, the former Lenin museum was transformed into the new historical museum. This overt political statement overlooked the lack of suitability of the original Lenin Museum for such an important political project.

The Lenin Museum was opened in 1970 to celebrate the 100-year anniversary of Vladimir Lenin's birth. Each Soviet city of significance or capital of a Soviet republic was required to have a Lenin museum. Tashkent's large Lenin museum was a mark of the status and importance of the city. Previous Lenin museums often tried to suggest Lenin's physical presence, for example by recreating his childhood home or sites where his revolutionary activities had taken place, such as his office in the Kremlin. Those museums kept some artifacts and documents related to Lenin which had historical value. Tashkent's Lenin museum similarly faithfully reproduced other Russian museum displays of all twenty of Lenin's rooms, with their contents. Amongst those contents included a reproduction of Lenin's coat complete with bullet holes.[13]

However, this particular Lenin museum was specially acclaimed for its artistic merit both in its displays and in the building itself.[14] The museum's creation took four years and the best Soviet architects, sculptors, artists and craftsmen were invited to contribute. Two prominent Russian architects, Rozanov and Shestopalov, designed the project. The museum consisted of a white cube divided into two floors. In the core of the building was a central staircase next to a six-meter tall statue of Lenin created by Tomski. Behind the statue there was a ten by eight meter mosaic made by Zamkov and Ionin which was devoted to the establishment of Soviet power in Uzbekistan and depicted the rise of the multiethnic revolutionaries of Uzbekistan. Two of the best Uzbeki craftsmen, Usmanov and Haidarov, decorated the interior of the building. The Lenin Museum was incorporated into the existing architectural ensemble of the Concert Hall, the Theatre of Ballet and Opera, and the hotel Tashkent in the centre of Tashkent.

The Lenin Museum also became a part of the city's social life. On Lenin's birthday (22 April) children who wanted to become members of the Pioneer Organization took the Pioneer's oath in a ceremony on the staircase in this museum. This organization which existed between 1921 and 1990 was a preparatory organization for the Young Communists or *Komsomol* and was responsible for the political orientation of children aged between ten and fifteen. In a photograph from the Tashkent Encyclopedia, a square of children can be seen surrounding the statue of Lenin with the mosaic serving as a background. It was a highly staged procedure with speeches and music within an impressive surrounding and for those children who became Pioneers it was a memorable moment in their life.[15] The poignancy of the Lenin Museum was that for younger generations it turned into an iconic image of the continuation of Marxist ideas. To the newly independent state of Uzbekistan, though, the Lenin Museum was an irritating reminder of the communist past; it could not to continue to exist in its present incarnation.

Yet transforming the Lenin Museum into the Museum of the History of Uzbekistan was a daunting task. At the start, there was a massive clearout of all the artifacts regardless of their historical or artistic merit. The statue of Lenin was removed and the mosaic was taken down and plastered over. All that remained were the Uzbeki craftsmen's plaster carvings on the ceiling, leaving an empty shell which urgently needed to be filled. Seventy other Uzbeki museums were required to share their collections to help to build up the displays in the new museum. Based on the wealth of those artifacts collected from all over Uzbekistan, the exhibitions were to present a new version of national history: that of the independent nation state of Uzbekistan.

The two-floor division dictated a display divided into two parts. The first floor covered history from the Stone Age until Russian colonization, whereas the second floor focused on Russian Tsarist colonial history followed immediately by the current independent period — completely erasing the Soviet period. These two floors were massive open spaces, which had previously been arranged to facilitate the faithful reproduction of the twenty Lenin rooms and nothing else. Each floor being a single wide-open space, the various historical periods became mixed up, and there was considerable debate over the placement of each artifact. For example, some clerics on the Uzbeki Arts Council objected to a display about the Stone Age that made reference to the theory of evolution. Because of issues such as this, white boards were placed separating viewers from some parts of the displays on every floor. The clerics were thus satisfied that certain disputed artifacts would be hidden from open view by these boards. However, the massive boards were shaped in strange white configurations, which detracted attention from the main display. The overall impression of the new museum exhibition was one of chaos. The museum was intended to be open for the celebration of the first decade of independence in 2001, but the opening to the general public took place only in 2003. The entire process took twelve years which reflects the complexity in the formation and conceptualization of the museum displays. The commissioning of paintings for this museum further illustrates the complexities and problems surrounding interpretations of Uzbekistan's history in the post-independence period. It is this that I will now turn to.

Painting commissions for the Museum of the History of Uzbekistan

In order to highlight the long journey towards independence, the state intended to commission the best Uzbeki artists to design three monumental frescoes. The state commission was going to be monitored by the president's advisors, the Arts Council, and the museum administration (listed in order of importance). These three frescoes had to provide cohesiveness to the narration of the glorious history of Uzbekistan. The frescoes were not there for merely decorative purposes: they were supposed to clarify what the displays could not achieve and to simplify the history of the nation state within the aforementioned ideological framework of 'independence'. Each of the frescoes had a precise goal depending on its location. The first fresco, located on the wall of the staircase, was supposed to introduce visitors to the glory of the ancient state of Uzbekistan. The two other frescoes, on the first and second floors, were to emphasize important events in the ensuing historical periods: from the medieval, Tsarist and post-independence periods, but not the Soviet period.

Two Uzbeki artists, Bakhodyr Jallalov (b.1949) and Alisher Alikulov (b.1963) were commissioned to create the three frescoes. The first artist, Bakhodyr Jallalov, was the last head of the local Union of Artists before independence. Jallalov's single commission was finished in 1995 and destroyed by 2002. The second artist, Alisher Alikulov, came to prominence working in the genre of inspirational military painting. His art reflects the present situation of art in Uzbekistan. Two of Alikulov's commissions were finished by 2001. These two projects illustrate the difficulties for Uzbeki artists in dealing with the various readjustments resulting from the changing ideological turns in the independent state of Uzbekistan.

Bakhodyr Jallalov

Prior to 1995, Jallalov was commissioned to create a very conspicuous fresco, measuring eight by ten meters, for the central stairs of the museum. Jallalov's fresco was supposed to fill the empty space previously occupied by the Soviet-era mosaic by Zamkov and Ionin. By the time Jallalov was ready to start his commission, there was a blank wall and a hole in the floor left after the removal of Lenin's statue. Jallalov intended to show the most glorious moments in Uzbeki history united in a single fresco entitled *Under the Vault of Eternity*. The composition was divided into three levels. The lowest level represented the great medieval past of the Timurid period: the rider Tamerlane looks down on the fruitful results of his own rule and on his descendants. In the middle is the contemporary independent period, with a huge portrait of President Karimov positioned between examples of medieval Islamic architecture and Hellenistic monuments of the pre-Islamic period. Behind the president is Uzbekistan's coat of arms, with branches of cotton and wheat wrapped in the flag's tricolor bands: blue, symbolizing water resources; white, for cotton; and green, representing the Islamic heritage. On the highest level of the fresco are the celestial signs of the twelve months.

Jallalov's version of Uzbeki history progressed immediately from the glorious medieval past directly to the jubilant independent present. It is not surprising that there is a direct link between the two rulers Tamerlane and Karimov, but what is confusing is what keeps them together. Jallalov has placed an open Qur'an between the medieval and the contemporary heads of state. The fresco was painted in 1995 when all Central Asian states were experiencing religious freedom and had high expectations of future economic prosperity. It was therefore possible to represent the president in a royal pose: pointing one hand towards the Qur'an and holding a golden globe as a symbol of power in the other hand. The globe shows only one country, Uzbekistan. The globe itself has two hidden meanings: one points to the replacement of the statue of Lenin in the main square of Tashkent by a globe; and the second refers to the replacement of Marxism-Leninism by the new ideology of 'independence' as directed by the president's advisers.[16] By 2001, however, the situation had changed: a terrorist campaign by religious extremists had begun in 1999 and an economic slowdown was taking place. It was now rather inappropriate to claim geopolitical and ideological superiority or to even mention political stability. Similarly, it was now not ideologically possible to use religious fervor, and especially Islam, to obtain legitimacy. As a result of this change in the political scene, the fresco was promptly changed in a number of ways.

In 2001, Jallalov immediately covered both hands of the president in the same way as the media covers undesirable images, with small dots. The president was therefore no longer pointing to the Qur'an and thus explicitly aligning himself with Islam. Those dots, joked another artist Vladimir Shevtsov, who participated in creating the museum's exhibition, could not hide however "either the abrupt movement both towards and then away from religion by the state, or the great expectations manifested on the geographical map."[17]

For me, what was noticeable in the fresco was not this sense of shame in using Islam as a political tool (the religion, once regarded as the pillar of traditional Uzbeki society, became marginalized by religious extremists opposed to Karimov's rule), but the conspicuous attempt to forget the Russian presence established during the Tsarist and the Soviet periods. By 2002, the movement of militant religious extremists, whose intention was to topple Karimov's regime and establish an Islamic state in the Ferghana Valley, became fuelled by growing social and economic unrest in the country. Uzbekistan urgently needed Russian military and diplomatic assistance in handling the issue of an Islamic threat on the home front. Russia, which had its own backyard Muslim insurgency in Chechnya, was glad to lend support to the increasingly feeble Karimov regime. The improved relationship between Russia and Uzbekistan led to more problems with the content of the fresco. With the new turn in foreign affairs between the two states the museum could no longer keep the fresco on display without any reference to a Russian presence in Uzbekistan's past. Therefore, the museum received an unusual order from the president's advisers to remove Jallalov's work. The museum administration could not simply destroy the fresco and leave a colossal empty space above the central stairs, it could only replace one fresco with another. The administration attempted to find an artist who would volunteer to paint over Jallalov's fresco. However, nobody would agree to do such a commission out of principle: artists are trained to produce their own creative works, not to destroy their colleagues' works. So the administration had no choice other than to approach Jallalov himself. The agreement was reached that Jallalov's fresco would be covered with a layer of paint.

The same year, Akmaldjan Ikramdjanov (b.1952) was commissioned to fill the blank space left after Jallalov painted over his fresco. Ikramdjanov proposed a project which was promptly accepted by all the interested parties: the advisors of the president, the Arts Council and the museum administration. However, Ikramdjanov was highly reluctant to complete his own commission alone, because he was not confident that his work would not be destroyed as Jallalov's work had been. In order to go ahead it became necessary to invite another artist, Azod Khabibulin (b.1957) to finish Ikramdjanov's project. Finally, a rather bland decorative tableau emerged. It was divided into three levels representing Uzbekistan's landscape: the lowest line portrayed flowering tulips; in the middle was apricot blossom; and on the top level were mountains under the blue sky. Despite the work's lack of either political or aesthetic value, the museum administration was satisfied. The administration was hopeful that this work would last longer than its predecessor, but if it also had to be destroyed, at least it would be a work of questionable merit.

Alisher Alikulov

Alisher Alikulov was commissioned to produce a fresco illustrating the medieval and early modern period on the first floor of the museum, representing Uzbekistan's history from the ancient world up to 1865. Alikulov proposed a three-part composition focused on the Timurid period, named *Timur*. Viewers could see the composition itself on the wall next to a reproduced architectural plan of the famous square of the Registan in the city of Samarkand which was built under Tamerlane's rule and recently declared by UNESCO a site of world heritage. This positioning of the fresco and the plan of the square in close proximity to each other was meant to enhance the connotation of the ruler's contribution to contemporary Uzbekistan.

In his first project Alikulov proposed the following themes: the left side of the composition would show wars and the results of those wars, namely the securing of east-west trade routes; in the middle the rider Tamerlane would be surrounded by flags; and on the right side Alikulov intended to place the entire dynasty of the Timurids. The Arts Council, which represented high government officials, bank managers, writers, historians, clerics of both Orthodox Christian and Sunni Muslim creeds, but not art historians, found the portrayal of only the Timurid family unacceptable and requested that Alikulov include some scholars, artists and poets as well. Furthermore, the historians from the Arts Council did not accept Alikulov's depiction of the physical appearance of the founder of the dynasty. Alikulov complied with their suggestions, but he convinced them that he could not portray the victorious rider as a seventy-year-old man, lame and with a crippled right arm. So the Arts Council, after much debate, agreed that Tamerlane could be rejuvenated back to his early fifties. Alikulov stated, "I am not happy with how my Tamerlane looks as a weak man, — he cannot lead an army. I wished to follow Gerasimov's 1941 reconstruction of Tamerlane's portrait." [18] The anthropologist Mikhail Gerasimov had been assigned to reproduce sculptural portraits of historical figures based on their cranial remnants. This work was considered important because there were often no images left of these leaders.

Alikulov was left in an awkward situation because of a hypocritical attitude towards Tamerlane. Alikulov's comment reflected the logical contradiction in the 'independence' ideology. The whole bulwark of this ideology was based on two claims. First, that the predecessor to the modern state was the Timurid Empire, and the second that Tamerlane, the founder of the Timurid Empire was a figurehead of Uzbeki-ness. These claims led to the assumption that the contemporary nation of Uzbekis are of the same ethnic and racial type as Tamerlane: that is they are both of the Ferghana-European race. However, true history is less straightforward and cannot fall neatly into a design by ideologists. There emerged a preoccupation with determining a correct racial type for the Uzbeki nation by the ideologists, who exercised their pressure on artists to visualize the 'correct' look of the Uzbeki race.

The main problem was that, despite the veneration of Timur or Tamerlane and his descendants by the official ideology, Tamerlane was also resented because of his ethnic origin. In 1941 the Timurid bodies were exhumed by anthropologists and on the basis of an analysis of the skeletal remains their appearance was described, reconstructed, and published in 1964.[19] Biological and anthropological research revealed that Tamerlane had the features of a Mongol: his ancestors were Mongols from the Barlas clan, who converted to Islam. Russian anthropologists therefore showed that the Timurids were of a Mongol racial type rather than the pure version of an Uzbeki defined as being of the Ferghana-European race. To the regret of a generation of Uzbeki scholars, even the skulls of Tamerlane's son Shakrukh and his two grandchildren, including the famous astronomer Ulugbeg, showed various degrees of Mongol descent. Contemporary ideology could not accept the portrayal of Tamerlane as a non-Uzbeki, or Mongol in the museum fresco. Thus his image was borrowed, not from the Gerasmov portrait, but from the artist Nabiev's version which was created for the celebration of the Tamerlane jubilee in 1996. It was very unpopular to ask all artists to copy the Nabiev version of Tamerlane's face. Previously, not even the Soviet ideological powers had exercised this kind of censorship based on the physical appearance of Uzbekis portrayed in art. The artists and art historians on the Soviet-era Arts Council would often control identifying ethnic attributes such as clothing, but restrictions on the depiction of the physical features of Uzbekis were never applied to Uzbeki images.

More comical moments occurred in relation to the fresco measuring five by seven meters on the second floor, which depicted nineteenth and twentieth century Uzbeki history. Alikulov named this fresco *Repressions and Uprising* or *Represii e Vostanie*. Alikulov produced a three-part composition: on the right-hand side there were Tsarist Russian rebels and the dates of important historical uprisings; in the middle was a poor Uzbeki woman with two children who had been left without support due to the persecution of the males in her family; and on the left-hand side there were the *Jadids*, or Young Bukharans, who supported the Russian 'civilizing mission,' but were executed during the Stalinist purges of 1937.[20]

According to Alikulov himself, the main problem was with the central woman who was meant to represent the outcome of the reprisals; left alone after everyone emigrated, perished, or was exiled as a member of a persecuted family. Alikulov told me, "I am not happy with her. I could not make a pretty happy face, but I could not also make her how she should look. So what I was able to do was to make her a bit disheveled and cover her head with a scarf."[21]

It was interesting to hear about Alikulov's attempts to make a realistic image of an Uzbeki woman of the mid-nineteenth and early twentieth centuries, because Uzbeki women at that time covered themselves with veils. He could not portray a pretty sufferer, but nor was he able to depict a more realistic sufferer under a heavy veil, hiding her face from outsiders. Alikulov again compromised: he put a scarf on the head of the woman. Despite the fact that she was meant to be an Uzbeki woman from Tsarist Russia, the scarf on her head made her appear more like a woman of the late Soviet period. Historically the scarf replaced the veil on an Uzbeki woman's head only after the mid-1940s. The replacement of the veil with the scarf in society took a mere twenty years and was regarded as one of the great Soviet achievements, freeing indigenous Muslim women from bondage.[22] Apparently, Alikulov had known about the battle over the veil, but he made his own statement by portraying an idealized Uzbeki past without controversial attributes.

Conclusion

The Museum of the History of Uzbekistan is incapable of producing a public display which can form a coherent connection between, and evaluation of the importance of, each of the nation's pasts: medieval, Tsarist and Soviet. Moreover, the Jallalov and Alikulov frescoes indicate that the local ideologists and artists could not complete even a single project of state importance in the new era of independence. These frescoes make one question the validity of national arts within the new state ideology. The subservient position of national arts, entangled in the uneasy twists and turns of the *mustakilik* ideology, typified the nature of independence period arts management. The new arts management system, represented by a triumvirate of the advisors of the president, the Arts Council and the museum administration, had to concentrate on the political demands of the regime rather than the artistic process of fulfilling a single state commission: the creation of the museum. The commission itself turned from the reinvention of the national past connected to the present to an attempt to cover up the instability of the new regime. Thus the present decline of state art in Uzbekistan raises the question: should the decrease in the quality and quantity of fine arts in the post-independence period be cause for lament, or does state art not justifiably deserve anything better than a complete decline?

Notes

[1] B. Groys, "The Struggle Against the Museum, or, the Display of Art in To-talitarian Space," in *The Museum Culture: Histories, Discourses, Spectacles* ed. D. J. Sherman and I. Rogoff (London: Routledge, 1994), 144-162.

[2] D. Darewych, "Soviet Ukrainian Painting (1955-1979): New Currents and Undercurrents," (PhD diss., University College London, 1990).

[3] I collected the ethnographic data for this article in Uzbekistan (1999-2001) while working on my doctorate in anthropology.

[4] See the analysis of Soviet period culture in Central Asia by E. Bacon, *Central Asians under Russian Rule: A Study in Cultural* Change (New York and London: Cornell University Press, 1980); H. Carrere d'Encausse, *Decline of an Empire: The Triumph of the Nations* (New York: Basic Books, 1982); N. Shahrani, "Soviet Central Asia and the Challenge of the Soviet Legacy," *Central Asian Survey* 12, no.2 (1993): 123-135.

[5] O. Roy, *The New Central Asia: The Creation of Nations* (London and New York: I. B. Tauris, 2000); L.L. Adams, "Invention, Institutionalization and Revival in Uz-bekistan's National Culture," *Journal of Cultural Studies* 2, no.3 (1999): 355-373; and M.M. Doi, *Gesture, Gender, Nation: Dance and Social Change in Uzbekistan* (Westport, Connecticut, and London: Bergin & Garvey, 2002).

[6] S. Krukovskaya, *Russkie Khudozhniki v Srednei Azii v 1890-1900 Godahkh* (1932); S. Krukovskaya, *Zhivopis' Sovetskogo Uzbekistana 1917-1932* (1951). These two hand typed manuscripts by S. Krukovskaya were never published and are kept in the library of the Tashkent Arts Institute.

[7] On this see, M. C. Bown, *Soviet Socialist Realist Painting (1930 s-1960s: Paintings*

from Russia, the Ukraine, Belorussia, Uzbekistan, Kirgizia, Georgia, Armenia, Azerbaijan and Moldova) (Oxford: Museum of Modern Art, 1992); M. C. Bown, *Socialist Realist Painting* (New Haven, Connecticut: Yale University Press, 1998).

[8] R. Taktash, *Khudozhestvenno-Kriticheskie Etudy* (Tashkent: Fan, 1992).

[9] Russian art which functioned outside of the arts institution and state patronage has various names such as "unofficial", "non-official" and "non-conformist" arts. See A. Erofeev, *Non-Official Art: Soviet Artists of the 1960s* (Australia: Craftsman House and G+B Arts International, 1995), 8; A. Kovalev, *Between the Utopias: New Russian Art during and after Perestroika (1985-1993)* (Australia: Craftsman House and G+B Arts International, 1995), 18.

[10] N. Akhmedova, *Zhivopis' Tsentral'noi Azii : Traditsee, Samobytnost', Dialog: Osobennosti Formirovanyia e Razvitiya* (Tashkent: Akademiya Khudozhestv Uzbekistana, 2004).

[11] "Iskusstvo Novogo Uzbekistana," *San'at* 2 (1999): 12-16.

[12] A.F. March, "The Use and Abuse of History: 'National Ideology' as Transcendental Object in Islam Karimov's 'Ideology of National Independence,'" *Central Asian Survey* 21, no.4 (2002): 371-384; A.F. March, "State Ideology and Legitimation of Authoritarianism: the Case of post-Soviet Uzbekistan," *Journal of Political Ideologies* 8, no.2 (2003): 209-232.

[13] N. Sadykova, *Muzeioe Delo v Uzbekistane* (Tashkent: Fan, 1975), 195-196.

[14] *Sovetskoe Dekorativnoe-Isskusstvo* [1945-1975] (Moscow: n.p. 1989), 249.

[15] *Tashkent Encyclopedia* (Tashkent: Glavnaiya Redaktsiya Uzbekskoi Sovetskoi Entsyclopedii, 1983), 90.

[16] J. Bell, "Redefining National Identity in Uzbekistan: Symbolic Tensions in Tashkent's Official Public Landscape," *Ecumene* 6, no.2 (1999): 183-213.

[17] Vladimir Shevtsov, interview 12 August 2001.

[18] Alisher Alikulov, interview 21 July 2001.

[19] L. Oshanin, "Antropologicheskoe Issledovanie Skeletov Timura e Timuridov," *Nauchnye Trudy: Arkheologiya e Antropologiya* 232 (1964): 74-189.

[20] On *Jadids* see A. Sengupta, "Minorities and Nationalizing States Central Asia," *International Studies* 34 (1997): 269-300.

[21] Alisher Alikulov, interview 20 September 2001.

[22] On freeing indigenous Muslim women from bondage see G. Massel, *The Surrogate Proletariat: Moslem Women and Revolutionary Strategies in Soviet Central Asia, 1919-1929* (Princeton: Princeton University Press, 1974); S. Keller, "Trapped between State and Society: Women's Liberation and Islam in Soviet Uzbekistan, 1926-1941," *Journal of Women's History* 10/1 (1998): 20-44; O. Gorshunova, "Vneshnii Oblik Uzbekskoi Zhenshchiny: Evolutsiya Esteticheskikh Predstavleniy Konets XIX- Konets XXv.," *Etnograficheskoe Obozrenie* 5 (2001): 12-17.

9

The Use of Byzantine Iconography
to Express National Aspirations and Identities in Bulgaria and Greece in the 1920s and 1930s. Phōtēs Kontoglou and Vasil Zakhariev

Sophia Hadjipapa

In this paper I will examine how two artists, one Greek and the other Bulgarian, used similar practices to transform Byzantine art into a secular 'national art.'[1] Both artists adapted key elements of a collective tradition of sacred art to make secular art which sought to give expression to notions of an exclusive national consciousness. During the 1920s and 1930s in Bulgaria and in Greece, two art movements emerged that appropriated European modernism in a peculiar way: artists from these countries, though drawing on Western artistic models, incorporated elements from their native artistic traditions. In this period, religious subjects or representations of monasteries and churches were quite popular in both countries; even for artists who were not directly influenced by the 'icon aesthetic.' Folk traditions and key elements of Byzantine art were used in paintings to create a native, 'national art.' This study, which is a comparative analysis, begins by sketching the context in which the idea of the creation of national art was developed in Bulgaria and Greece. It then goes on to examine specific practices used by two artists, Phōtēs Kontoglou and Vasil Zakhariev that drew from the common Byzantine tradition in an attempt to create a 'national art'. Parallels in the practices employed are made apparent by pointing out the common sources from which the two artists drew their inspiration and the similarities in their works. This is facilitated by the use of specific examples drawn from the two artists' oeuvres.

To understand why Kontoglou and Zakhariev, and the wider artistic movements in both countries, used the tradition of Byzantine ecclesiastical art in artworks with a modern, secular subject matter and an explicitly national character, we shall first look at the origins and development of the idea to create a 'national art.'

The Late Enlightenment and the feeling of "belatedness"

Modern scholarship views Bulgaria and Greece as part of a Balkan cultural community.[2] The Balkan cultural community (also known as the ecumenical community of Balkan Orthodoxy) refers to a perception of the Balkan peoples as a community that had similar social conditions and cultural expressions at the time when national communities were still inarticulate. With the fall of the Ottoman Empire, which was holding the Balkan cultural community together, smaller local communities became more and more self-aware and consequently felt the need to legitimise themselves before the world.[3]

During the Balkan national revivals, a period of time in the eighteenth and nineteenth centuries when the different communities in the Balkans, although still part of the Ottoman Empire, were starting to develop a national consciousness, a rapid period of westernisation and modernisation commenced.[4] At the same time there was a contra movement within the various cultures to rediscover their ancient roots and thus establish founding myths to substantiate and validate the new nations as existing in their own right. The first stages of a national consciousness occurred for both cultures during the period of the 'national revival' in Greece (eighteenth century) and that in Bulgaria (eighteenth and nineteenth centuries).

The aspiration to create a 'national art' emerged in the general context of the national revivals, when a sense of national consciousness began to develop. In the eighteenth century enlightenment ideas were gradually introduced to both Greece and Bulgaria via intellectuals who were studying or living in Europe. Consequently, enlightenment ideas developed with some delay in Greece and Bulgaria in comparison to Western Europe and were not fully integrated into the local culture. This created a sense of 'belatedness' in both countries and a feeling that they had to catch up with the rest of Europe. Furthermore, the mediated nature of the introduction of enlightenment ideas caused the Greek and Bulgarian revivals to have a reflected character as opposed to a native or indigenous one.

Moreover, a sense of discontinuity in Balkan history has often been discussed: the bond between modern culture on one hand and antiquity and medieval culture on the other was interrupted through the domination of Bulgaria and Greece by the Ottoman Empire. This gave rise to a perception of cultural discontinuity, which had perhaps arisen from the strong perception of discontinuity of state authority.[5] In that sense, the Ottoman Empire was considered a foreign interruption to the cultural development of both Greece and Bulgaria.

What were perceived as 'oriental' elements in the culture were discarded because they were considered responsible for a certain backwardness. At the same time intellectuals sought for links to a glorious past: a classical period that would affirm the continuous and historically founded existence of a nation that justified patriotic sentiments.[6] This oscillation between their own past and the western culture motivated the revival artists of both Greece and Bulgaria to create a hybrid art that combined Byzantine and western artistic influences.

After the establishment of the Greek and Bulgarian states (1833 and 1885 respectively) the idea of creating 'national art' in both countries was expressed through paintings of a similar genre by means of an imported Academism.[7] Genre realism offered the possibility to include elements from the national culture, such as folk customs and national dresses. Even though artists aimed to create a 'national art' this way, often they painted these national scenes from the perspective of external observers rather than placing themselves in the idyllic peasant atmosphere. Critics at the time pointed out that these did not have an authentic national character.

In Greece in the middle of the nineteenth century there was a turn towards historical paintings that exalted the Greek nation by depicting scenes from the War of Independence. A desire to create a continuous Greek past together with the Western Europe philhellene interest in the Greek classical period led to artists directly associating events of the modern period with the past of ancient Greece. Typical of this trend is the painting of Geōrgios Margaritēs, Geōrgios Karaiskakēs Dashes Galloping towards the Acropolis (1844). In this painting the national hero Geōrgios Karaiskakēs is galloping in the foreground dressed in his national costume, but in the background we see the ruins of the ancient civilization (see Fig. 10, page 156).

At the outset of the twentieth century however, the demand to create a 'national art' in terms of content and form became more pressing and was facilitated by the rediscovery of Byzantium and its (re)-integration in the national cultural past of each country, which had already occurred in the late nineteenth century.

To whose history does Byzantium belong?

In Greece the Byzantine past (312-1453) was at first overlooked in favor of the classical period. In Bulgaria Byzantine culture was often associated with the Greeks, because of the ecumenical patriarchate, which during the Ottoman Empire used and imposed the Greek language in all orthodox churches. The Byzantine Empire was nevertheless an important chapter in the history of both cultures. The question of continuity, which is of critical importance in this region, was behind attempts to include and integrate the Byzantine culture in a modern understanding of the cultural history of the region as a whole.[8] Greek historian Antonis Liakos demonstrates the challenge of tracing genuinely ethnic elements in Balkans culture, in a region where several national histories are markedly intertwined and therefore the construction of any national identity becomes an extremely complex process. Liakos asks "[to] whose history does Byzantium belong? … Is it Greek or does it belong equally to Bulgaria and Serbia? Is the Ottoman period an integrated part of Balkan and Arab history or a foreign interruption of it?" [9]

The Greek and Bulgarian appropriation of the Byzantine heritage

The claim of modern nineteenth-century Greek nation builders that they descended directly from ancient Greek civilization ignored the living Orthodox tradition and downplayed Greece's recent history.[10] The eighteenth-century Greek scholars, who received their education in Europe and often spent their entire life outside of Greece, could easily identify themselves with ancient Greeks whereas the local population felt much closer to the Byzantine heroes that had survived through folk songs.

The re-discovery and appropriation of the Byzantine heritage in Greece, while it had some roots in Greek academia itself, was largely inspired by a shift of focus in Europe around 1850. During this period the interest of European intellectuals shifted from classical antiquity to the medieval period. The rediscovery of medieval culture was connected with the Romantic movement and inspired the neo-Gothic style. The fascination with the medieval period had a direct impact on the Balkan Peninsula since interest in the Crusades led scholars to rediscover the riches of Byzantium.[11]

Of particular significance in the introduction of the Byzantine period in the Greek past is the work of the historian Constantinos Paparrigopoulos, who in his late nineteenth century *History of the Greek Nation* was the first to talk about the triple nature of Greek identity: ancient, Byzantine and modern.[12] Still, professors in Byzantine art and Byzantine history were not appointed to Athens University until 1912 and 1924 respectively.[13]

A clearly political reason for the appropriation of the Byzantine past was, according to Cyril Mango, the appearance of "the Great Idea, that is, the dream of incorporating within the Greek Kingdom both Constantinople and the Turkish provinces that had substantial Greek settlements."[14] Mango cites another, more political, reason for the nineteenth century Greek appropriation of the Byzantine past: "Bulgaria was awakening under Russian prodding and claiming her substantial share of the Byzantine heritage, including all of Macedonia. To counteract such a claim it was necessary to show that Byzantium had been thoroughly Greek, not only in language, but also in spirit, in the very essence of its civilization."[15]

While in Greece the process of incorporating the Byzantine past into the national culture came via the West, in Bulgaria it came from the opposite direction: Bulgaria's traditional ties with Russia played an important role in both the formation of an ethnic identity and also facilitated the inclusion of Byzantine culture into a developing Bulgarian national identity. After the fall of Constantinople in 1453 Moscow increasingly became known as the "Third Rome" and thus was seen as the heir of the Byzantine Empire. It also perceived itself as the natural centre of the Slavic community. This permitted scholars to associate Slavdom with Byzantium and also to imagine Byzantium as "an antidote to the diseases of Europeanization."[16]

While Greece had succeeded in including both its ancient heritage and the Byzantine tradition in the narrative of its creation Bulgaria differentiated herself from this by identifying Byzantium with the spiritual yoke of the Ecumenical Patriarchate: the main opponent in Bulgaria's fight for ecclesiastical independence. This spiritual battle however, did not hinder Bulgarian attempts to "underline Slavic elements in Byzantium and incorporate these elements into her own legacy."[17] As such the use of the Byzantine legacy was initially justified through Russia and its Slavic elements.

While the Byzantine legacy was monopolized by the Greeks until the end of the nineteenth century this was all set to change during the twentieth century. Writings of the time claimed that Bulgarians also had a right to this legacy—and not through Russia.[18] The Byzantine Empire soon came to be perceived by Bulgarians as a multicultural community and thus Byzantine art as a pictorial style, was understood as being not exclusively Greek.

Under these conditions at the outset of the twentieth century, artists in both countries attempted to create a "native modernism": a modernism that would be an authentic expression of their modern society equal to western models, but at the same time different, original and not an imperfect imitation of them. While modernism in European art sought inspiration in pre-academic art—especially that of non-European civilizations. Balkan artists drew from their own traditions instead to create a 'native Modernism.' Having now embraced their 'eastern' identity, artists re-evaluated their own local traditions and looked back to them for inspiration.

These movements for 'national art' were moreover manifestations of a late Romanticism. Romanticism was a fitting ideology to embrace for the artists that strove to achieve a 'national art' since it politicized art for the first time and placed it firmly in the arsenal of national aspirations and aims.[19] While Romantics in Western Europe sought for a transcendental mysticism in Gothic art and the Pre-Raphaelites and the Nazarenes found it in western medieval religious art, Balkan artists found a home-grown, potent mysticism in Orthodoxy and its associated art. The link between these local art movements and western Romanticism is further confirmed by the fact that the works of the leading Romanticist Ruskin were quite familiar to artists in both countries: articles by him were extensively published in Greece in the 1930s and evidence exists that his doctrines were celebrated among the circle of the Bulgarian artists and intellectuals that strove for the creation of a successful 'native art' during the 1920s.[20]

Byzantine art: the vehicle for the creation of a 'National Art'

Artists 'borrowed' iconographic models from the Byzantine past and by putting them in a new context and using subjects infused with national significance they altered their meanings and connotations as well as simultaneously creating a cultural continuity with the past in a nationalist context. In Greece, Phōtēs Kontoglou (1896-1957) is the best example of this artistic endeavor. While in Bulgaria, efforts to revive old icon representations, but with secular subjects, made their appearance repeatedly in the works of Vasil Zakhariev (1895-1971).

To fully understand what this means we must first clarify the nature of Byzantine art. In Byzantine art a common stylistic and iconographic language was created over the centuries. A very concrete vocabulary was articulated for every subject matter and every character mentioned in the Bible. Each saint or holy person is depicted with specific characteristics, clothing and attributes. Each scene from the Bible is portrayed in a pre-determined manner: the characters are placed in conventional postures executing specific actions. Furthermore, each character and biblical scene has an allotted place in the church. For example the Almighty (the Pantokratōr) is always placed in the dome while Mary, the mother of God, is in the niche of the altar. It is this system that is meant by the terms Byzantine iconography and iconographic cycles. This regulated manner of depicting holy figures and scenes was initially defined by merely copying older representations. During the sixteenth century the visual paradigms were set down in books, the so-called hermeneias. Moutafov describes the hermeneas as "not just a manual on icon painting, rules of composing various religious subject-matters and common characteristics for figures, but an attempt to represent them in the pictorial sacred language, called iconography."[21] In the hermeneas iconographers were given instructions on icon painting techniques and also descriptions of figures of saints, Old and New Testament events, and the decoration of churches.

Byzantine iconography, which was used in all parts of the Byzantine Empire, was further disseminated through such manuscripts during the Ottoman period. In this sense, we could say that the art produced was more or less the same throughout the entire region, with some local variations, alterations or innovations introduced by individual masters. This iconography, with its very specific rules and conventions, was put in a totally different context in the beginning of the twentieth century, especially by the two artists under examination.

Kontoglou and Zakhariev did not just revive an old pictorial style; they were both emotionally engaged ideologists of this movement that sought tradition and cultural roots and they tried to promote these ideals through their research, writings and even their own everyday life. They both visited old monasteries, namely the Mount Athos monastic community, where they believed the old simple and pure kind of Christian life had survived. In many of his articles, Kontoglou attempted to revive the spirit and way of thinking of the old icon masters as if he wished to become one of them. Through his book entitled *Ekphrasis* in which he gave advice on how to paint icons he hoped to establish a new *hermeneia*.[22] This work was probably inspired by one of his numerous trips to Mount Athos, where he discovered the manuscript of Dionysius of Fourna, the author of the most famous *Hermeneia*: *The Hermeneia of Dionysius of Fourna*.[23] In *Ekphrasis*, Kontoglou strives to systemize the canons of Byzantine art that had survived through the centuries in the various *hermeneias* and to purify and remove all western elements that had entered orthodox iconography. He gives advice on practical techniques, descriptions of the iconographic types of saints, biblical scenes, and advice on the spirit that every modern icon painter should try to infuse in his icons. Moreover, in numerous books and articles Kontoglou examines both Byzantine and post-Byzantine art often juxtaposing Byzantine or eastern art, with western, Renaissance art.[24] Kontoglou also undertook the painting of many churches in the traditional Byzantine iconography and the restoration of many Byzantine monuments, for example the church of Mistra. He was also one of the first curators of the Byzantine museum in Athens.

Zakhariev similarly contributed to the studies of Byzantine and revival art in Bulgaria, he was the author of monographs on various Bulgarian revival masters and also published articles on medieval Bulgaria and the national revival movement in general.[25] He was constantly replenishing the Museum of the Fine Arts Academy, where he taught, by energetically collecting icons, church objects, embroidery, national costumes and woodcarvings.[26]

National heroes become saints

In 1926 Kontoglou created a painting that was to become emblematic of his future work. *Fighter of Macedonia (Makedonomakhos)* represents a young man dressed in the typical costume of the region and painted in the Byzantine manner. The homespun cape, the breeches tied in the waistband and the shallow cap are all typical of the national costumes of the entire region and can be found in the ethnographic museums of Greece, Bulgaria or the Former Yugoslav Republic of Macedonia. This young man could therefore easily have been Bulgarian or of any other Balkan origin, but in this case he is a Greek fighting for the liberation of Macedonia (see Fig. 11, Page 157).

The painting is tempera on board and has a gilded frame, which is typical for icons both of Bulgaria and of Greece. Here we see how the Byzantine style is associated with an entirely national subject. This painting is similar to the illustrations that Kontoglou did for Natalia Mela's book *Pavlos Melas* where there is an abundance of such fighters.[27] The creation of these works was motivated by the Macedonian conflict known as the Macedonian struggle in Greek historiography (1904-1908). Although the historical and political dimensions of this conflict are not part of this study it is interesting to observe how the conflict was reflected in art and how it was used in the formation of 'national art'.

In one of Kontoglou's illustrations we see the figure of Pavlos Melas, a protagonist of the Macedonian conflict who died during it and subsequently became a folk hero in the Greek consciousness, dressed in the traditional costume of those fighters. It is interesting to notice here the hand of God in a blessing gesture, a common iconographic type in Byzantine art. In Byzantine icons, the hand of God placed in the upper right corner, signifies God revealing himself to the depicted person and at the same time God's blessing of this person. It is followed by the subsequent inscription,

> God, do not abandon me before I proclaim Your hand to all the coming generations. For You have shown me a great deal of sorrows and ordeals. But returning to me, You gave life to me. For as if a great monster to many were born, [against which] You have been a powerful aid to me.

A reasonable interpretation of these allegoric words could translate into the following: God has revealed himself to Melas and thus shown him support. God, who often puts Christians to the test, has given the Greeks much grief in the past by depriving them of their liberty and by putting them through the ordeals of slavery, but now He has returned to the faithful and infused life again to Greece by liberating it from the Ottomans. However, a new danger or enemy has appeared, the Bulgarians which Melas, with God's help, manages to defeat. Kontoglou's Byzantine iconographic and stylistic devices were to become his strategy *par excellence* in the construction of a national imagery: the 'Byzantinised' images take on a divine quality, they become sanctified.

Zakhariev attempted something similar in *Marincho Bimbelov the Frightful,* a wood engraving from 1935. His legendary hero from the Bulgarian Independence battles is depicted in the style of the old eighteenth and nineteenth-century revival prints. These prints had educational or patriotic subjects and their style was a combination of western renaissance elements (introduced by revival masters that had lived abroad) with the existing medieval stylistic tradition of flatness, two-dimensionality, and non-naturalistic representation. The national hero here obtains the appearance of a religious image. Imperiously he rides on his horse, creating associations with the Byzantine warrior-saints, possibly Saint George or Saint Demetrius (see Fig. 12, page 158).

These works both use a style that was initially developed to address the supranational orthodox Christian community of the Byzantine Empire in order to create a national style and to embody the national imagery of each country. National heroes or intellectuals were represented as iconographic types of saints. The Byzantine style effectively infused the notion of nationhood with a mystic quality. By using the sacred language of the Orthodox tradition painters were able to sanctify their subjects and imbue them with a transcendental quality. More examples of how this was achieved will be examined below.

Another very popular theme in the attempt to create a sacred national art through the use of Byzantine iconography was the placement of historically important people in the role of an evangelist. A good example of this practice is a painting called *Father Paisiĭ* by the Bulgarian artist Ivan Penkov, who was also quite involved in the creation of a 'national art' that was based on older religious and folk art. In 1935 Penkov depicted Paisiĭ Hilendarski, the cleric who in 1762 was the first to write a history of the Bulgarian nation, in the iconographic type of the evangelist Luke. Paisiĭ Hilendarski is considered to be the most important figure in the process of the national awakening of the Bulgarians. He spent a lot of time at the Mount Athos monasteries and while there came into contact with Greek and Serbian Enlightenment ideals that no doubt inspired him to "revive the glorious past of Bulgarians" and to "awaken their national identity, to fill them with the idea that they rightfully deserve to have a high national confidence and pride."[28] In Penkov's painting, the figure of Paisiĭ

Hilendarski is represented using the iconography traditionally reserved for saints (see Fig. 13 and 14, page 159).

The Christian story of how the evangelists were inspired by the Holy Spirit to write the gospels, is used here as an allegory: Hilendarski is presented as a new evangelist writing about the deeds and the passions of his people. In Hilendarski's book, one can find the history of the Bulgarian people as well as the path to their salvation.

The image of the evangelist is employed by artists in both countries to represent national heroes: intellectuals, philosophers, and writers. For example, the Greek artist Nikos Engonopoulos in 1933 depicts Phtōhoprodromos, a Byzantine poet of the twelfth century, in a painting. The posture of the poet and elements in the composition directly link this painting to representations of the evangelist Mark in twelfth-century manuscripts.

In the Bulgarian painter Boris Kotcev's proposed illustration for a stamp of 1939 the place of the evangelist is occupied by a writer: the Bulgarian medieval writer Chernorizec Hrab"r. Again, the choice of the model is not accidental. His writings gave later Bulgarians the belief that they had a significant culture they could rightly celebrate. The posture of the writer in the illustration is again closely linked to the old Byzantine prototypes (see Fig. 15 and 16, page 160).

Bulgarian painter Tsanko Lavrenov also uses this iconography in his painting *Iconopisets* (The Icon Maker, 1926). The icon maker is again linked to the image of the evangelists who narrated the life of Christ: possibly Luke, who according to a legend was the first icon maker and is often represented as a painter in Byzantine art. In his icon-like picture of the icon maker Lavrenov subtly suggests that painters of his day could use the old style to make contemporary icons for the nation.

Zakhariev was no exception to this trend: His miniature *Ivan Rilski Writes his Testament* (1946) again uses the iconography of the evangelists and is no doubt influenced by Penkov's painting of Hilendarski. In this miniature created for the jubilee chronicle of the Rila Monastery we see a representation of Ivan Rilski (ca. 876 - 946), the first Bulgarian hermit saint. Zakhariev used the iconography of the evangelists to represent the saint who is the patron and protector of Bulgarians and Bulgaria. The similarity with medieval miniatures is more than obvious here and illustrates the use of allegory in the works of many artists who were related to the 'national art' movements in both countries as well as the conscious intention to transform religious art into national.

The representation of Ivan Rilski is a subject that is constantly repeated in the works of Zakhariev. In the engraving *Ivan Rilski* from 1946, the similarity with the old is quite apparent. Here Zakhariev used a composition, which is characteristic of icons: he framed the central scene with smaller scenes from the life of the saint. Another representation of a figure of national importance is the engraving by Zakhariev, depicting the bishop Sofroniĭ Vrachanski (1739-1813). In his portrait, *Sofroniĭ Vrachanski* (1951), Zakhariev used an older prototype: an oil portrait of the bishop from 1812 found in the city gallery of Plovdiv. The pose, the clothes, the accessories of this figure are all found in Zakhariev's copy. The choice of the model here is very important. Vrachanski was the first to make a copy of the first *History of the Bulgarian Nation* written by the aforementioned Paisiĭ Hilendarski, and in addition, he helped disseminate the national ideals infused in the book. He fought for the ecclesiastical independence of Bulgaria and introduced the Bulgarian language into schools to replace Greek, which until then had been the language of learning and education. It is now commonly believed and taught in Bulgaria that he was a key figure in the national awakening of the Bulgarian people.

A mainstay of Bulgarian historiography is the idea of the double yoke: the physical and political yoke of the Ottomans and the spiritual yoke of the Greeks. The Bulgarians keenly felt in danger of being assimilated by Greek culture, of being Hellenised. The historian Maria Todorova has gone as far as to say that this was perceived as a greater threat to their identity than oppression by the Ottomans.[29] It is for these reasons that Zakhariev's choice of subject is significant (see Fig. 17, page 161).

While Zakhariev *iconized* a historical figure of national importance, in contrast Kontoglou accurately copied whole iconographic models, but completely changed their meaning and connotations. The iconographic types of saints were used by Kontoglou to embody the figures of national heroes: ancestors of the nation. In this way, both ancient Hellenes and heroes from recent Greek history took on the shape of Byzantine saints. The best examples of this practice are the murals painted in his home and the ones in the municipality of Athens. In both cases he constructed his compositions imitating the arrangement of iconographic cycles in Byzantine churches and gave a Byzantine look to heroes and subjects from different epochs, from the distant past of ancient Greece up to the present. In the murals in his home he created a personal pantheon that consisted of philosophers, scholars and painters. He represented his idols as Byzantine saints, by positioning them in medallions and placing in their hands their attributes, or instruments of their craft, analogous to the practice in Byzantine churches (see Fig. 18, page 162).

Kontoglou used the same strategy of replacing the religious subject with a secular one in the municipality murals. He had already constructed his principles and simply had to adjust them to the new task, which was, according to the protocols of the Athenian municipal council, "to imply the unity of the Race"(see Fig. 19, page 163 and Fig. 20, page 164).[30]

The creation of these murals took place in 1938, when Metaxas was ruling the country. The quest for national identity in the arts that had begun as early as the beginning of the twentieth century now gained a new impetus to serve the goals of the totalitarian regime. Artists who had already striven after Greekness in art, found themselves launched into the wider sphere and in demand for big state commissions. Those who did not wish to mix their art with 'Greek' elements and preferred to pursue a pure version of European modernism were marginalized and forgotten.[31]

The compositions in the municipality murals are developed in a frieze. The subject matters include not only the entire historical course of the Greek nation, from antiquity until 1821 (the year when the Greek War of Independence began), but also the ontological birth of the nation, according to ancient Greek mythology. The blending of all epochs, history and mythology suggests the cultural continuity of the Greek nation, and the connections within its triple identities, as presented in the historian Paparrigopoulos' *History of the Greek Nation*. In the archetypal and mythological cycles, Kontoglou once more indulged in a practice of substituting and replacing: ancient Greek myths are reproduced with loans from Byzantine and Post-Byzantine iconography.

Ancient Greek mythology is used here to suggest continuity with an even earlier period in mythological times. A lucid example is the scene representing Iapetos and Graekos. According to the mythology, Iapetos was one of the Titans, son of Gaea and Uranus, which makes him the first man. Kontoglou positions him next to Graekos, who was the first Greek. In the inscription we read: "Iapetos, the most ancient man" and "Graekos, the forefather of Greeks." By placing them next to each other, Kontoglou suggests that the Greek nation is as old as the creation of the world. Iapetos and Graekos are presented as white-bearded old men that remind us of the Byzantine hermit saints. Especially Graekos who, according to art historian Antōnēs Kōtidēs, has his prototype in the figure of Saint Peter, as depicted by the famous Byzantine painter Panselēnos in the Prōtaton Monastery, in Mount Athos.[32] Panselēnos is considered by many to be the father of monasticism and can therefore be seen as a religious forefather of the nation. Kontoglou gives a sacred quality to the ancient ancestors by reincarnating them in the image of this much-cherished saint. Furthermore, he is using a model created by Panselēnos, one of his favourite Byzantine painters, who occupies a central medallion in his home Pantheon.

In the scene *Ikarius, King of Athens Offering Wine to the Shepherds*, the iconographic types of the shepherds derive from the shepherds as they are represented in the Byzantine iconography of the Nativity of Christ. The God of wine Dionysus taught Ikarius the craft of making wine. Dionysus then offered it to some shepherds who, experiencing the unknown feeling of inebriation, killed him thinking he had poisoned them. The inclusion of this myth in the municipality murals is again related to Kontoglou's desire to show cultural continuity and coherence in the Greek past. Although the cult of Dionysus came from Thrace it later became quite popular in Greece. In the municipality murals, Kontoglou is including and combining different cults, cultures, and myths just as Paparrigopoulos was comprising different periods and cultures in his *History of the Greek Nation* (see Fig. 22, page 166).

Kontoglou followed the same principle in the historical cycle as well: The iconographic type of the Pantokratôr as depicted in the fourteenth century church of Omorphoklçsia near Athens served to inspire Kontoglou in a series of Pantokratôrs he painted in numerous churches. In the municipality, *The Almighty* embodies the national hero from the War of Independence: Athanasios Diakos. The same subject is repeated in a panel work in 1946. If one is not acquainted with Kontoglou's deep religiousness, one might well think this is blasphemy. On the other hand, some researchers believe it was quite natural for Kontoglou, being an icon painter and muralist, to search for his iconographic models in the Bible.[33] Yet this method of substituting and replacing is neither accidental nor unconscious. By re-embodying the saints and even Christ with images of the ancestors that had safeguarded the Greek nation, Kontoglou sanctifies them. The Pantheon he constructs this time is the *Nation's Pantheon*. The nation acquires a transcendental and mystical quality (see Fig, 24, page 168 and Fig. 25, page 169).

Kontoglou is unquestionably the artist who best embodies this attempt to transform religious art into national art. His ability to transfer the artistic means of religious art to the sphere of secular art is definitely his most interesting achievement. However, this transformation of religious art into national art was subject to serious criticism. In the book *Neobyzantinism, Avant-garde or Kitsch?* Spuridōn Marinēs comments that the evolvement of religious art into a national ideology is completely atypical of the traditional understanding of Orthodoxy and its art, since the Orthodox Church is an intercultural phenomenon.[34] According to Marinēs, Kontoglou and the whole group of Neo-Byzantinists completely appropriated religious art. It was taken out of context, and was recruited to sanctify whatever it depicted, thus acting as a crutch to an ideology; namely nationalism.[35]

Indeed, these artists aimed to construct a national imagery through their use of the cultural heritage that Byzantium offered them. Condemning the blending of diverse artistic means to create a new art is problematic. Perhaps what is most disturbing in such cases is the bringing of religion into the secular sphere. If we accept it is inappropriate, we should also condemn the works of the Pre-Raphaelites, the Nazarenes and other artistic movements that used the stylistic language of medieval art.

What we should focus on instead is how these artists of Greece, Bulgaria and other Balkan countries, who are bonded by a common historical past and artistic heritage, managed generally to transform religious into secular art, and specifically Byzantine into national art. From the comparative analysis carried out above, it becomes obvious that similar practices were used in both countries. Furthermore, the strategies employed by the two artists together with the evidence of the art itself demonstrate clearly the similarities in the process of constructing 'national art' in the two countries. This leads one to speculate as to whether similar processes were at work in neighboring Balkan countries which shared the same traditions and faced the same issues as they entered into the twentieth century.

Notes

[1] All translations from Greek and Bulgarian sources are done by the author. Transliterations of Greek and Bulgarian bibliographies are done according to the transliterations of the Greek and the Cyrillic alphabet as they are presented in *The Chicago Manual of Style*, 13th ed., (Chicago and London: The University of Chicago, 1993).

[2] N. Genchev, *B"lgarskata Kultura, XV-XIX v* (Sofia: Universitetsko izdatelstvo Kliment Okhridski, 1988), 101, 130; N. Aretov, *B"lgarskoto V"zrazhdane i Evropa* (Sofia: Kralica Mab, 2001), 11; M. Todorova, "Self image and ethnic stereotypes in Bulgaria," *Modern Greek Studies Yearbook* 8 (1992): 147; P. Kitromilides, "Imagined Communities and the Origins of the National Question in the Balkans," in P. Kitromilides, *Enlightenment, Nationalism, Orthodoxy: Studies in the Culture and Political Thought of South-Eastern Europe* (U.K.: Variorum, 1994), 151, 154, 156. Originally published in the *European History Quarterly* 19/2 (London: Sage publications, 1989).

[3] Aretov, *B"lgarskoto V"zrazhdane*, 3.

[4] For the shaping of national ideals and the reception of the Enlightenment in the Balkans see P. Kitromilides, "The Enlightenment East and West: A Comparative Perspective on the ideological Origins of the Balkan Political Traditions," in P. Kitromilides, *Enlightenment, Nationalism, Orthodoxy: Studies in the Culture and Political Thought of South-Eastern Europe* (U.K.: Variorum, 1994), 53, 54. Originally published in the *Canadian Review of Studies in Nationalism* 10/1 (1983). Aretov, *B"lgarskoto V"zrazhdane* 9.

[5] Genchev, *B"lgarskata Kultura,* 180.

[6] A. Liakos, "The Canon of History and the Strategies of Response," (forthcoming).

[7] Academism is a style in painting and sculpture which was produced under the influence of the European academies and which embraces the movements of Neoclassicism and Romanticism. See Rafael Cordoso Denis and Colin Trodd eds, *Art and the Academy in the Nineteenth Century* (New Brunswick, NJ: Rutgers University Press, 2000).

[8] A. Liakos, "The construction of National Time: The Making of the Modern Greek Historical Imagination," *Mediterranean Historical Review* 16/1 (2001): 28.

[9] Ibid., 29.

[10] Ibid., 30-31.

[11] C. Mango, "Byzantinism and Romantic Hellenism," *Journal of the Warburg and Courtauld Institutes* 28 (1965): 40.

[12] C. Paparrigopoulos, *Istoria tou Ellēnikou Ethnous: Ē Prōtē morfē*, ed. K. Th. Dēmaras (1860–74; reprint, Athens: Ermēs, 1970).

[13] Liakos, "The construction of National Time," 34. Byzantine art was taught long before the actual history of the empire because the painters associated with the "native art" or "Greek art" movements were more interested in the Byzantine artistic legacy and pictorial system than in Byzantine history itself. See E. Vakalo, Ē fysiognōmia tēs Metapolemikēs Technēs stēn Ellada; O mythos tēs ellēnikotētas" (Athens: Kedros, 1983), 16.

[14] Mango, "Byzantinism and Romantic Hellenism," 40.

[15] Ibid., 40-41.

[16] Aretov, 53. See also: K. Leontiev, *Vizantinizmŭt i slavyanstvoto* (Moscow: n.p. 1876), 40-41 and T. Zhechev, *B"lgarskiyat Velikden ili strastite b"lgarski* (Plovdiv: "Christo.G.Danov", 1985), 132, 134.

[17] Aretov, 53-54.

[18] See: B. Filov, *Starob"lgarsko izkustvo* (Sofia: Naroden myzei, 1924); I. Lazarov, "Edin chas pri skluptora Lazarov," *Literaturen glas* 63 (1930): 3; I. Lazarov, "Izkazvane na I. Lazarov," *Zhivo Slovo* 4 (1936): 7; G. Milev, "Yubileina Izlozhba," *Vezni* 2 (1921): 19-20.

[19] À. Hauser, *The Social History of Art* (London: Routledge and Kegan Paul, 1962). Here cited from the Greek edition, Koinōnikē Istoria tēs Teknēs, vol. 3. (Athens: Kalvos, 1980) 182, 188.

[20] One of the most eminent representatives of the movement of "Native art", Nikolai Raynov begins his article "Eastern and Western Art" with a citation from Ruskin. See: N. Raynov, "Iztochno i zapando izkustvo," *Vezni* 8 (1919): 231.

[21] E. Moutafov, *Evropeizaciya na khartiya; S"chineniya za zhivopista na gr"cki ezik prez p"rvata polovina na XXVIII v.* (Sofia: Aba, 2001) 16-17.

[22] Ph. Kontoglou, Vivlos kaloumenē Ekphrasis tēs Orthodoxou Eikonographias (Athens: Astēr, 1960).

[23] The English title of the book is: *The painter's manual, of Dionysius of Fourna, 1728/1733* trans. Paul Hethertington, (California: Oakwood Publications, 1988).

[24] For example Ph. Kontoglou Ē tekhne tou Athō (Athens: Chrusostomos Ganiaris, 1923); *Icones et Fresques d' Art Byzantin* (Athens: n.p., 1932); Ē leitourgikē Tekhnē ē ē Vizantinē Xōgrafikē (Athens: n.p., 1956); "Ē Ponemenē Rōmiosunē" in *Erga*, vol 3 (Athens: Astēr, 1976); and Vivlos Kaloumenē Ekphrasis tēs Orthodoxou Eikonographias (Athens: Astçr, 1960).

[25] For example, Vasil Zakhariev, *Stanislav Dospevski* (Sofia: B"lgarski Hudozhnik, 1971); and *Zakhari Zograf* (Sofia: B"lgarski Hudozhnik, 1957).

[26] I. Genova, "Kulturnata situatsia ne tsent"r na b"lgarskoto izkustvo prez 1920-te godini," in I. Genova and T. Dimitrova, *Izkustvoto v B"lgariya prez 1920-te godini. Moderniz"m i natsionalna ideya* (Sofia: B.A.N., Institut za izkustvoznanie, 2002) 17. The article was originally published in the periodical *Problemi na Izkystvoto* 1 (1994).

[27] N. Mela, *Pavlos Melas*, (1964; reprint, Athens: Dōdōnē, 1992).

[28] Quoted from *Kirilo-metodieva entsiklopediya*, Vol.3, downloaded from the virtual library of Bulgarian literature–Slovoto, http://www.slovo.bg/showbio.php3?ID=15 (accessed June 21, 2005).

[29] Todorova, "Ethnic Stereotypes", 140.

[30] In N. Zias, Phōtēs Kontoglou, zōgrafos (Athens: Emporikē Trapeza Ellados, 1991) 85. Also published in English as, N. Zias, *Photis Kontoglou, Painter* trans. David Turner (Athens: Commercial Bank of Greece, 1993).

[31] Kōtidēs, Monternismos kai "Paradosē" 274.

[32] Ibid., 164.

[33] N. Zaganiarēs, "Ē muthologikē Paradosē stē Zōgrafikē tou Ph. Kontoglou," in Phôtçs Kontoglou, Sçmeion Antilegomenon. Gia ta Ekato Khronia apo tç Gennçsç kai ta Trianta apo tçn Koimçsç, ed. I. Vivilakçs (Athens: Armos, 1998), 193.

[34] S. Marinçs, Neovuzantinismos. Prôtoporia ç Kitsch? (Athens: Armos, 1996),74.

[35] Ibid., 55-7.

Figure 10. *Geōrgios Karaiskakēs dashes galloping towards the Acropolis*, painting by Geōrgios Margaritēs, 1844, oil on canvas, 94 cm × 117 cm. National Gallery and Museum of Alexandros Soutsos, Greece.   Reprinted from *Ethnikē Pinakothēkē, 100 Chronia* (Athens: Ethnikē Pinakothēkē kae Mouseio Alexandrou Soutsou, 2000), 62.

Figure 11. *Makedonomakhos*, painting by Phōtēs Kontoglou egg tempera on board, 70 cm × 45 cm. Collection of C. Konstandenēdēs, Greece. Reprinted from N. Zias, *Phōtēs Kontoglou, zōgrafos* (Athens: Emporikē Trapeza Ellados, 1991).

Figure 12. Marincho Bimbelow the Frightful, engraving by Vasil Zakhariev, 1935, wood engraving 50 cm × 65 cm., City Gallery of Dobrich, Bulgaria. Reprinted from V. Svintila, *Vasil Zachariev* (Sofia: Bŭlgarski Hudozhnik, 1972).

Figure 13. "Father Paisiĭ," by Ivan Penkov, 1932, City Gallery of Stara Zagora, Bulgaria. Courtesy of the City Gallery of Stara Zagora.

Figure 14. *Phtōhoprodromos*, painting by Nikos Engonopoulos, 1933 egg tempera on board, 30 cm × 20 cm. Reprinted from *o Phōtēs Kontoglou kae oi mathētes tou* (exhibition catalogue), (Thessaloniki: Dēmotikē Pinakothēkē Thessalonikēs, 2002).

Figure 15. *Chernorizec Hrabur,* illustration for a stamp by Boris Kotcev, 1939. Reprinted from K. Krŭstev, *Boris Kotcev* (Sofia: Bŭlgarski Hudozhnik, 1963).

Figure 16. *Iconopisets,* painting by Tsanko Lavrenov watercolour on paper, 32.5 cm × 22.5 cm. Temporary exhibition of Tsanko Lavrenov, Plovdiv, Bulgaria (Photo by the author).

Figure 17. *Sofroniĭ Vrachanski*, engraving by Vasil Zakhariev ,1946 lino engraving, 54 cm × 36.4 cm. Reprinted from V. Svintila, *Vasil Zachariev* (Sofia: Bulgarski Hudozhnik, 1972).

Figure 18. Murals from the house of Phôtçs Kontoglou, 1932, now exhibited in the National Gallery and Museum of Alexandros Soutsos, Greece. Reprinted from *Ethnikē Pinakothēkē, 100 Chronia* (Athens: Ethnikē Pinakothēkē kae Mouseio Alexandrou Soutsou, 2000).

Figure 19. Scenes from the Greek Mythology, murals from the Municipality of Athens, Greece, by Phōtēs Kontoglou, 1938. Reprinted from N. Zias, *Phōtēs Kontoglou, Zōgrafos* (Athens: Emporikē Trapeza Ellados, 1991).

Figure 20. *Iapetos, and Graekos,* (detail) murals from the Municipality of Athens, Greece, by Phōtēs Kontoglou, 1938. Reprinted from N. Zias, *Phōtēs Kontoglou, Zōgrafos* (Athens: Emporikē Trapeza Ellados, 1991).

Figure 21. *Saint Peter the Athonian* (detail) mural from the Prōtaton Monastery, Mount Athos, Greece, by Manuel Panselinos, 1290. Reprinted from *Diary of 199; Prōtaton; Kyr Manuēl Panselēnos* (Thessaloniki: Organismos Politistikēs Prōteyousas kae Ierē Koinotēta Agiou Orous, 1996).

Figure 22. *Ikarius, King of Athens Offering Wine to the Shepherds*, mural from the Municipality of Athens, Greece, by Phōtēs Kontoglou, 1938. Reprinted from N. Zias, *Phōtēs Kontoglou, Zōgrafos* (Athens: Emporikē Trapeza Ellados, 1991).

Figure 23. *The Nativity of Christ* (detail), icon, first half of the fifteenth century, 52 cm × 40 cm., Museum of Byzantine Art, Athens. Reprinted from M. Acheimastou-Potamianou, *Eikones tou Vuzantinou Mouseiou Athinōn*, (Athens: n.p., 1988)

Figure 24. *Pantokratōr* (detail) mural from the church of *Omorphoklēsia* near Athens (fourteenth century). Panselinos, 1290. Reprinted from Ph. Kontoglou, *Vivlos Kaloumenē Ekphrasis tēs Orthodoxou Eikonographias* (Athens: Astēr, 1960).

Figure 25. *Athanasios Diakos* (detail), mural from the Municipality of Athens, Greece, by Phōtēs Kontoglou, 1938. Reprinted from N. Zias, *Phōtēs Kontoglou, Zōgrafos*, (Athens: Emporikē Trapeza Ellados, 1991).

THE REMEMBERING OF THE PAST

To Construct the Nation in

Post-Ottoman States

10
The Patron Saints of Turkish Humanism
Religion and the Formation of Turkish National Culture

Mark Soileau

Nationalist movements are necessarily concerned with culture, attempting to define the particular constellation of linguistic, artistic, material, habitual, moral, and spiritual elements which would best represent the unity and uniqueness of the social entity they seek to delineate. A recurrent problem in this pursuit of the strongest case for a national culture is the fact that most societies, even some that possess a relatively high degree of uniformity in terms of language, religion and traditions, nevertheless contain variant elements that are associated with local ethnic groupings, social classes, or other divisions within the intended society. Part of the nationalist project, then, often involves a choice—whether conscious or unconscious on the part of those in power—between rival dialects, sects, or other cultural fragments, in the formation of the national culture. This process carries the risk of creating division rather than unity, but as the choices are usually made with privilege toward one particular cultural matrix—usually that to which those with political power and/or the majority of the population ascribe—the process tends to result in a dominant national culture which allows for local variation, or to which variations are assimilated. While some cultural elements that are selected for national use more or less accurately represent the majority of the population, others are taken from local traditions, and their adoption involves a transformation from a local into a national relevance. Concomitant with its use of culture, the nationalist movement is obliged to incorporate or create a national history, in order to show that its nation possesses a cultural identity that has persisted in time, and the formulation of this history likewise involves a selection from various possible elements.

The late Ernest Gellner was aware of the use of culture by nationalist movements, setting the advent of the consciousness of culture at the transition from the agrarian to the scientific or industrial stage of mankind's history.[1] In the agrarian stage, according to Gellner, communities were fairly stable and, concerned primarily with the production of food, were thus tied to the land. They were dominated by a military-political ruling elite and a clerical hierarchy who had access to literacy and used a written language that was distinct from the spoken dialects of the communities within their realm. The communities were immobile and insulated, and thus had little need for inter-communal communication, a standard language and a common culture. In the industrial stage, however, increases in technology and the advent of industrialization which rendered food production less dominant resulted in a society that was more mobile and literate, and thus in need of more diverse communication. This need led to an educational system that promoted a cultural homogeneity, which in turn allowed the individual to participate in the new social system. As a result, there arose a consciousness of culture:

> So culture, which had once resembled the air men breathed, and of which they were seldom properly aware, suddenly becomes perceptible and significant. The wrong and alien culture becomes menacing. Culture, like prose, becomes visible, and a source of pride and pleasure to boot. The age of nationalism is born.[2]

The same process had the effect, in Gellner's analysis, of bringing about a decline in the authority of religion, since the cognitive growth that accompanied economic growth was not willing to be limited by any stable world-view. Gellner links the decline of religion with the rise of culture:

> So at the very same time that men become fully and nervously aware of their culture and its vital relevance to their vital interests, they also lose much of the capacity to revere their society through the mystical symbolism of a religion. So there is both a push and a pull towards revering a shared culture *directly*, unmediated in its own terms: culture is now clearly visible, and access to it has become man's most precious asset. Yet the religious symbols through which, if Durkheim is to be believed, it was worshipped, cease to be serviceable. So— let culture be worshipped directly in its own name. That is nationalism.[3]

While the historical process that Gellner sketches may offer some insight into the rise of culture-conscious nationalism in the modern period and along with it a relative decline—in some cases—in the efficacy of religious symbols, it involves, as does much of Gellner's greater theory of nationalism, a generalization which overlooks many possible counter-examples. Religious symbols have in fact been incorporated by nationalist movements, such as those in India, Ireland and Israel—nations which are conceived as including religion as an integral part, if not the defining aspect, of their shared culture. But even in the case of nationalist movements which develop in opposition to religious authority—such as in Turkey—traditional religious symbols can reappear in new forms. It is highly debatable whether 'culture' can be 'worshipped' directly, without mediation; it is more likely that societies in the modern era continue to express their distinction through symbols. Those symbols that in the past were linked primarily to a religious identity can in the national period be used to form a religious-national identity, or be transformed in a non-religious national context to symbols of a secular national culture.

Before he fully formulated his model of the development of nationalism, Gellner had conducted ethnographic fieldwork among Berber tribes in the Atlas Mountains of Morocco, and he placed these tribes in opposition to the more literate, urban Arabs of the Moroccan towns. His findings on the role of saintly lineages in arbitrating between the tribes and thus in maintaining the social structure were published in his early book *Saints of the Atlas*, and were later to appear in his collection of essays entitled *Muslim Society*.[4] In this latter work, he had this to say about the tribal saints he had observed:

> The saints were, in modern conditions, useless: they were essentially local or particularistic. A shrine is tied to a locality, to specific patterns of pilgrimage; a saint is linked to the performance of this or that service, the curing of this or that ailment. Their magic has a functional and territorial specificity. For a tribal society well-articulated in terms of clans and segments, they were for this very reason admirably suited; and they were also well adapted for mediation between such tribesmen and the towns. But for an atomised, mobile, uprooted population, their usefulness was limited, at best. As a banner under which a whole large population, a latent nation, is to recognise its own identity, they were useless, both through their fragmentation and through the fact that the practices they stood for—ecstasies, rural festivals, the mingling of the profane and the sacred—are scarcely usable as a modern ideology or as a basis for national pride. By contrast, the purified, literacy-stressing Islam of the reformers was very well suited for this end.[5]

Gellner here sets up a series of dichotomies: tribal versus urban, local versus universal, popular versus literal Islam, and saint versus scholar. While there may, at the time and in the particular context that he examined, have been some truth and analytical utility in making such juxtapositions, the model that Gellner establishes for a general Muslim society is static, seemingly impervious to change, and presents an over-generalization based on limited data.[6] His model moreover represents a very narrow and idiosyncratic understanding of the possibilities for national identity. Gellner was referring specifically to tribal saints, and living ones at that. It is obvious that counter-examples can be found in the Christian context of saints who have become associated with nations—such as St. Patrick in Ireland and St. Denys in France. But it is even possible for Islamic saints, though they are not normally considered 'patron saints' of nations, to move beyond a relevance to strictly local communities and become symbols of 'modern ideology' and the foci of 'national pride.' This is in fact what has happened in the case of certain medieval Islamic mystics who have come to play a role in the formation of Turkish national culture.

How they came to play such a role was not a result of an invention of tradition with no basis in historical reality. In fact, understandings of saints (the term 'saint' here referring to a variety of historical figures in some way associated with Islam and/or Sufism, and venerated by some segment of society) have changed form throughout the centuries, in response to changing political and social exigencies. The secularist, modernist, nationalist ideology of the early twentieth century in Turkey certainly had a major effect on how these saints came to be represented, but what these modern representations reflect is a shift of emphasis, a transformation of pre-existing cultural material. This is change, but at the same time continuity.

Three mystics in particular stand out in modern conceptions of the Turkish national heritage: the illustrious poet Mevlana Jalaluddin (known in the West as Rumi); the "saint of saints" Haji Bektash Veli; and the first great Anatolian Turkish poet, Yunus Emre. Rumi lived, composed poetry and danced his ecstatic dance in Konya during the thirteenth century. While the dates of Haji Bektash and Yunus Emre are not known definitely, Haji Bektash was probably contemporaneous with Rumi, and Yunus Emre a generation younger. All three were mystics, all were connected in some way with the Turkish language and culture, and all reflect in their poetry or legends values such as peace, tolerance, brotherhood, and love of mankind – values which in the right circumstances could be linked to the notion of humanism. The Turkish and humanist associations have proven to be the most useful to the nationalist ideology, and are in fact the aspects that dominate the way these figures are commemorated in Turkey today.

As a symbol of Turkish culture, Rumi (1207-1273) poses the greatest problem, since his inspiring and voluminous poetry was composed in Persian, as were his father's writings. Turkish scholars and writers influenced by nationalist ideology argue that he was in fact ethnically Turkish and only wrote in Persian because that was the high-cultural language of the time. Rumi lived in Konya during the rule of the Seljuks, and was closely tied to the Seljuk court—the Seljuks having the equivocal distinction of being the first great Turkish dynasty in Anatolia, but one which used Persian as its court language, since its early rulers had been influenced by Persian administrators. The claim to Rumi's Turkish ethnicity derives from the fact that he was born in the Khorasan region of Central Asia, which is considered by Turks as the homeland of Turkish mysticism.[7]

Leaving aside the question of Rumi's own ethnicity and native language, an important connection with Turkish culture is made by the fact that the Mevlevi order that was founded in his name developed into its classical form during the Ottoman period and under the influence of Turkish Sufi culture, using many Turkish terms in its ritual language, much of which is shared with the Bektashi order.[8] The Mevlevi order was of course famous for its 'whirling dervish' dance, or *sema*, which was documented by European travelers and residents in the Ottoman Empire, particularly in the capital Istanbul. Besides the mystical dance, the order was known for its fostering of arts such as poetry, music and calligraphy, supplying many of the greatest poets, composers and calligraphers of the high Ottoman culture. It also maintained cordial ties with the Ottoman state. Because of the prominence of the Mevlevi order and its cultural production, the mystic whom it had commemorated for more than six centuries took on a national relevance when the cultural heritage of the Turkish nation began to be formulated and institutionalized in the early twentieth century under the Republican state. While his poetry was widely known in elite, Persian-speaking circles, in the modern period Rumi was transformed from being the founding saint of one dervish order among many to being what one recent commentator refers to as "one of the spiritual architects of the Turkish nation."[9]

Though he lived around the same time as, and not far geographically from, Rumi, the life and influence of Haji Bektash was somewhat different. Since he settled in a village, it is certain that his influence during his life was directed more towards the Turkmen peasants of the area rather than to the urban, literate elites of a major cultural center like Konya. Beyond this, there is little historical record of his life, so for details we have to rely on the legendary account contained in his hagiography, the *Vilayetname*.[10] Haji Bektash is said to have migrated from Khorasan to Anatolia, where he landed in the form of a dove, and settled in the village which was eventually named after him. He worked many miracles such as multiplying food for those who showed him kindness and outdoing the lesser miracles of those who failed to accept his mystical authority, and in the process attracted many followers. Such was his renown that many other saints, especially of the non-orthodox variety, were later said to be his spiritual disciples. Most of these non-orthodox mystics were eventually absorbed into the pantheon of saints of the Bektashi order, which formed around the tradition of Haji Bektash and took definite institutional form under Balim Sultan around the year 1500. The Bektashi order was probably the most 'Turkish' of the dervish orders that thrived during the Ottoman period in that it relied to the greatest extent on Turkish as a ritual language, though it also quickly spread among non-Turkish peoples in the Balkans. It was also the least orthodox among the orders, Bektashis being known for not outwardly following the prescribed Islamic norms of praying in mosques, fasting during Ramadan, separating women from men in ritual, and refraining from the consumption of alcoholic beverages. In addition to the Bektashi order, a vast population of Turkmens and Kurds who were never fully assimilated into orthodox urban forms of Islam—known after the Safavid-inspired rebellions of the sixteenth century as Kizilbash, and in the present day as Alevi—generally venerated Haji Bektash over their various local saints.

Haji Bektash was thus remembered throughout the Ottoman centuries primarily by religious groups of a heterodox nature, most of whom were peasants with little influence on elite urban culture. The Bektashi dervish order did eventually establish a presence in Istanbul and other urban centers, so the cult of Haji Bektash would have been somewhat known there, as a result of contact between Bektashi dervishes and those of other orders. Another factor which early on universalized to some extent the originally local cult of Haji Bektash was the importance of the Janissaries, the elite standing infantry of the Ottoman Empire. When the Janissary corps was formed in the fourteenth century, the troops were said to have been blessed by Haji Bektash himself, though this was probably an anachronism. It is known, though, that the troops were levied from Christian families through the *devshirme* system and Islamized through the Bektashi order, and Bektashi *babas* served as chaplains to the troops. Haji Bektash thus had some level of fame throughout the Ottoman period. He was also mentioned by scholars allied to the Ottoman state such as Taşköprüzade in the sixteenth century, although they tended to represent him as an orthodox religious figure, denying any direct connection between the saint and the heterodox groups who venerated him.[11]

In the early twentieth century, however, when nationalist writers were turning to Turkish peasant culture as a source for elements to be used in the promotion of a Turkish national identity, the Alevis were 'discovered,' and the cult of Haji Bektash came to be known to Istanbul intellectuals.[12] Many of the nationalist intellectuals who were secularist in outlook took an interest in the Alevis and Bektashis since they represented a form of religion that was other than the Sunni orthodoxy that had long dominated Ottoman society. More importantly, these groups used the Turkish language in their rituals and prayers, and so appeared to represent an indigenous, Turkish form of spirituality. The fact that many of the poets who had composed verse in Turkish through the Ottoman period, during which elite literature was dominated by Persian and Arabic vocabulary and structures, were Alevi or Bektashi led nationalists to see them as representing the persistence of Turkish culture through a kind of cultural dark ages. The Bektashis were praised for having Turkified members of other nations where the order spread in the Balkans, partly through the Janissaries. While it is reasonable to assume that Haji Bektash himself was ethnically Turkish since he lived among Turkmen peasants, in the nationalist interpretation of history he becomes someone who came to Anatolia *for the sake of* spreading Turkish culture. This 'mission' thus ensures his place in Turkish national heritage.

The nationalist utilization of Yunus Emre has been the least problematic of these three, since his poetry is all in a Turkish dialect that despite its antiquity is readily understandable by speakers of modern Turkish. As with Haji Bektash, the paucity of historical data has rendered any account of Yunus Emre's life dependent on legendary materials; and these are only scanty at best. However, 1320 is generally accepted as the year of his death, and his voluminous poetry includes many references to Tapduk Emre as his *shaykh*. Bektashi tradition appropriates Yunus Emre as an early Bektashi, and maintains a legendary connection between him and Haji Bektash: during a period of famine Yunus Emre comes to Haji Bektash's lodge seeking wheat for his family, and offers a load of wild fruit in exchange. Haji Bektash offers him his spiritual breath in lieu of the wheat, but Yunus Emre takes the wheat. When he realizes what he has passed up, he returns to seek the breath, but Haji Bektash sends him instead to Tapduk Emre. Since this is the most detailed narrative linking Yunus Emre with another historical figure, and moreover accounts for his discipleship under Tapduk Emre, it has also been repeated by non-Bektashis, especially those who are willing to accept Haji Bektash as the grand saint of Anatolian Turkish Sufism. But other dervish orders also count Yunus Emre among their spiritual forebears, and his poems have been sung in the rituals of all Turkish orders (at least those that use music in their rituals), where they are among the most cherished of mystical poems.

The spread of Yunus Emre's influence across the spectrum of dervish orders gave him a broad recognition which in the modern era made him acceptable as a national figure, but at the same time has meant that he is subject to a variety of representations. This is compounded by the diversity of modern ideologies that interpret him today. Yunus Emre can thus be shown to be: a pure humanist speaking to all peoples at all times, without much concern for the particularities of Islam; a cultural missionary whose main goal was to promote the Turkish language; or an orthodox poet voicing the tenets of Islam.[13] More often, however, writers rely on some combination of these trends, since Yunus Emre's poetry certainly contains a latent humanism and many Islamic references, while being expressed in the Turkish language. His use of Turkish rather than the dominant literary languages of Islamic culture at that time—Arabic and Persian—was a result of his developing within a certain socio-cultural milieu, yet this is often represented as if he refused to compose verse in anything other than his own national language, rebelling against the cultural imperialism which had denied his native tongue.[14] Any understanding of a Turkish national cultural heritage—i.e. that of a nation consisting of the Turkish-speaking peoples of present-day Turkey—would have to include Yunus Emre as a foundational figure, since he was the first great poet in the Turkish language in Anatolia. In addition, his greatness as a poet has ensured that he is still meaningful for modern-day Turks, no matter what particular approach they take in interpreting his importance. One modern commentator sums up his relevance with a link to nationalist values:

> Yunus, with his simple and effective artistry, his faith, his sincerity, and an enthusiasm and vitality that are respectful towards religious principles and towards humanity, has shown the way for Turkish humanity; he is a torch that for centuries has not gone out. Even today we have much to take from Yunus. By developing this sacred homeland and culture that we took over from our Yunuses and our ancestors, by preserving our Turkishness, by protecting our unity and togetherness, we can embellish them and provide for an everlasting Turkish homeland.[15]

Clearly, Yunus Emre, Rumi and Haji Bektash can still inspire modern Turks.

In Ottoman times, none of these figures were remembered as humanists; they were known as poets, mystics, religious leaders, bearers of Islamic teachings, foundational saints of dervish orders, miracle-workers, or manifestations of God on earth. Their tombs have for centuries been sites of pilgrimage and animal sacrifice, but it is unlikely that anyone before the modern period sacrificed a sheep to them out of admiration for, say, their views on the need for tolerance among the different religious communities. But today the dominant understanding of these three mystics is as humanists, and it is not difficult to find in them elements that can be associated with humanist values: poetic references to love, brotherhood, the cosmological centrality of man, and a disdain for rigid religious ortho-doxy and the intolerance it leads to. Many scholars and popular writers have picked up on these, and, seeking to represent Turkish history and culture in a modern, secular light, have depicted these saints as the great Turkish humanists. This particular mode of representation has caught on and become reproduced so often that it now seems an unquestionable his-torical truth.

The state has certainly been influential in the development of this un-derstanding. The website of the Ministry of Culture (and Tourism), for example, describes Rumi as believing in the "brotherhood of all human-ity," and as attaching great importance to women.[16] Haji Bektash is there described as a philosopher who taught a love of humanity and tolerance, and this is then linked to modern conceptions of humanism, especially those espoused by the Turkish republic:

> His philosophic thought has been based on existence of human being and love of human being. This thought has been reflecting the same understanding with 1948 Human Rights Universal Dec-laration. Thoughts of "Hacı Bektaş-ı Veli" have been taken into consideration in 1923 by M. Kemal Atatürk approximately after 600 year[s], and a republic which is secular, democratic, respectful to human rights has been established. Despite such a long time passed, his thoughts have been preserving their effectiveness and proceeding to enlighten the path of humanity.[17]

Yunus Emre is also regarded as having developed a system of thought based on love of mankind. In 1991, the supposed 750th anniversary of Yu-nus Emre's birth, Yunus Emre was honored by UNESCO with an "Inter-national Yunus Emre Year" on the basis of "his call to universal friendship and solidarity, his tolerance, and his spirit of love and peace"—a tribute that was initiated by the Turkish Minister of Culture at the time.[18] All three saints are also commemorated annually in festivals supported by the Min-istry of Culture, and the discourse of politicians and officials who speak at them is centered around these humanist values. Because of their human-ism, their Turkishness, and their greatness, these three mystic saints are relevant in modern, national Turkey, and have taken an important place in the pantheon of Turkish cultural heritage.

While the shift in emphasis from religious values to humanist ones is closely tied to the particularities of the nationalist movement, the trans-formation of the memories of saints in the Anatolian Turkish milieu is not a new phenomenon. Hagiographies of the fourteenth and fifteenth centuries focused on the miracle-working powers of saints; early Ottoman chronicles were especially interested in the close relations between saints and the Ottoman sultans; in the sixteenth century, the Ottoman capture of the Islamic holy lands and struggles against the Shi'ite Safavids led to an increased emphasis on Sunnism, and thus orthodoxy, which had an effect on the way heterodox saints were represented; the Sufi orders had mystical interpretations of the lives of their founding saints; and the common people saw them as sources of spiritual beneficence and intercession in fulfilling personal wishes. So the ways saints are understood and represented can vary among different interest groups, and can change in time and in response to historical events and changing attitudes. Certain interpretations can then be more or less solidified by the institutions that are formed around them.

When individuals venerate a saint, they establish a connection with him and to some extent identify themselves with him. But more important sociologically, they come to identify themselves with other individuals who also venerate the saint. This occurs perhaps most powerfully in pilgrimages and other rituals around the saint's shrine, in which venerators see themselves acting in unison with others, and toward a common focal point. When the saint then, for whatever historical or political reasons, comes to be relevant to a larger collectivity, the number of people who share in veneration of the saint increases, and the form of his veneration will necessarily change in accordance with their expectations. Rumi, Haji Bektash and Yunus Emre early on moved out of their local contexts; mostly through the institutionalization of Sufi orders. In the modern era, they have taken on the aura of humanism and were thereby allowed to reach the height of universalism. And because they are indelibly linked to Turkey as a land, Turkish history and Turkish culture, they have become national icons.

It is interesting that mystic saints long associated with popular forms of Islam have taken on such an important role in a nationalist republic that is avowedly secular and self-consciously modern. Among the reforms initiated by Atatürk, of course, were many that, directly or indirectly, limited the role of Islam in the state and in social life. The caliphate was abolished, Islamic law was replaced with a secular civil code, the Arabic script was replaced with a modified Latin script, women's rights were advanced, the Qur'an and the call to prayer were translated into Turkish, and even the men's head covering that represented the East, the fez, was forbidden. In 1925, in response to a rebellion led by a Naqshbandi *shaykh*, a law was passed closing the Sufi orders, along with titles used in the orders, positions, dervish garments, and shrines. Most of the practices listed in the law—shrine visitation, the use of charms and amulets, even fortune-telling—were considered superstitious and thus contrary to the rationalist, modernist ideology of the republic. But an important reason underlying the closure of the orders was the political threat posed by these highly structured institutions, which demanded their adherents' devotion to their leaders. Organized Islam was a possible rival to the nationalist project, and the "purified, literacy-stressing Islam" that Gellner saw as being conformable to a national identity was considered by the secularist Turks under Atatürk as a danger.

However, it can be argued that the secularists sought not to eliminate Islam, but to bring it under state control. Though Islamic law was no longer in effect, a Directorate of Religious Affairs was instituted in order to ensure that the Islam taught in mosques was of the kind permitted by the state—and this did not include Sufism. Interestingly, however, Atatürk in his speeches incorporated language from the Sufi orders to differentiate between the old superstitious system and the new modern ideology. One of his most famous dictums is: "The truest guide in life is science" (*Hayatta en hakiki mürşid ilimdir*)—using the term mürşid, which refers specifically to a spiritual guide in Sufism. In another speech he proposed a *Tarikat-ı Medeniyye*—"Civilized Order"—co-opting the term used for Sufi orders, *tarikat*, in highlighting how his new system was more modern, rational and civilized than its predecessor. If the institution of the orders, their offices, their beliefs and their practices were banned and vilified, it might be expected that their founding saints would likewise be condemned. But, in fact, they turned out to be useful.

There is a process undertaken by many nationalist movements of using elements from the past to reconstruct the present, a kind of "political archaeology," to borrow a term from Anthony D. Smith."[19] This was an important part of the Turkish nationalist project, as evidenced by the formulation of the Turkish History Thesis in the 1930's.[20] The need was felt to promote Turkey's indigenous history and culture, and, as in many nations, great importance was placed on literature, music and folk dancing. But because of the concomitant emphasis on secularism, much of religious ritual and belief was also secularized into culture, particularly those elements deriving from Sufism. The dervish orders were now closed, but the rituals they had performed were in many cases widespread, recognizable, and aesthetic examples of Turkish cultural heritage, so they began to be performed as folklore. The best example is the 'whirling dervish' dance of the Mevlevi order. Though the order which developed this dance is officially closed and performance of the *sema* dance by dervishes is illegal, it is regularly performed as a folklore spectacle. The Ministry of Culture actually funds a Sufi Music Orchestra in Konya, Rumi's center, complete with a troupe of *sema* dancers in Mevlevi costume. So, even though it is illegal for dervishes to whirl for God, the state has no problem paying state employees to whirl for tourism and Turkish culture. Recognizing the importance of the saints themselves in Turkey's cultural heritage, the Ministry of Culture has also taken over the administration of the tomb complexes of Rumi and Haji Bektash, which are now museums, and constructed a large complex near a grave purported to be that of Yunus Emre. Other tombs, those of the less humanist, more orthodox, or less socially and culturally useful saints, are controlled by the Directorate of Religious Affairs. So, though expression of religion has been restricted in the secular republic, a way has been opened up for some saints to be remembered in national terms; as cultural figures. However, this is only possible for dead, medieval saints. The modernist republic has prevented the acceptance of modern saints and religious figures, like Said Nursi, whose links with the Naqshbandis and widespread appeal have made the state suspicious of his followers,[21] and Zöhre Ana, a faith healer in Ankara who refers to herself as an *evliya* (saint), but has been persecuted by the police, the secular media, and the Islamist media as well.

So, the three mystic figures who have been the most important for the formation of Turkey's cultural heritage are: Rumi, because of his immense fame as a poet, the stature of members of the Mevlevi order and their role in the development of arts such as poetry, music and calligraphy, and the particular beauty of the *sema* ritual and the music which accompanies it; Haji Bektash, because of the progressiveness of members of the Bektashi order and the Alevis and their use of Turkish in poetry and rituals, and his importance for a large section of the population; and Yunus Emre, because of his stature as a poet of the Turkish language. Since these three can also be shown to represent humanist values, they are that much more useful. As the Turkish nationalist movement involved a shift from religion to culture, humanism marks a shift from religion to the human, which constitutes a secular and progressive outlook. The fact that such a humanism can be found in Turkish history is used in part in order to put Turkey on a par with Europe. The earliest depictions of these saints represent them as working miracles, which at the time was what was expected of a saint. The greater the saint could be made to sound, the more successful the order would be in attracting new disciples. Today, an image of a thirteenth-century saint flying in the air, multiplying food, or changing into the form of an animal is not likely to impress many people, because it would not seem credible. But showing the saint as great in terms of humanism establishes a connection with the values people today cherish, and raises the nation whose cultural heritage he symbolizes to a higher moral level, which then satisfies the need of individuals who consider themselves part of that nation to feel morally elevated.

The representation of these saints as humanists has become institutionalized through repetition, and is the dominant paradigm for understanding them, but this does not preclude contestation over how they are to be remembered; there are rival understandings of these saints. In particular, Islamist writers tend to stress the saints' piety and roles as propagators of Islam. Even Haji Bektash, who was represented in the earliest narratives as heterodox, and has been venerated almost entirely by the unorthodox Bektashi order and Alevi sect, is seen in Islamist eyes as a missionary who had sought to teach orthodox Islam to the half-pagan Turkmen nomads. There is also a strictly nationalist approach, which sees Haji Bektash and Yunus Emre especially as having been engaged in a mission to Turkify Anatolia. Then there is a leftist view, which, while it focuses more on rebel saints such as Shaykh Bedreddin and Pir Sultan Abdal, also sees Haji Bektash as being a kind of proto-Marxist.[22] But it is a sign of the strength of humanism as a set of positive values that the humanist thesis works its way into all of these interpretations. Thus, the saint was a humanist and Muslim, or a humanist and Turkish hero, or a humanist and Marxist. Throughout them all, the saint is made to fit present ideologies while maintaining his humanism.

The mystic saints are taken from a remembered history, but are given an interpretation in line with the aims of the nationalist movement. These saints are artifacts from the cultural heritage, crystallizations of what society considers important. Their use in modern nationalist discourse is a reconstruction, but not necessarily a fabrication. It is the result of a construction decision, a practical response to the need for a Turkish nationalist narrative and a limited availability of materials. Since there is a clear continuity with the past—in content if not in form—it is more an innovation than an invention of tradition, or a transformation. Some Turkish nationalist ideas constructed solely by intellectuals—like the Sun Language Theory, and the theory that world civilization developed out of Anatolia, whose original inhabitants were supposedly Turkish—either did not take hold at all or remained marginal, in part because they were not based on memories from the collective experience of the people. The tradition must have resonance, as Anthony Smith points out: that is, it must touch on some memory, while simultaneously fulfilling specified nationalist goals.[23]

Notes

[1] On Gellner's three stages of the history of mankind and the modernity of nationalism see his *Nations and Nationalism* (Ithaca: Cornell University Press, 1983); and *Nationalism* (New York: New York University Press, 1997).

[2] Ernest Gellner, *Culture, Identity, and Politics* (Cambridge: Cambridge University Press, 1987), 16. For the full treatment of this historical change, 13-17.

[3] Ibid., 16.

[4] Ernest Gellner, *Saints of the Atlas* (Chicago: University of Chicago Press, 1969); *Muslim Society* (Cambridge: Cambridge University Press, 1981).

[5] Gellner, *Muslim Society*, 166.

[6] For a critique of Gellner's model of Muslim society in this work see Sami Zubaida, "Is There a Muslim Society? Ernest Gellner's Sociology of Islam," *Economy and Society* 24, no.2 (1995): 151-188.

[7] For a comprehensive study of the life of Rumi and the different ways he is represented see Franklin Lewis, *Rumi: Past and Present, East and West* (Oxford: Oneworld, 2000). For his discussion of the Turkish appropriation of the poet, 547-550.

[8] For a list of Mevlevi terms see Abdülbaki Gölpınarlı, *Mevlana'dan Sonra Mevlevilik* 2nd edition (Istanbul: İnkılap ve Aka, 1983), 433-38.

[9] Sinan Yağmur, *Mevlana Celaleddin Rumi: Tennure ve Ateş* (Konya: Esra Yayınları, n.d.), 7.

[10] Abdülbâki Gölpınarlı, *Manâkıb-ı Hünkâr Hacı Bektâş-ı Velî "Vilâyetnâme"* (Istanbul: İnkılap Kitabevi, 1958).

[11] Mecdi Mehmed Efendi, *Şaka'ik-i Nu'maniyye ve Zeyilleri: Hada'iku'l-Şaka'ik*, ed. Abdulkadir Özcan (Istanbul: Çağrı Yayınları, 1989), 44.

[12] See for example the articles by Baha Said Bey collected in Nejat Birdoğan, *İttihat-Terakki'nin Alevilik Bektaşilik Araştırması* (Istanbul: Berfin, 1994).

[13] For an analysis of the various modern interpretations of Yunus, Rumi, Haji Bektash and other religious figures, see the articles in Ahmet Yaşar Ocak, *Türk Sufiliğine Bakışlar* (Istanbul: İletişim, 1996).

[14] For example Sabahattin Eyuboğlu, *Yunus Emre* (Istanbul: Cem Yayınevi, 1971), 7-9.

[15] Ahmet Vehbi Ecer, "Yunus Emre'nin Yaşadığı Çağda Anadolu'da Kültür Hayatının Ana Hatları," in *Uluslararası Yunus Emre Sempozyumu Bildirileri* (Ankara: Atatürk Kültür Merkezi Yayını, 1995), 51.

[16] http://www.kultur.gov.tr/portal/kultur_en.asp?belgeno=1592 (accessed on 15 August 2005).

[17] Ibid.

[18] Talât Halman, *A'dan Z'ye Yunus Emre* (Istanbul: Yapı Kredi Yayınları, 2003), 40.

[19] Anthony D. Smith, *Myths and Memories of the Nation* (Oxford: Oxford University Press, 1999), 12 and 181.

[20] An excellent analysis of the development of the official Turkish history is found in Büşra Ersanlı Behar, *İktidar ve Tarih: Türkiye'de "Resmi Tarih" Tezinin Oluşumu (1929-1937)* (Istanbul: Afa, 1992).

[21] See Şerif Mardin, *Religion and Social Change in Modern Turkey: The Case of Bediuzzaman Said Nursi* (Albany: State University of New York Press, 1989); also Camilla T. Nereid, *In the Light of Said Nursi: Turkish Nationalism and the Religious Alternative* (Bergen: Center for Middle Eastern and Islamic Studies, 1997).

[22] See for example Âdil Gülvahaboğlu, *Hacı Bektaş Veli: Lâik-Ulusal Kültür* (Ankara: Yorum Yayınları, n.d.) – a strange mix of Turkist and Marxist rhetoric.

[23] Smith, *Myths and Memories of the Nation*, 181.

11
Narrating the 'Yoke of Oppression'
Twentieth-Century Hungarian Scholarship of the Ottoman-Hungarian Borderlands

Claire Norton

Introduction

One of the consequences of the teleological nature of history is the tendency of historians to retrospectively imagine past communities in accordance with contemporary, dominant geo-political cartographies. The nation state as the current pre-eminent unit of geo-political division is thus frequently employed as a prism through which to examine and define past events and communities. The nation state's concomitant emphasis on ethno-linguistic or religious homogeneity as criteria for belonging and a principle basis of identity therefore commonly results in the imagination of past communities distinguished in these terms and thus obscures alternative sites for the construction of collective identity.

Evidence of the anachronistic employment of nation-state cartographies in twentieth-century historians' imagining of earlier, sixteenth and seventeenth century communities is illustrated in scholarship of the Hungarian-Habsburg-Ottoman marches or border lands. Many twentieth-century histories of this border zone project current geo-political realities and divisions back onto the early modern communities which inhabited this area. Consequently they tend to be imagined as ethnically, linguistically and religiously discrete (and antagonistic) communities that conveniently provide a direct and unbroken social and cultural link with present-day nation states. The Ottoman Turkish presence in the Balkans is thus often seen as an aberration, an occupation which is almost exclusively viewed negatively as a "yoke of oppression" which stifled the development of the 'natural' communities in the area.[1] However, numerous primary sources suggest another perspective and present different articulations of identity and ontologies of community. Tales, muster records, and personal and official correspondence all attest to the existence of more integrated and diverse border communities in which imaginations of self and other were not constructed solely and rigidly in terms of religious, ethnic or linguistic criteria, but were more complex and fluid.

This chapter will examine the depiction of these border communities by twentieth century, mainly Hungarian, historians of the Ottoman Empire. Specifically, it will analyze their construction, understanding, and use of the term Hungarian. It will focus on how, through their histories of the Ottoman Empire, historians have essentially depicted Hungarians as constituting a singular, unchanging socio-political entity which preserved a pre-Ottoman fifteenth century ethnic, linguistic, cultural and religious identity throughout the period of Ottoman 'subjugation' until its eventual emancipation and coterminous awakening as the nation state of Hungary. Through a deconstruction of their use of the term Hungarian it will be argued that it is an implicit assumption of these historians that 'Hungarian-ness' did not change over time, it remained pure and unsullied by the culture of their Ottoman 'oppressors' thus subsequently legitimizing their claim to be a genuine nation. The chapter will begin with a brief overview of Ottoman involvement in Hungary in the sixteenth and seventeenth centuries. It will then explore a number of sources that suggest that this border area was a culturally fluid zone in which communities did not necessarily, or solely, define themselves in terms of a common religious, linguistic or 'ethnic' heritage. Lastly, the depictions of the various communities in the Ottoman-controlled border zone by twentieth century Hungarian historians will be examined in greater depth.

Ottoman Hungary

Following the Ottoman conquest of Istanbul in 1453 the Ottomans gradually expanded further west into the Balkans. Throughout the second half of the fifteenth century and the first decades of the sixteenth century they maintained generally peaceful relations with the kingdom of Hungary. In 1520 this period ended when Sultan Süleyman I sent his envoy to Buda to renegotiate the peace treaties with the Hungarian government. The envoy was imprisoned by the Hungarian king, Louis II; an action which precipitated a belligerent military response from Süleyman. The Ottoman army returned again to Hungary in 1526 and at the battle of Mohacs decisively defeated the Hungarian kingdom's army, killed the king and 'occupied' the southern regions of the kingdom. The ensuing succession struggle for the Hungarian throne between the Austrian Archduke Ferdinand of Habsburg and János Zapolya, the constitutionally elected king of Hungary, led to a period of conflict which precipitated continued Ottoman involvement in Hungarian affairs through their support of Zapolya.[2] Following Zapolya's death in 1541 Archduke Ferdinand sent Habsburgs troops to Buda in accordance with a secret agreement signed in 1538 between himself and Zapolya which named Ferdinand as heir to the kingdom. However, just before his death Zapolya had apparently wished to rescind the agreement following the birth of his son, and when two Hungarian envoys arrived at Istanbul requesting that Süleyman act in accordance with Zapolya's last wishes and acknowledge his son as his heir, and ruler of Hungary, Süleyman was more than happy to comply. Responding to Ferdinand's military presence in Buda, Süleyman led a campaign into Hungary and permanently occupied Buda, creating a new Ottoman province. This intervention resulted in the division of the old fifteenth-century kingdom of Hungary into three areas: the directly controlled province of Ottoman Hungary in the south; the Ottoman vassal principality of Transylvania in the east governed by the prelate Georg Mönch Martinuzzi on behalf of János Zsigmond, Zapolya's underage son; and Habsburg controlled Hungary (Royal Hungary) in the north.[3] Süleyman commanded a number of campaigns in the region in the following years capturing Pécs and Esztergom in 1543 and finally Szigetvár in 1566. Whether the Ottomans always intended to incorporate Hungary into their empire from the beginning of the sixteenth century, or whether they would have preferred to maintain it with vassal status as a buffer between themselves and the Habsburgs is subject of much debate among historians.[4] The Ottomans remained in Hungary for approximately 150 years until the end of the seventeenth century when, following the disastrous second Ottoman siege of Vienna, they were routed by a Habsburg-led relief army that was able to take advantage of the confusion of the retreating Ottomans and occupy much of Hungary.

During the sixteenth and seventeenth centuries, the fifteenth-century kingdom of Hungary was thus divided into Ottoman Hungary, Habsburg Hungary and the semi-autonomous vassal state of Transylvania. But what happened to the communities that had lived in the fifteenth-century Hungarian kingdom during the period of Ottoman rule? Were they, as Hungarian scholars have frequently asserted, divided along ethno-linguistic and religious lines into separate, discrete and often antagonistic groupings? Was the pre-fifteenth century Hungarian kingdom essentially preserved dormant until its modern re-awakening as a nation state? Or is there evidence of significant mediation, linkage and transfer between communities, of cultural synthesis, and of a blurring of the boundaries of division?

A zone of mediation, synthesis and transfer?

There is a significant amount of evidence that suggests that collective identities in Ottoman Hungary, like the border itself, were not fixed and immutable, but were fluid and porous. A variety of primary sources attest that the allegiances of border communities did not orient exclusively and deterministically around loyalty to a particular religion, language or state, but were frequently defined in terms of class, locale, shared practices and customs, work, or allegiance to a local lord or commander.[5] Many people changed allegiances at their convenience; others integrated themselves and formed new hybrid communities that transcended the boundaries of ethnicity, religion and language. For example, Western European Christians fought together with Muslim and Christian Ottomans against other Christians: Hungarians, Habsburg Austrians, Poles and Transylvanians all fought both against and alongside the Ottomans at various times. An event from the Long War (1593-1606) between the Habsburgs and Ottomans at the turn of the seventeenth century illustrates this military fluidity: a number of French and Walloon mercenaries garrisoned at the frontier fortress of Pápa in Habsburg-Hungary mutinied over a delay in the payment of their wages and defected to the Ottoman army which they subsequently assisted in its capture of Habsburg-held Nagykanizsa castle in 1600. According to Ottoman military records these soldiers continued to fight in the Ottoman army in subsequent years in Moldavia, on the Hotin (Chotin) campaign and also against the Safavids and Cossacks.[6] While one of the French captains from Pápa converted to Islam in the winter of 1600-01 and was rewarded with a position in the military-administrative hierarchy many of his men did not convert and remained Christian. Moreover, even after the captain converted he maintained his command over the Pápa mercenaries and thus adopted dual identities; as an Ottoman Muslim in his relations with the Ottoman state, but as a French military commander in the context of his command over his men. There is further evidence from Ottoman campaign treasury account books that during this same war Christians from Poland, Transylvania and some Austrians were also paid by the Ottomans for military service. In particular, the latter were involved in the Ottoman attempt to recapture Esztergom from the Habsburgs in 1605.[7]

It was not just Christian European mercenaries who fought for the Ottomans on this border though: the multi-ethnic, poly-lingual, interdenominational Ottoman border garrisons provide ample evidence of more permanent alliances. Despite imperial Ottoman rhetoric that Christians were not permitted to fight in the Ottoman army, Christian (Orthodox and Catholic) *sekban* soldiers clearly participated in the Ottoman military as has been noted by a number of authors.[8] Pakalın, for example mentions the large number of Christian *sekban* soldiers among the Ottoman forces during the second siege of Vienna in 1683.[9] Moreover, Stein, through an analysis of military registers and rolls has demonstrated that Christians were a significant and important presence in Ottoman border fortresses from the fifteenth century until the end of the seventeenth century. These Christian soldiers not only undertook garrison duties in the fortresses, but they also accompanied their Muslim comrades on raids across the frontier and shared the proceeds. In some border fortresses up to a third of the non-janissary (that is the local permanent garrison) were Christians.[10] Although the predominately Christian units were commanded by Muslims, this situation should not be understood as one divided by ethnicity; that is Muslim Turks commanding Christian Hungarians, because, as Stein has argued, many of the Muslims were newly converted local people.[11] The existence of mixed Christian and Muslim garrison units and the conversions among Christian border soldiers indicate that religion was not necessarily a strong determiner of community allegiance and identity. Instead shared occupations, languages, cultural traditions and practices, or loyalty to a local commander seem to have been at least as, if not more, important as criteria of identity. A similar example occurs with regard to the Belgrade gypsies. Hertz notes that they formed a mixed Muslim and Christian community in Belgrade: their identity as gypsies was more significant than their religious affiliations. In fact the Belgrade domesday book (*defter-i mufassal*) provides evidence that there were both Christians and Muslims in the same family unit.[12]

Other sources suggest that the Habsburg-Hungarian-Ottoman border zone existed largely outside the sphere and rhetoric of central imperial authority and that consequently border communities developed, co-existed and integrated according to local conditions rather than the political and religious dictates of the centre. There is evidence that between the local commanders on either side of the border zone there existed a sense of shared values reflecting both the particularities of the local geo-political context and a common social status and occupation which often transcended factional, religious or imperial divisions and animosities. The different commanders frequently corresponded with each other in friendly terms and exchanged presents.[13] They were also more than prepared to co-operate and work together, often defying their respective imperial orders, if they believed it suited their interests. For example, the local Ottoman border authorities tolerated the collection of taxes by Habsburg agents from peasants in Ottoman territories because in return they received one per cent of the total collected sum.[14] Likewise, both sides smuggled and traded goods across the border area with no regard for existing imperial treaties or orders.[15] They also frequently agreed to exchange prisoners who had been captured as result of continuing border raids that violated Ottoman-Habsburg peace treaties, but made no attempt to stop the illegal raids themselves.[16]

Bracewell describes a similar environment existing on the Croatian borderlands surrounding Senj on the Adriatic coast. Here the Christian Uskoks were nominally engaged in a holy war against the Muslim Ottomans: raiding their territory, burning settlements, and enslaving or ransoming the local population. However, in practice the situation was more complex and the Uskoks' interactions with both Muslims and Christians in this border zone were prescribed more by the exigencies of the frontier locality and common interests than imperial or state pronouncements or the rhetorics of holy war. That religious difference was not the only motivating criteria behind Uskok raids and military endeavors is evidenced by their persecution of Christians living in Ottoman lands as well as Muslims.[17]

The Uskoks and local Ottoman garrisons inhabited a shared world. They possessed a common language and participated in a culture with shared concepts of honor, heroism, vengeance and ties of kinship. There were often familial ties between the Uskoks and Ottoman state officials. In 1588 an Ottoman delegation in Venice requested that six captured Uskoks not be executed because one of them was a close relative of an eminent Ottoman captain.[18] In addition to such family connections there also existed ties of kinship based upon a shared notion of blood brotherhood. This institution helped to create identities that transcended religious divides and connected commanders and soldiers on both sides of the border. As on the Hungarian marches, in the border areas around Senj, when the interests of local Uskok and Ottoman commanders coincided they often acted independently of orders from the imperial centre. In 1588 the Ottoman government proscribed the practice of ransoming Ottoman captives from the Uskoks in an attempt to decrease Uskok raids by removing a key financial incentive. However, as the exchange of captives was a critical part of the frontier economy the local commanders on each side were reluctant to implement this decree and instead concluded an independent agreement which culminated in an exchange of gifts and a ceremony joining the two commanders as blood brothers.[19] Furthermore, there was often collaboration between local Ottoman commanders and Uskoks on the matter of border raids. Ottoman officials in the town of Karin agreed to allow the Uskoks to cross their territory without hindrance in order to raid other Ottoman settlements and even undertook to mislead any Ottoman troops sent to pursue the raiders in exchange for a guarantee that the Uskoks would not raid Karin.[20]

Habsburg official documents also attest to the flexibility of border communities and to the weakness of ties based solely upon religion, ethnicity and loyalty to a particular state. A report to the Aulic War Council in 1718 suggests that the Habsburgs were concerned about Christian peasants settling in Ottoman lands because the Ottomans were generally offering lower taxes and longer periods of tax exemption. However, much more seriously, they were concerned that these Christian Habsburg subjects, having moved to Ottoman lands might fall upon hard times and resort to raiding or brigandry in the country they had left; that is against their former compatriots.[21]

Narrations of the Ottoman-Hungarian border zone by twentieth-century Hungarian historians.

In contrast to the depiction of socio-cultural synthesis or interaction described above a number of twentieth-century, predominantly Hungarian, scholars who work in the field of Ottoman history have described the Ottoman-Hungarian-Habsburg border area as one of isolation and hostility between the different communities living there. While many of these historians acknowledge the theory that borders are areas of mediation, linkage and transfer, where material and cultural exchanges occur, they then go on to assert that the Hungarian-Habsburg-Ottoman border lands are an exception to this rule.[22] They note the unique cultural character of the marches, but then argue that despite this inimitability very little, if any, interaction occurred between the communities living there. For example, Dávid and Fodor argue that the Hungarian border was a unique area of military acculturation and transfer, but deny that there existed any long-lasting interaction between the various communities in the area.[23] Sugar similarly argues for the existence of a common military code and patterns of behavior between the various border communities, but then comments that in the Ottoman-Hungarian marches there was no revival of the old *gazi-akritoi* confrontation and symbiosis which had existed in Anatolia in the thirteenth and fourteenth centuries.[24] Fekete is even more direct when he comments that "[D]uring the one hundred and fifty years of Ottoman occupation in Hungary, they [the Ottomans and Hungarians] cohabited in such a way that no ties of cohesion were established between them."[25]

Klara Hegyi reinforces this idea that there existed a lack of interaction between the various communities by arguing that Ottoman rule in Hungary never amounted to more than a military occupation and that the Ottomans always lacked the strength to control civilian life.[26] She thereby hypothesizes the presence of a significant divide between the Ottoman military occupiers and a continuing Hungarian social, political and cultural community. This depiction of the Ottomans as solely an occupying military force is echoed by Dávid who notes that there was "almost no civilian Muslim population" in Ottoman Hungary and the castles "bristled with Ottoman soldiers" which created a hostile situation that ultimately drove the Hungarian civilian inhabitants "to other places where they felt less threatened by the Ottoman presence."[27] Bayerle presents the Ottomans as being both physically as well as culturally isolated from the Hungarian population when he states that by the end of the sixteenth century the Ottomans were forced to live barricaded in the cities.[28] These constant allusions to Ottoman Hungary as a hostile environment emphasize again the lack of cooperation, cultural synthesis and integration between the various communities.

These comments imagine an environment in which Ottoman Turkish Muslim soldiers occupied Hungary, but remained distinct and separate from the local Hungarian civilian population. They also link religion to assumed ethnicity and status: all Muslims are Ottoman Turks (and soldiers) whereas all Hungarians are Christians (and civilians). For these authors the possibility that Hungarians could have either converted to Islam or served the Ottoman state apparatus in a military or bureaucratic function as Christians is virtually inconceivable. Dávid and Fodor argue that the numbers of Hungarian converts to Islam or 'renegades' were insignificant.[29] Dávid reiterates this point and further asserts that newly converted Muslims in cities in Ottoman Hungary were definitely not Hungarian, but had different ethnic backgrounds and reportedly spoke Slavonic.[30]

Thus, when interaction between Christian and Muslim communities is acknowledged by the aforementioned scholars it is generally depicted as being between non-Hungarian Christians and Muslim Ottomans. Dávid argues that of the few non-Muslim *timar* holders in Ottoman Hungary many were Slavs or Jews and only a few were Hungarian and these appointments were "infrequent and temporary."[31] He also clearly states that the non-Muslims who served in the border garrisons were not Hungarian.[32] Hegyi more explicitly states that various forms of co-operation existed between the Ottomans and the southern Slavs living in Hungary, but *not* between the Hungarians and Ottomans.[33] Moreover, when inter-communal interaction is acknowledged it is relegated to an instance of financially-motivated cooperation: the motivation behind the interaction is always given in terms of a desire for monetary reward rather than based in any genuine co-operation and symbiosis among communities. Dávid argues that the loyalty of "Christian auxiliary troops ... can be partly explained by the fact that they received significant tax exemptions and often a piece of arable land (*baştina*) for life."[34] Needless to say this acknowledgement of non-Muslim involvement in the Ottoman military structure in Ottoman Hungary contradicts the image of an Ottoman Turkish Muslim military occupation existing in isolation from a local Hungarian and Slav, Christian civilian society presented above by these scholars.

Occasionally, as has been demonstrated in the preceding paragraph, a connection between the two communities (and they always are imagined by historians as two communities; the Hungarians and the Ottomans) is noted. However, the significance of these interconnections is consistently minimized. For example, the existence of translations of Turkish songs into Hungarian or the use of Turkish tunes by Hungarian minstrels is dismissed by Dávid and Fodor as demonstrating the existence of "a—probably small—group of minstrels on both sides of the frontier familiar with both Ottoman and Hungarian poetry."[35] These two authors also argue that despite Hungarians adopting some Ottoman food and clothing items, embroidery patterns, musical motifs, instruments and building styles, the Ottomans had no lasting cultural impact on Hungarian communities.[36] In a similar manner, a number of historians including Dávid have stressed the insubstantial or decentralized nature of the Ottoman 'occupation' of Hungary; "the occupation of Hungary remained unconsolidated throughout, thus encouraging variations in procedure."[37] It seems to be implied that this 'unconsolidated occupation' permitted a greater degree of autonomy for the Hungarians thus allowing them to retain a greater degree of their pre-existing cultural, political and religious practices and identity than that of other Balkan communities.

To summarize, the above historians generally portray these marches as consisting of separate ethnic and religious communities. In particular they imagine a Hungarian community that is essentially a continuation of a pre-Ottoman collectivity - namely the fifteenth and sixteenth century Hungarian kingdoms of King Matthias Corvinus and King Louis II respectively. Their emphasis on the lack of interaction, interconnectedness and symbiosis between various communities, but particularly between the Christian Hungarians and Muslim Ottoman-Turks seems designed to accentuate that this pre-sixteenth century Hungarian community remained intact throughout the Ottoman occupation of the land. The preservation of an unchanging, constant Hungarian ethnic, cultural and religious identity throughout the early modern period is crucial if one wishes to argue that the Hungarians as a distinct community have continuously occupied the same territorial space from the fifteenth century until the present day.

This however raises some questions: what constitutes the religious, cultural and ethnic identity of this Hungarian community? How homogeneous was it? Did it really not change over time? Dávid and Fodor mention that the percentage of the late fifteenth-century population of the Hungarian kingdom which consisted of "Hungarians properly speaking" was between 60-70%.[38] But, what determines one's status as a Hungarian, "properly-speaking"? The term Hungarian or *Magyar* is never adequately defined by these historians and similarly, the question of how communities resident in the fifteenth century Hungarian kingdom and later communities imagined themselves is never discussed. The implicit assumption throughout many of these histories seems to be that religion (Christianity), language (Hungarian) and the indefinable and ever-elusive ethnicity are the key determinants of Hungarian-ness. Not only is this very anachronistic, but it is also confusing and problematic: do Hungarians who convert to Islam cease being Hungarians? Are Christians resident in the province of Buda who are not native speakers of Hungarian, Hungarians? Are 'proper' Hungarians Catholic, Protestant or Orthodox? Moreover, there appears to be an attempt in these histories to partially define Hungarian-ness in contrast to Ottoman-ness where Ottoman is defined as Turkish (linguistically and ethnically) and Muslim. It is uncritically assumed that Muslims can not be Hungarian—Muslims are either Turks or 'renegade' Bosnians and Serbs. For example, Dávid and Fodor ask how far Muslim culture affected sixteenth and seventeenth century Hungarians: they therefore imagine Hungarians as being Christian and not Muslim.[39]

The dominance of a nation-state dominated cartography in these histories is again foregrounded by the ubiquitous references by such scholars to the Ottoman 'occupation' of Hungary. Such references however raise the question: where were the Ottomans not occupying? Which people were they not subjugating beneath their yoke? Over what territory did the Ottomans exert legitimate sovereignty? That the answer to this latter question by a number of different historians is variously, not Greece, Hungary, the Balkans, the Hejaz nor the Arab states, implies that the only territory the Ottomans were not illegally occupying was Anatolia: a territorial landmass conveniently coterminous with the present-day nation state of Turkey. Thus the dominance of the nation state paradigm retrospectively conditions and dictates the extent of legitimate Ottoman sovereignty, and determines whether the Ottomans were 'occupying' a particular place or not.

Similarly, the treatment of rebellions, revolts and uprisings in the early modern Balkans by twentieth-century historians reveals the prevalence and dominance of the nation-state paradigmatic framework. Intra-empire violence within the European territories of the Ottoman Empire is frequently read teleologically by historians as evidence for proto-nationalist struggles for independence: as a desire by the dormant nations to throw off the Ottoman "yoke of oppression."[40] In a Hungarian context, the Bocskai rebellion in the early seventeenth century is often depicted as a proto-national movement: Bérenger comments that it "quickly assumed a war of national liberation."[41] Bocskai's alliance with first the Habsburgs and then the Ottomans is therefore interpreted as an attempt by the peasants to assert their Hungarian independence from both the imperialist Habsburgs and Ottomans.

Conclusion

Despite the dominant narrative of separation, exclusion and difference articulated by these historians, both primary sources and the gaps in these historians' narratives divulge other stories which attest to the existence of more integrated and diverse border communities: communities in which the criteria for inclusion or exclusion were not constructed solely and rigidly in terms of the nation-state identity markers of religion, language or ethnicity. As noted at the beginning of this chapter, there is considerable evidence in sixteenth and seventeenth-century muster records, personal correspondence, eyewitness accounts, histories and official documents that indicates that the formation and identification of communities in the multi-lingual, religiously diverse, and culturally complex context of the Habsburg-Ottoman-Hungarian marches was a lot more complicated and fluid than is suggested by these historians' accounts. It was not a place where Christian Austrians, Hungarians, Serbs, and Muslim Turks lived totally isolated from each other in distinct communities — or separate proto-nation states.

Inhabitants of the Ottoman Balkans, including Ottoman Hungary participated in plural communities and had multiple identities. Peasants while identifying as Christian or Muslims, Hungarian or Turkish speakers may have been more closely brought together by their common employment by the Ottoman state, by their serving under a particular commander in a border fortress, by their shared social status, comradeship, or occupation.

So why then have the above historians overlooked these more assimilative stories in favor of a narrative describing separate and largely antagonistic communities? I suggest that historians are imagining the past and writing histories within a framework dominated by a nation-state orientated cartography or way of mapping political and social relations. Implicitly they are trying to explain or justify the existence of the nation state of Hungary through their teleological construction of the past. By defining the Hungarian community as a distinct entity and by emphasizing not only its cultural and social isolation from contaminating sources, but also its continuation from an earlier kingdom, the Hungarians are presented as constituting a 'natural' community and thus nation state. In other words they are depicted as linguistically, ethnically and culturally different to other peoples and thus they can more easily be imagined as a nation. As Breuilly notes in his introductory chapter in this volume, such historians by demonstrating a particular 'was' about the past, are in fact trying to facilitate the assertion of an 'ought' in the present: because Hungarians have constituted a distinct and autonomous community from earliest times they are therefore now entitled to nation-state status.

I do not want to suggest that Hungarian historians are in any way more prone to narrating past events within a nation-state dominated discourse than any other historian—I have previously explored how twentieth century Turkish-language popular narrations of military encounters on this border have been re-written within a Turkish nation-state orientated discourse.[42] Instead I want to argue that the lure of the nation-state paradigm as a framework for interpreting and constructing geo-political space and social relations is so great that it affects the way we all construct the past. Our histories, rather than isomorphically corresponding to a past reality, instead create this reality according to our own concerns, interests and interpretative strategies. Historical narratives are not neutral and impartial, in contrast, they reflect and help constitute particular views of sovereignty, and since the nineteenth century they have been instrumental in naturalizing a territorial, or nation-state orientated mapping of geographical and political space.

Notes

[1] M. R. Hickok, *Ottoman Military Administration in Eighteenth Century Bosnia* (Leiden: Brill, 1997), 114-5 discusses how various histories of the Balkans have tried to demonstrate how a Slavic heritage survived underground during the Ottoman 'occupation' until finally evolving into the struggle for 'national' independence at the end of the eighteenth and nineteenth centuries.

[2] Jean Bérenger, *A History of the Habsburg Empire 1273-1700* English translation (London and New York: Longman, 1994), 159.

[3] Ibid., 190.

[4] Pal Fodor, "Ottoman Policy Towards Hungary 1520-1541," *Acta Orientalia Academiae Scientiarum Hung.* Tomus XLV 2-3 (1991): 271-345 argues in support of the former thesis whereas, Géza Perjés, *The Fall of the Medieval Kingdom of Hungary 1526-Buda 1541* War and Society in East Central Europe vol. XXXI. Social Science Monographs, (Highland Lakes, New Jersey: Boulder Colorado Atlantic Research and Publications, distributed by Columbia University Press, 1989) and Halil Inalcık, *The Ottoman Empire: The Classical Age 1300-1600* (London: Phoenix, 1994 (1973)), 35-6 argue for the latter explanation.

[5] For a more detailed discussion of the fluidity of identities on this border area see, Claire Norton, "'The Lutheran is the Turks' Luck': Imagining Religious Identity, Alliance and Conflict on the Habsburg-Ottoman Marches in an Account of the Sieges of Nagykanizsa 1600 and 1601," in *Das Osmanische Reich und die Habsburgermonarchie in der Neuzeit. Akten des internationalen Kongresses zum 150-jährigen Bestehen des Instituts für Österreichische Geschichtsforschung, Wien, 22.-25. September 2004* ed. Marlene Kurz, Martin Scheutz, Karl Vocelka and Thomas Winkelbauer MIÖG Erg. Bd. 49, (Wien: Mitteilungen des Instituts für Österreichische Geschichtsforschung, 2005).

[6] Caroline Finkel, "French Mercenaries in the Habsburg-Ottoman War of 1593-1606. The Desertion of the Papa Garrison to the Ottomans in 1600," *Bulletin of the*

School of Oriental and African Studies 55, no.3 (1992): 451-471, 465-8.

[7] Ibid., 452.

[8] Luigi Ferdinando Marsigli, *Stato militare dell'Imperio Ottomano* I (Amsterdam: n.p., 1732), 85, quoted in Mark Stein, "Seventeenth-Century Ottoman Forts and Garrisons on the Habsburg Frontier (Hungary)," (Ph.D. diss., The University of Chicago, 2001), 152; and Mehmet Zeki Pakalin, *Osmanlı Tarih Deyimleri ver Terimleri Sözlüğü* III (Istanbul: 1993), 146.

[9] Mehmed Zeki Pakalın, "Sekbân," *Islam Ansiklopedisi* 10 (1966): 325-27, 326.

[10] Stein, "Seventeenth-Century Ottoman Forts," 147-149.

[11] Ibid., 145 and 147.

[12] A. Z. Hertz, "Muslims, Christians and Jews in Sixteenth Century Ottoman Belgrade," in *Mutual Effects of the Islamic and the Judeo-Christian Worlds* ed. Abraham Ascher, Tibor Halasi-Kun and Béla Király (New York: Brooklyn College Press, 1979).

[13] Ludwig Fekete, *Türkische Schriften aus dem Archive des Palatins Nikolaus Esterhazy 1606-1645* (Budapest: n.p., 1932), 21 letter no.6.

[14] Gustav Bayerle, *Ottoman Tributes in Hungary: According to Sixteenth Century Tapu Registers of Novigrad* (The Hague, Paris: Mouton, 1973), 22.

[15] Ibid.

[16] Peter Sugar, "The Ottoman 'Professional Prisoner' on the Western Borders of the Empire in the Sixteenth and Seventeenth Centuries," *Études Balkaniques* 7 (1971): 82-91, 82 citing a letter from the chief janissary *ağa* of Nagykanizsa fortress to Count Adam Batthyany at Körmend, located in the Hungarian National Archives, Batthyany Family archives, Collection No. P1313 Fascicle 249 Document 226a.

[17] Catherine Wendy Bracewell, *The Uskoks of Senj: Piracy, Banditry and Holy War in the Sixteenth-Century Adriatic* (Ithaca, N.Y.: Cornell University Press, 1992), 188.

[18] Ibid., 181.

[19] Ibid., 182.

[20] Ibid., 184-6.

[21] Report by Petrasch to the Aulic War council in 1718 cited in Kurt Wessely, "The Development of the Hungarian Military Frontier Until the Middle of the Eighteenth Century," *The Austrian History Yearbook* 9-10 (1973-4): 55-110, 91; Finkel, "French Mercenaries," 452 also mentions that the Ottomans tried to encourage those living in the border lands to settle in their region with tax incentives.

[22] Geza Dávid and Pal Fodor, "Introduction" in *Ottomans, Hungarians, and Habsburgs in Central Europe: The Military Confines in the Era of Ottoman Conquest* ed. Geza Dávid and Pal Fodor (Leiden: Brill, 2000), xii.

[23] Ibid., xviii and xix-xx.

[24] Peter Sugar, *South Eastern Europe under Ottoman Rule, 1354-1804* A History of East Central Europe Vol. v. (Seattle and London: University of Washington Press, 1977), 63.

[25] Lajos Fekete, *Budapest a törökkorban* (Budapest: 1944), 308. Translated by and quoted in Geza Dávid and Pal Fodor, "Hungarian Studies in Ottoman History," in *The Ottomans and the Balkans: A Discussion of Historiography* ed. F. Adanir and S. Faroqhi (Leiden: Brill, 2002), 318-9.

[26] Klara Hegyi, *Egy világbirodalom végvidékén* (Budapest, 1975) quoted in Dávid and Fodor, "Hungarian Studies in Ottoman History," 319.

[27] Geza Dávid, "Administration in Ottoman Europe," in *Süleyman the Magnificent and his Age. The Ottoman Empire in the Early Modern World* ed. Metin Kunt and Christine Woodhead (London, New York: Longman, 1995), 87-8.

[28] Gustav Bayerle, *Ottoman Diplomacy in Hungary* (Bloomington: Indiana University, 1972), 9-10.

[29] Dávid and Fodor, "Introduction," xx.

[30] Dávid, "Administration in Ottoman Europe," 86-7.

[31] Ibid., 83. A *timar* was a fief that provided an income for the holder in exchange for military-administrative service to the Ottoman state.

[32] Ibid., 85 quoting the work of Antal Velics and Ernő Kammerer, *Magyarországi török kincstáari defterek I: 1546-1635* (Budapest: 1886), 6, 9, 17, 19-21, etc.

[33] Klara Hegyi, *Török berendezkedés Magyarországon* (Budapest: Histöriá Könyvtár, Monográfiák, 7 1995) quoted in Dávid and Fodor, "Hungarian Studies in Ottoman History," 320.

[34] Dávid, "Administration in Ottoman Europe," 78.

[35] Dávid and Fodor, "Hungarian Studies in Ottoman History," 343.

[36] Dávid and Fodor, "Introduction," xx.

[37] Dávid, "Administration in Ottoman Europe," 89.

[38] Dávid and Fodor, "Hungarian Studies in Ottoman History," 333.

[39] Ibid., 345.

[40] Hickok, *Ottoman Military Administration* 154 has noted that the transformation of Ottoman border officials from state administrators into local potentates has often been re-interpreted within the paradigm of nation-state geo-political divisions as evidence of the emergence of proto-nationalist movements rather than examples of intra-Ottoman power negotiations.

[41] See Bérenger, *A History of the Habsburg Empire*, 249-50.

[42] Claire Norton, "The Remembrance of the Sieges of Kanije in the Construction of Late Ottoman and Modern Turkish Nationalist Identities," *Parergon* 21, no.1 (2004): 133-53.

12
The Re-Construction of the Past in the Greek Left
The Case of Five Special Issues Published in *Art Review*

Matrona Paleou

This paper focuses on the special issues of the left-wing literary periodical *Art Review* (*Epitheorisi Technis*) published between 1955-1962 which were dedicated to the 1821 Greek Struggle for Independence and the National Resistance movement against the Axis occupation in Greece (1941-1944). In view of the social and political framework of that period, this paper will explore first, how left-wing discourse was affected by the discourse of nationalism and then, how the commemoration of national struggles served the objectives of the Greek Left at that time. Before proceeding to an examination of these issues, it is necessary to give a brief picture of the historical and ideological framework of the 1950s and 1960s in Greece and a few words on the periodical *Art Review* itself.

The 1950s and 1960s are considered one of the most crucial periods in Modern Greek history. The successes in the Albanian war (1940), the cruelty of the Axis occupation, and the rise of the resistance movements (1941-1944) had been followed by a devastating Civil War (1946-1949), the roots of which lay in the inter-war period and in the resistance to the occupation.[1] The 'Democratic Army', which was of Communist origin, was defeated in the Civil War (1949).[2] The abstention of the communists and some liberals from the elections held in March 1946, coupled with the instability of other moderate political coalitions, paved the way for a clear victory for the right-wing party in elections held in November 1952. The demand for reconstruction after two successive wars was more urgent than ever. The dominance of the Right over the next twelve years (1952-1963) provided a period of stability, reinforced by support from the USA, which began with the proclamation of the Truman Doctrine (March 1947) followed by the implementation of the Marshall Plan. However, the price for this stability was high. Economic development between 1952 and 1963 deepened social inequalities, a state of affairs which resulted in increased emigration.[3] Moreover, the so-called 'national conviction' ($\varepsilon\theta\nu\iota\kappa\sigma\phi\rho\sigma\sigma\acute{\nu}\nu\eta$) and a fierce anti-communism were two key features of the Right's ideological discourse, which aimed at preserving the much sought-after social and political stability. Policy was backed up by the predominance of the army and police in every aspect of political life during this period. It is noteworthy that police clearance was necessary wherever the public sector was involved. The hopes for change generated by the massive victory of the Centre Union in February 1964 were soon shattered by the tension between the palace and the Prime Minister George Papandreou, which reached a climax in July 1965. The period of political instability that followed resulted in the military coup of April 1967. This period of containment lasted for seven years and its repercussions were reflected in every aspect of political and social life.

Focusing now on the Greek Left, it is worth mentioning certain aspects of its development on a political level that made a significant contribution to the formation of its ideological discourse in that period. The Communist Party of Greece (KKE) was outlawed in December 1947 and shortly thereafter the party newspaper *Rizospastis* was banned. There were a variety of reasons for the isolation of the Left from Greece's political life during this period: their refusal to participate in the elections held in 1946; the reference to the 'Macedonian problem' in the fifth plenum of the Communist Party Central Committee (January 1949); the decision of the exiled leadership of the KKE to affiliate itself with the Soviet Communist Party (especially after Yugoslavia's expulsion from the Cominform in 1948); and the propaganda against the Communists after the Civil War. This isolation led to a hardening of the political line taken by the party both against their opponents and within the party itself. The rigorous stance taken against those who had signed a 'declaration of repentance' (δήλωση μετάνοιας) was a decision which seriously weakened the party.

Even so, in 1951, the United Democratic Left (EDA) was formed and functioned mainly as a cover for the Communist Party. However, some of its cadres have been described as moderate socialists.[4] The party's very name, which carefully conceals its Communist origins, underlines how cautious the Greek Left was in facing the increasingly anti-Communist tide of opinion. The formation of this party provided the Greek Left with a route to parliamentary representation. In the elections held in May 1958, EDA was elected as the main opposition party despite the fact that at the time some members of the Left were being harshly persecuted for their political beliefs. However, it was also in the 1950s that the first signs of the tension between the outlawed and exiled communist leadership and the communists remaining in Greece occurred. In the years to come, these tensions were to increase and would eventually lead to a split in the party in 1968, the year which saw Czechoslovakia's invasion by the Warsaw Pact.[5] The split within the Greek Communist Party came under a dictatorship, which bore down harshly on left-wingers condemning them to exile, placing them under house arrest or depriving them of political rights. Other left-wingers were forced to leave Greece. For such people the situation would change only after the fall of the junta in 1974, an event which opened the way for the legalisation of the Communist Party and the abolition of the monarchy.

These political developments had a great impact on the ideological discourse of the Greek Left during that period.[6] The circumstances of repression and the radical positions adopted by the opposing political sides contributed to silencing both liberal and left-wing intellectuals and also impeded access to the ideas being shaped in the rest of Europe after World War II. It is worth mentioning that the radical divisions were not just a Greek phenomenon. The same sharp divide could also be seen in France just after the war.[7] However, the phenomenon lasted longer in Greece, fuelled by memories of the Civil War as well as by the establishment of the dictatorship, and to some extent surviving into the post-dictatorship period, the so-called *metapolitefsi*. These developments show the formation of the left-wing ideological discourse during the 1950s and 1960s to have been a long process of opposition to the dominant right-wing discourse as well as a balancing act between the orthodox and revisionist tendencies within the Greek Left.[8]

Art Review was one of the most significant left-wing periodicals at that time and mirrored the tension within the post-war Greek Left. It represents a graphic example of the distinctions between orthodox and revisionist trends within the Greek Left, which were to re-define its ideological discourse in the years to come. The appearance of periodicals such as *Art Review* (1954-1967) and *Panspoudastiki* (1955-1966) in Athens, with their undisguised links with EDA, marked a turning point in the formation of the ideological discourse of the Greek Left. *Art Review* and *Panspoudastiki* attempted to bridge the gap between the opposing tendencies and paved the way for a more open-minded approach to art without, however, seriously challenging the party line. As will be shown below, the case of *Art Review* is typical, as it had to face restrictions imposed by the party line especially during the period 1961-1965.

The first issue of *Art Review* came out in December 1954 and the last in February 1967, two months before the military coup, making a total of 146 issues altogether. The military regime put a stop to nearly thirteen years of uninterrupted publication.[9] Although the Greek Left was marginalised in the 1950s and left-wing militants harshly persecuted, *Art Review* had a readership from a variety of ideological backgrounds insofar as the prevailing social and political circumstances permitted.[10] Nevertheless, in the web of social, political and ideological developments in Greece, *Art*

Review had to overcome a number of obstacles over and above persecutions brought by its political opponents such as the one after the publication of the special issue dedicated to the USSR.[11] The periodical also had to face opposition from within the Greek Left. This opposition was driven on a political level by the existence in that period of two different representations of the Communist party and on an ideological level by the co-existence of orthodox Marxist criticism, still attached to the doctrine of socialist realism, and revisionist Marxist criticism.[12] Accordingly, the relationship between *Art Review* and EDA was quite problematic as is confirmed by the diversity of opinions on this topic. What emerges from the numerous articles referring to this relationship is that the editorial board of *Art Review* – initially composed of three different overlapping groups indicative of the innovative and broad-based character of the new periodical– tried especially in the 1950s to revise key points of left-wing criticism as far as they could under existing social and political circumstances.[13]

In an attempt to maintain a balance, *Art Review* incorporated a wide range of contributions from both orthodox and revisionist critics, published articles by intellectuals of different political persuasions and provided information about debates taking place in Western and Eastern Europe insofar as this was possible.[14] What the representatives of the revisionist tendency within *Art Review* actually demanded was a kind of repositioning of their relationship to the two positions in the party in order to obtain a degree of autonomy as far as aesthetics were concerned. However, this was not enough to avert the strict control by EDA, which was imposed after the publication of the "heretical" short-story "Silence" by Daniel Granin and which lasted from about 1959 to 1964.[15] Even so, EDA never banned *Art Review* outright, as it was the most prestigious left-wing periodical of the time and much needed during that period of harsh persecutions.[16]

It is necessary to turn now to the three special issues of *Art Review* dedicated to the 1821 Struggle for Independence. The first one, which was the longest, was published in 1955; the other two were published in 1958 and 1961 respectively, and highlight only some aspects of the Struggle.[17] As it would be difficult to deal with all the articles, I have singled out certain points that characterise the way the Greek Left set the 1821 Struggle against the background of its own social aims. The major categories of articles included in these three issues are: studies on the national and social role of the 1821 Struggle and the art and major figures that contributed significantly to the national cause; source texts (e.g. public appeals, public records and official documents); literary texts (e.g. folk songs, memoirs, poetry and prose fiction inspired by the struggle).

Before concentrating on the special issues themselves, it may be useful to refer to the period of Ottoman rule, the so called *Tourkokratia*. The fall of Constantinople in 1453 and the capture of Crete in 1699 are two crucial events in the long sequence of Ottoman conquests in the region that started in the fourteenth century in Asia Minor and continued until the eighteenth century with the recapture of the Peloponnese (1715). Apart from the Ionian islands, the whole Balkan peninsula, with its majority Christian Orthodox population, was under Ottoman rule. The Struggle for Independence that broke out in 1821 in both Walachia and Greece was the result of a long period of economic progress, social and political developments, intellectual revival and national awakening that had started almost a century before.

To turn now to the Struggle for Independence, the years 1821-1823 were very successful in terms of military operations. This contrasts with the subsequent period (1823-1824) which was marked by conflict in the Greek camp and led to a devastating civil war between provincial notables and military leaders with the latter questioning the 1822 constitution and claiming an active part in the governance of the recently captured territories. The following years (1825–1827) were even worse for the Greek cause because the Ottoman Empire entered into an alliance with Egypt, a coalition that threatened to shatter every hope of liberation. At this crucial stage, the intervention of the Great Powers (Britain, France and Russia) led to the Battle of Navarino (October 1827) where the Ottoman - Egyptian fleet was defeated by the combined fleets of the Great Powers. Accordingly, the outbreak of war between Russia and the Ottoman Empire in April 1828 was a major blow for the already seriously weakened Ottoman Empire. Autonomy was granted to Greece in 1829 and its independence under a hereditary monarchy declared in February 1830. As a result, the Ottoman Porte acknowledged the independence of the Greek state in May 1832. This new state included the Peloponnese, central Greece and some islands. Its northern boundaries were defined by an imaginary line drawn between Arta in the west and Volos in the east. As far as the internal affairs of Greece were concerned, the third Constitution was enacted in May 1827 and Kapodistrias, former Foreign Minister of Russia became its first President. His assassination in 1831 brought about a period of anarchy, which the Great Powers attempted to rein in by the installation of seventeen-year-old Otto of Wittelsbach as king.

The foreword entitled "The Heritage of 1821", which was published in the first special issue of *Art Review*, stressed that the 1821 Struggle had involved two main objectives: the national uprising against Ottoman rule as well as an aspiration to social liberation and justice. The tone and choice of words are interesting as are the echoes of left-wing discourse employed,

> Our fathers, who shed their blood and sacrificed themselves,
> fighting with heart and mouth to give us Freedom, had a broad
> agenda: redeeming the nation from bondage, social liberation, de-
> mocracy, equality on all fronts as well as cultural advancement.[18]

The desire to associate the 1821 Struggle with an agenda of social
liberation is evidenced in Y. Kordatos's 1955 article entitled "A People's
Fight…"[19] Kordatos was a fervent advocate of the social character of the
1821 Struggle, arguing that it had been directed both against Ottoman rule
and the Greek landowners, who, in his opinion, had been very submissive
to foreign powers and aimed only to keep their privileges, to the detri-
ment of the national cause.[20] At this point, it is worth mentioning that the
readers of *Art Review* had also been acquainted with the Marxist point of
view on historiography, as presented in Svoronos's study "Thoughts on
an Introduction to Modern Greek History."[21] Nevertheless, Kordatos's attitude is harsh, and perhaps even biased, against the provincial notables.
The sharpness of his criticism is further emphasized when reading his
article in conjunction with Asdrachas's "On the *Armatoloi* under the Ottomans and During the War of Independence" published in 1958.[22] Asdrachas examines the role of the Christian militia, known as *armatoloi*, that
were formed by the Ottoman forces in order to protect the mountain passes from dangers including groups of *klefts*, or bandits. It is noteworthy that
the *klefts* often attacked both Greeks and Ottomans; their attacks against
the Ottomans eventually evolved into a disorganized national resistance
movement. Unavoidably, Asdrachas refers to the relationship between the
armatoloi and the provincial notables as well as the Ottomans. However,
he is not as harsh regarding the role of provincial notables. Although he
admits that there were cases in which *armatoloi* and provincial notables
supported their vested interests through special agreements, he looks at
their role during the period under examination more dispassionately. Accordingly, he characterizes contemporary radical left-wing views on this
matter as graphic examples of the so-called 'moralizing historiography'
and 'modernizing criticism.'[23]

This association between national and social liberation is continued in
the articles in *Art Review* on the 1941 resistance against Axis occupation.
The common denominators of a struggle for national independence and
resistance to social inequality is located in both uprisings. This connection
between the two events explains why Gritsi-Milliex's chronicle "A History
of the Resistance", finds a place in the 1961 issue dedicated to the 1821
Struggle.[24] Another common thread running through *Art Review*'s special
issues on both the 1821 Struggle and the 1941 resistance is the contention
that the yearning for national and social liberation that motivated both

these struggles still remains unfulfilled. According to the foreword in the 1961 special issue on the 1821 Struggle the fact that the 1941 national resistance movement was still not officially recognized—a status realized only in the 1980s—was a further proof that the Greek state was repeating the errors of the past, when the fighters of the 1821 Struggle who, marginalized from the current socio-political developments in Greece, ended up leading a wretched life.[25] The parallel being drawn between the two uprisings is obvious in the following lines:

> All our fellow countrymen are united in demanding recognition of the sacrifices made by the people. The spirit of 1821 is turned to advantage when we acknowledge the National Resistance which, like a shining deed, is raised ever higher above our blood drenched land. And the twentieth anniversary should be the occasion 'to raise the sun over Greece'.[26]

The role and position of art in society is another major topic treated by the post-war Greek Left. Ideological commitment, a thorny question for left-wing intellectuals, was one of the key concerns raised in the process of interpreting and evaluating art. According to Gramsci, engagement in the left-wing cause must be based on certain 'moral' principles that assure the homogeneity and the unity of the struggle.[27] How this 'morality' was interpreted created many problems in the left-wing camp not only in Greece, but also internationally, especially after the introduction of the doctrine of socialist realism in the USSR in 1934. The problems generated by the issue of ideological commitment in Greece were further aggravated by the turbulent social and political situation following the Civil War. The three articles in the special issues that comment on art in relation to national demands epitomise the way left-wing discourse aimed at combining national and social aspirations in the post-war period.

The article by Kallergis, "Makriyannis's Pictures—a Sacred National Trust" exhibits the influence of socialist realism in the appreciation of art.[28] Makriyannis, one of the best-known military leaders during the 1821 Struggle for Independence, learned to read and write only in order to commit his experiences to his *Memoirs*; a work that remained highly influential throughout the twentieth century.[29] The reception of Makriyannis's *Memoirs* is varied.[30] For example, although it became a point of reference for Greek Modernism, Makriyannis's work as a whole did not escape Marxist criticism, which saw in its essential features another occasion for a programmatic account of the evaluation of art. According to Kallergis, the content of a work of art must be *progressive*, meaning left-wing, its form must be *popular*, meaning easily comprehensible, and it must serve *national aims.* In this way, art is able to work for people's rights and restore historical truth. Taking a critique of Makriyannis's paintings—or rather Panayiotis and Dimitris Zografos's paintings under Makriyannis's supervision—as its starting point, this article constitutes an example of orthodox Marxist criticism imbued with the optimism of socialist realism as first introduced into Greece in the mid-1930s. As mentioned above, there had been a long story of alignment of the Greek Communist Left with developments taking place in the USSR on a political level, which illustrates, to a certain extent, why the doctrine of socialist realism was still prevalent in Greece up to the late 1950s. The long-standing dominance of socialist realism explains why left-wing literary criticism still tended to privilege ideological criteria over the aesthetic in the evaluation of art and in certain cases reveals another significant problem; a lack of proper education concerning Marxism and cultural issues, in general.[31]

In the same issue, Kostas Varnalis, a left-wing poet, wrote a brief article on Dionysios Solomos, Greece's national poet, acknowledging the key position of his oeuvre in the canon of Modern Greek literature.[32] Varnalis stressed that the aims of the 1821 Struggle had not yet been accomplished and insisted on the distinction between *progress* and *reaction,* in other words, between left- and right-wing ideology. He also underlined the duty of the poet to promote the didactic and social character of his art and thus become a guide for his compatriots. Lastly, the article "The 'Collective Myth' of Modern Greece" written by Kouloufakos, a moderate left-wing critic and published in 1958, evaluated the potential of the 1821 Struggle to function as a *collective myth* in modern Greece.[33] Kouloufakos argued that it could, insisting that the struggle could inspire authors, poets and directors to create original works, drawing on that period, with the aim of illustrating some of its crucial moments and recreating the historical truth, though not at the expense of artistic insights.

The importance of the 1821 Struggle is also highlighted in the two special issues dedicated to the National Resistance movement, published in 1955 and 1962.[34] The forward to the 1955 issue, for example, draws a clear parallel between the 1821 Struggle and the National Resistance of the 1940s. Moreover, the study "Folk Elements in the War and the Occupation" focuses among other things on the imitation of folk versification that flourished in the 1940s.[35] The appreciation of folk songs by the Greek Left goes back to the 1930s, when their use was in accordance with the tenets of socialist realism. In the 1940s, drawing on traditional roots was a common practice among left-wing and other poets, who aimed in many cases to associate the wartime resistance with the earlier struggle for national independence.[36] The passage from Yannis Ritsos's poem "Global neighbourhoods", and the selection of resistance poems also published in the

1955 issue, represent another kind of poetry inspired by war, which directly responds to the adverse socio-political circumstances.[37] It is significant that an article on the national poet Solomos is incorporated in the same issue, suggesting that the poet's social awareness is most appreciated by the Greek Left and plays an important role to the evaluation of his oeuvre.[38]

It may be helpful at this point to mention certain key dates in the national resistance that will serve as a background to the examination of the 1955 and 1962 special issues dedicated to this event. Following the fall of Athens (April 1941) and Crete (May 1941), the whole of Greece was under Axis occupation by June 1941. Meanwhile the Greek government-in-exile initially escaped to London and then to Cairo (March 1943). No later than September 1941 the first resistance group was established, namely the National Liberation Front (EAM) and shortly afterwards its military wing the National People's Liberation Army (ELAS) emerged. It is worth mentioning that, although the leadership of EAM consisted of Communists, most of its members came from other political persuasions. There were also other non-Communist resistance groups, such as National Republican Greek League (EDES), acting in parallel with EAM, although the pre-eminence of the latter was obvious. The resistance moved into the mountains from 1942 onwards, but it was plagued by internal conflicts, which at this stage did not last long (October 1943—February 1944), but which nevertheless foreshadowed the harsh civil war that was to follow liberation. EAM never hid its political aims including the fact that the Political Committee of National Liberation (PEEA), which was intended to act as a government in free "mountain" Greece, should eventually form the basis of a national unity government. However, it was at the Lebanon Conference in 1944 that a government of national unity was finally formed under British supervision with George Papandreou as its prime minister. Despite initial disapproval by EAM, which was under-represented in the new government, in the end the Lebanon agreement was accepted (August 1944). The liberation of Athens in October 1944 provoked an outburst of enthusiasm, which, however, did not last long. A new round of conflicts soon started which were to continue until the end of 1949.

One of the major aims of both these special issues was to rescue the reputation of the left-wing struggle of the 1940s and to keep its memory alive. It is noteworthy that the special issue in 1962, the most lengthy, was one of the few attempts by the Greek Left between 1950 and 1974 at a historical summary of that period. Thus the following account will initially refer to studies dealing with various subjects (e.g. art and education) and then to texts that function as testimonies to the wartime ordeal (e.g. chronicles, and diaries).

The studies in both the 1955 and 1962 special issues demonstrate not only the national, but also the intellectual alertness in the 1940s. Kallergis writing on art during the resistance in the 1955 issue reaffirmed his belief in the national character and social function of art, especially under adverse circumstances. He suggested that the left-wing orientation of art as developed in the 1940s should be continued in the years to come and that realism should be the answer to what he saw as the prevalence of formalism in contemporary art.[39] These views are not surprising in Kallergis; in the article mentioned above on Makriyannis's paintings he had argued against *poésie pure* as reflecting bourgeois decadence favouring realism instead. The same line was taken by Eleutheriou, who also referred to the major characteristics of literature during the resistance comparing them to those in the post-war period.[40] Roger Milliex, in the 1962 issue, emphasized the contribution of intellectuals to the resistance at the same time as Sotiriou and Kalatzis were highlighting the progressive character of certain educational and legislative regulations compared to pre-war examples, especially those under Metaxas's dictatorship.[41] It is significant that these regulations were introduced by PEEA, which had seen itself acting as a government in free 'mountain' Greece under the occupation.

The large number of chronicles and personal testimonies gathered in both these issues confirm the attempt to give a historical account of the period from a left-wing point of view and to praise the contribution of left-wing forces to the national cause. The Greek Left emphasized its overwhelming primacy in the wartime resistance and thus managed to serve its social aims in the post-war period. By drawing attention to wartime experiences, left-wing intellectuals highlighted what Kallergis in his second article had regarded as a precondition for creating art in the post-war period: the restoration of historical truth. The extracts from Voutyras's "My Occupation Diary", Panselinos's "Carceri Militari (A Prisoner's Diary)"—a title echoing Gramsci's *Prison Notebooks*—and Damianos's "Faith" in the 1955 issue, as well as a significant number of chronicles and testimonies by, among others, Alexiou, Vournas and Theodoridis collected in the 1962 issue are characteristic examples of how the Left tried to save major moments of the 1940s resistance from oblivion.

This brief presentation of five special issues of *Art Review* exposes the main characteristics of the left-wing discourse on national struggles in that period. Before exploring the role and position of these special issues, it may be useful to remember Gellner's observation on the views of Marx and Engels, who eventually did not provide a way to realize the ideal of the nationless, classless and "religionless" future they had envisaged.[42] The presentation of the national struggles in *Art Review* is an additional example of the difficulty of realizing this ultimate aim. A central element in these issues is the attempt to link national aims with left-wing objectives. Thus the 1821 Struggle was presented as being not only against Ottoman rule, but also against the Greek landowners, with the aim of rehabilitating the landless peasantry. The same reasoning was followed in the presentation of the wartime resistance. The two special issues, and particularly the second one, underline the major contribution of EAM and PEEA to the anti-fascist struggle. In this way the editors tried to give a left-wing slant to the history of that period. There was an attempt at convergence, or at least mutual appropriation, between left-wing views and national objectives: a strategy designed to strengthen the position of the Greek Left and broaden its appeal. This provided the framework in which the focus on warfare and the treatment of cultural issues must be seen. It is also worth mentioning that the accounts of national uprisings in *Art Review* reveal some of the long-standing tensions in the post-war Greek Left and illustrate the essential elements of left-wing criticism at that period.

Warfare, and not religion, for example, occupied a central position in these accounts of national struggles. These special issues underlined the fact that the outbreak of the 1821 Struggle and the wartime resistance inspired national sentiments, strengthened national consciousness, provided memories and fashioned collective myths that would have the potential to mobilize people in the future.[43] As shown above, memories of the 1821 Struggle proved to be particularly important in the issues dedicated to the wartime resistance. All five issues illustrate the attempt to create a 'map' for the Greek nation taking into account its glorious past, defining its place internationally, and unavoidably providing a moral code which could play a guiding role in times of hardship. As Smith notes, "In these ways the new nation could be endowed with a cognitive basis and moral purpose that would ensure the continued renaissance of its distinctive cultural heritage and vision."[44]

The accounts of national struggles provided in these issues of Art Review endorse the notion that "nationalism is primarily a cultural doctrine or, more accurately, a political ideology with a cultural doctrine at its centre."[45] Art inspired by national achievements and the response of artists and intellectuals, not only during these crucial periods, but also in their aftermath, occupies a central position in these special issues. The association of social with cultural, common in left-wing criticism, especially concerning literature and art, is here maintained and sometimes accentuated, revealing that socialist realism was still influential. One should not forget that the main aim of the Left was to gain a secure position in respect to political and social issues in Greece at that time. Art had always been one of the main concerns of left-wing intellectuals, but during the 1950s and 1960s this concern was intensified. For example, left-wing intellectuals attempted to compensate for the defeat in the Civil War by focusing on art in order to gain a prestigious position in cultural developments in Greece. Their left-wing discourse attempted to offer an alternative perspective on matters of art, while at the same time remaining consistent with the principles of the Greek Left and its political aims.

These special issues show that historical continuity, which is central to the rationale of nationalism, was maintained.[46] A significant number of left-wing intellectuals did not depart from the broadly used concept which sees in the succession of past, present and future an unbreakable continuity. At the same time, internationalism was underplayed in favour of the interests of the Greek nation. The difference is that this was achieved under conditions set by a left-wing ideology, which has always associated social, national and cultural objectives. On the one hand, the power of 'the people', usually gained through revolutionary acts – which, according to Sugar, characterises Eastern nationalism – is emphasized in the re-construction of the past presented in these issues of *Art Review*.[47] On the other hand, apart from some concessions to the nationless ideal of Marxism, these special issues represent both a significant departure from the introverted development of nationalism in Eastern Europe, which contrasts with the individual, cosmopolitan and rational character of nationalism in Western Europe, and furnish a pattern of re-construction adapted to the needs of the Left in Greece at the time.[48]

Notes

[1] Richard Clogg, *A Concise History of Greece* (Cambridge: Cambridge University Press, 1992), 100-168. See also Nikos G. Svoronos, Επισκόπηση της νεοελληνικής ιστορίας trans. by Aikaterini Asdracha, 13th edition (Athens: Themelio, 1999), 113-153, originally published as *Histoire de la Grèce Moderne,* (Paris: Presses Universitaires de France, 1972); and Mark Mazower, *Inside Hitler's Greece: The Experience of Occupation 1941-44* (New Haven and London: Yale University Press, 1993), 123-143.

[2] For the reasons behind the defeat see, John O. Iatrides, "Civil War, 1945-1949: National and International Aspects," in *Greece in the 1940s: A Nation in Crisis* ed. John O. Iatrides (Hanover and London: University Press of New England, 1981), 195-219; and Nikos Svoronos, "Greek History, 1940-1950: The main problems," in *Greece in the 1940s*, 1-14.

[3] Kostas Tsoucalas, Η Ελληνική τραγωδία, trans. by K. Iordanidi, (Athens: Nea Synora, 1981), 115-139. Originally published as *Greek tragedy,* (London: Penguin Books, 1969); and Kostas Vergopoulos, "The emergence of the new bourgeoisie, 1944-1952," in *Greece in the 1940s*, 298-318.

[4] Manolis Glezos, "Η ΕΔΑ ως «Ιδιορρυθμία Ελληνική»," in Η Σοσιαλιστική Σκέψη στην Ελλάδα από το 1875 ως το 1974: Τα ρήγματα της τριτοδιεθνιστικής ορθοδοξίας και οι νεωτερικές συλλήψεις της σοσιαλιστικής θεωρίας (1956-1974),

ed. Panayotis Noutsos, vol. 4, (Athens: Gnosi, 1994), 340-342, originally published as "15 χρόνια αγώνων της ΕΔΑ," in Ελληνική Αριστερά, vol. 23 (1966): 16-18. Ελληνική Αριστερά was the official monthly periodical of EDA.

⁵ See Panos Demetriou Η διάσπαση του ΚΚΕ vol.2 (Athens: Politika Provlemata, 1975).

⁶ See Alex Argyriou, Η Μεταπολεμική Πεζογραφία Από τον πόλεμο του '40 ως τη δικτατορία του '67, vol. 1 (Athens: Sokolis, 1988).

⁷ Tony Judt, Past Imperfect: French Intellectuals, 1944-1956 (Berkeley: University of California Press, 1992), 45-74; and Dimitris Raftopoulos, "Επιθεώρηση (στρατευμένης) Τέχνης," Mandragora 6-7 (1995): 126-127.

⁸ See Argyriou, Η Μεταπολεμική Πεζογραφία; and Constantine Tsoucalas, "The Ideological Impact of the Civil War," in Greece in the 1940s, 319-341.

⁹ Zisimos Synodinos, "Χρονολόγιο 1954-1967," Mandragora 6-7, (1995): no page number.

¹⁰ Takis Kayalis, "Ποίηση, Ιδεολογία και Λογοτεχνική Κριτική στην Επιθεώρηση Τέχνης," in Επιθεώρηση Τέχνης. Μια Κρίσιμη Δωδεκαετία (29 και 30 Μαρτίου 1996) ed. Maria Stefanopoulou, (Athens: Etaireia Spoudon Neoellinikou Politismou kai Genikis Paideias, 1997), 59-61; and Christos Cheimaras, "Η «Επιθεώρηση Τέχνης» και η εφηβεία ενός επαρχιώτη," Diavazo 67, (20/4/1983): 34-37.

¹¹ Yannis Ritsos et al., Αφιερωμένο στα σαράντα χρόνια από την Οκτωβριανή Επανάσταση, [special issue] Art Review 6, no.34 (1957).

¹² Panayotis Noutsos, ed., Η Σοσιαλιστική Σκέψη στην Ελλάδα από το 1875 ως το 1974, vol. 4, 68-77.

¹³ Kostas Kremmydas, "Επιθεώρηση Τέχνης και Κώστας Κουλουφάκος: Βίοι Παράλληλοι," in Επιθεώρηση Τέχνης. Μια Κρίσιμη Δωδεκαετία, 17-25; Titos Patrikios, "Αναλάβαμε κάθε ρίσκο μέχρι το τέλος," Mandragora 6-7 (1995): 135-136; Dimitris Raftopoulos, "Της μακρινής μας νιότης ιστορίες," Mandragora 6-7 (1995): 173; and Nikos Siapkidis, "Κάπως έτσι έγιναν τα πράγματα," Mandragora 6-7 (1995): 121-123.

¹⁴ Yannis Kalioris, "Μάχες από στενά χαρακώματα," Mandragora 6-7 (1995): 151-154; and Raftopoulos, "Επιθεώρηση (στρατευμένης) Τέχνης,," 126-127; Argyriou, Η Μεταπολεμική Πεζογραφία vol. 1, 148-149.

¹⁵ Daniel Granin, "Η σιωπή," trans. from the Italian by Manolis Fourtounis, Art Review 9, nos 50-51 (1959): 125-132; and Dimitris Raftopoulos, "Εξέγερση και «νομιμότητα» στην Επιθεώρηση Τέχνης," in Επιθεώρηση Τέχνης. Μια Κρίσιμη Δωδεκαετία, 283-290.

¹⁶ Dimitris Raftopoulos, "Επιθεώρηση (στρατευμένης) Τέχνης," 131.

¹⁷ Yanis Kordatos et al., Αφιέρωμα στο 1821, [special issue] Art Review 1, no.3 (1955); Th. Petsalis–Diomidis et al., Μικρό αφιέρωμα στο '21, [special issue] Art Review 7, no.39 (1958); Th. Fotiadis et al., Αφιέρωμα στο 1821 [special issue] Art Review 13, no.75 (1961).

¹⁸ Editorial Board, "Η Κληρονομιά του 1821," Art Review 1, no.3 (1955): 163.

¹⁹ Yanis Kordatos, "Όταν ο Λαός πολεμούσε…," 1, no.3 (1955): 164-168.

²⁰ See also Yanis Kordatos, Η κοινωνική σημασία της Ελληνικής Επαναστάσεως του 1821, (Athens: Epikairotita, 1999), first published in 1925.

²¹ N. G. Svoronos, "Σκέψεις για μια εισαγωγή στη Νεοελληνική ιστορία,"

Art Review 1, no.3 (1955): 208-212.

²² Sp. Asdrachas, "Γύρω από τον αρματολισμό κατά την Τουρκοκρατία και το 21," *Art Review* 7, no.39 (1958): 107-111.

²³ Ibid., 111.

²⁴ Tatiana Gritsi-Milliex, "Μια ιστορία της αντίστασης,," *Art Review* 13, no.75 (1961): 220-222.

²⁵ Editorial Board, "«Εικοσιένα» και Εθνική Αντίσταση," *Art Review* 13, no.75 (1961): 145-146.

²⁶ Ibid., 146.

²⁷ Antonio Gramsci, *Η οργάνωση της κουλτούρας,* trans. by Thanasis Papadopoulos, (Athens: Stochastis, 1973), 65-67.

²⁸ S. Kallergis, "Οι ζωγραφιές του Μακρυγιάννη - Ιερή εθνική παρακαταθήκη," 1, no.3 (1955): 201-207.

²⁹ General Makriyannis, *Memoirs (Απομνημονεύματα)* ed. Yannis Vlachoyannis, (Athens: Damianos, [n.d.]), first published in 1907.

³⁰ See Takis Kayalis, "Ο Μακρυγιάννης του Σεφέρη," in *Μοντερνισμός και Ελληνικότητα* Nasos Vayenas et al., (Irakleion: Crete University Press, 1997), 31-64 offers a review of Makriyannis's reception up to the 1940s; see also Sp. Vassileiou, "Σκέψις Μακρυγιάννη – Χείρ Δ. Ζωγράφου," in *Elefthera Grammata* (22/3/1946); Yanis Kordatos's "Η λαϊκή μούσα για τους δημοκρατικούς αγώνες του Στρατηγού Μακρυγιάννη," in *Eleftheri Ellada* (7/2/1947). The articles by Vassileiou and Kordatos are also published in Makriyannis, *Memoirs*.

³¹ See Christina Dounia, *Λογοτεχνία και Πολιτική* (Athens: Kastaniotis, 1996), 313-324; Foula Chatzidaki, "«Αληθινή Τέχνη» και «Τέχνη των μαζών»," in *Η Σοσιαλιστική Σκέψη στην Ελλάδα από το 1875 ως το 1974* vol. 4, 383-386; Chrysa Prokopaki, "Τα τείχη της αριστεράς και ο Καβάφης," *Mandragora* 6-7 (1995): 179.

³² Kostas Varnalis, "Σολωμός - Το μεγάλο μάθημα," *Art Review* 1, no.3 (1955): 192-193.

³³ Kostas Kouloufakos, "Ο «κοινός μύθος» της νεώτερης Ελλάδας," *Art Review* 7, no.39 (1958): 99-104.

³⁴ See Yannis Ritsos et al., *Αφιέρωμα στην Εθνική Αντίσταση,* [special issue] *Art Review* 2, no.10 (1955) and Yannis Imbriotis et al., *Αφιέρωμα στην Εθνική Αντίσταση,* [special issue] *Art Review* 15, nos 87-88 (1962).

³⁵ Editorial Board, "Λαογραφικά στοιχεία του πολέμου και της Κατοχής," *Art Review* 2, no.10 (1955): 289-292.

³⁶ Elli Alexiou, ed., *Ανθολογία Ελληνικής Αντιστασιακής Λογοτεχνίας, 1941-1944, Τόμος II: Ποίηση,* (Athens: Iridanos, [n.d.]), first edition published in Berlin by Akademie – Verlag in 1971.

³⁷ The poems gathered under the title "Αντιστασιακή Ποίηση" in the special issue 2, no.10 (1995): 279-288 are: "Ένας στρατιώτης μουρμουρίζει στο Αλβανικό μέτωπο" by Nikiforos Vrettakos, "Η αδερφή μου" by Rita Boumi-Pappa, "Ο Γερμανός λοχίας Αύγουστος Κραους" by Nikos Pappas, "Είδα μια νύχτα το Χριστό…" by L. Koukoulas, "Αθήνα" by Kostas Thrakiotis, "Μάνα" by Giorgos Karatzas.

³⁸ Giorgis Valtinos, "Ο Πατριωτισμός του Σολωμού και οι υβριστές του," *Art Review* 2, no.10 (1955): 325-327.

[39] S. Kallergis, "Η Τέχνη στην Αντίσταση," *Art Review* 2, no.10 (1955): 274-278.

[40] A. Eleutheriou, "Η λογοτεχνία της Αντίστασης," *Art Review* 2, no.10 (1955): 294-295.

[41] R. Milliex, "Οι διανοούμενοι της Ελλάδας στην υπηρεσία της Αντίστασης," trans. by K. Kouloufakos (original title in French not provided), *Art Review* 15, nos 87-88 (1962): 416-433; K. D. Sotiriou, "Το Εθνικό Συμβούλιο και η Παιδεία," *Art Review* 15, nos 87-88 (1962): 300-304; Chr. N. Kalatzis, "Ιδεολογική επιτομή της νομοθεσίας της Εθνικής Αντίστασης," *Art Review* 15, nos 87-88 (1962): 366-375.

[42] Ernest Gellner, *Encounters with Nationalism* (Oxford: Blackwell Publishers, 1994), 5-6.

[43] Anthony D. Smith, *National Identity* (London: Penguin Books, 1991), 27.

[44] Ibid., 65.

[45] Ibid., 74.

[46] See Pantelis Lekkas, "Εθνικιστική ιδεολογία και παράδοση," *Diavazo* 323 (10/11/1993): 46-50.

[47] Peter Sugar, "Nationalism in Eastern Europe," in *Nationalism* ed. John Hutchinson and Anthony D. Smith (Oxford: Oxford University Press, 1994), 171-177.

[48] Hans Kohn, "Western and Eastern Nationalisms," in *Nationalism*, 162-165.

About the Authors

Professor Breuilly is Professor of Nationalism and Ethnicity at the London School of Economics. He is the author on numerous monographs and articles on the subject of nationalism and German history including most recently an edited volume: Ronald Speirs, and J. Breuilly, eds, *Germany's Two Unifications: Anticipations, Experiences, Responses* (Palgrave, 2004) and an article "1848: Connected or Comparable Revolutions?" in *1848: A European Revolution? International Ideas and National Memories of 1848*, ed. A. Körner (Macmillan, 2004). His research interests include modern urban history, the history of socialism, and theories of nationalism and of modernization

Joshua Arthurs is a doctoral student in modern European history at the University of Chicago. His forthcoming dissertation, "A Revolution in the Idea of Rome: the Archaeology of Modernity in Fascist Italy," explores the intersection of ideology, the historical disciplines and romanità under Mussolini's regime. His research interests include critical theories of fascism, nationalism, and modernity, the classical tradition, and the history of historiography, monuments and urban space.

M.K. Flynn is a senior lecturer in politics at the University of the West of England. She specializes in the comparative study of nationalism, ethnic conflict, democratization, and contested history. Past publications have been on Spain, Ireland, and the Ukraine, as well as South Africa. She is on the editorial board for the journal *Ethnic and Racial Studies*.

Tony King is a visiting research fellow in the School of Politics, University of the West of England. He specializes in British imperial history, white settler society in Zimbabwe and South Africa, nationalism, and the politics of heritage, and has published in a variety of journals and edited volumes.

Eisuke Tanaka is a PhD student in the Department of Social Anthropology at the University of Cambridge. He is studying the issues surrounding archaeological objects marked as 'cultural property' and their movements across national or state boundaries, using cases from Turkey. His research interests include the articulation and elaboration of the concept of cultural property across different geographical and discursive spaces; national and local identity construction; and the deployment of cultural property in the constitution of locality.

Ulf Bruunbauer is an assistant professor at the Institute for Eastern European Studies at the Free University of Berlin. He is the author of the forthcoming book *"Die sozialistische Lebensweise." Politik, Ideologie und Alltag in Bulgarien, 1944-1989* and is the editor of *(Re-)Writing History. Historiography in Southeast Europe after Socialism* (Münster: Lit-Verlag, 2004). His main research interests include the social history of the Balkans, minorities and nationalism in the Balkans, and the historiography of Southeast Europe.

Tom Turner has taught political science in Rwanda, the Democratic Republic of Congo, Tunisia, and Kenya. He is a collector of African art. His recent publications include, "Images of Power, Images of Humiliation: Congolese 'Colonial' Sculpture for Sale in Rwanda," *African Arts* (Spring 2005).

Ulrike Stohrer teaches Social Anthropology in Frankfurt and Heidelberg. In 2004 she received her Ph.D. in Social Anthropology from the University of Frankfurt. She is currently preparing her Ph.D. thesis, "Bar'a-Dance, Nonverbal Communication and Identity in the Highlands of Yemen," for publication. Her research interests include ritual and performance, cultural identity, and media in the Middle East.

Kochi Okada is working on her PhD at the Anthropology Department, Goldsmiths College, University of London. Her thesis concerns the validation of artistic practices in Post-Soviet Uzbekistan. Her most recent publications include, the "Forward" to the *Catalogue for the Kyrgyzstan Arts Exhibition, Arts in Kyrgyzstan in the Grand Duchy of Luxemburg*, organized by the Cultural Office of Luxemburg (n.p.: Kyrgyzstan Embassy in Brussels, 2002) and "Social Changes in Kyrgyz Mortuary Practice," *Inner Asia* vol.1/2 (1999)

Sophie Hadjipapa is a lecturer at the Cyprus College, Nicosia. She has written articles on Konoglou and religious art for a variety of publications including Art Studies Quarterly of the Bulgarian Academy of Sciences.

Her research interests include Modern Greek and Bulgarian art, especially Byzantine and Post Byzantine reminiscences in the modern art of Bulgaria and Greece.

Mark Soileau is presently a Ph.D. candidate in Religious Studies at the University of California, Santa Barbara. His research focuses on religion and culture, collective memory, nationalism, and Islamic mysticism.

Claire Norton is a lecturer in Islamic history at St Mary's College, University of Surrey. She has published articles on Ottoman history in a number of edited collections and journals. Her research interests include, Ottoman literacy practices, identity formation, Christian-Muslim interactions, the rhetoric of conflict and representations of war, and questions concerning the epistemological status of history.

Matrona Paleou is a tutor in the history of European literature at the Greek Open University. She obtained her PhD degree at The University of Birmingham with a thesis entitled "Criticism, Poetry and Ideological Commitment: C.P. Cavafy and the Greek Left (1950-1974)." She has published articles on Modern Greek literature and culture and she is currently participating in a research program on women's contribution to literary and art periodicals of the period 1900-1940.